RHETORICAL MOVEMENT

RHETORICAL MOVEMENT

Essays in Honor of Leland M. Griffin

Edited by
DAVID ZAREFSKY

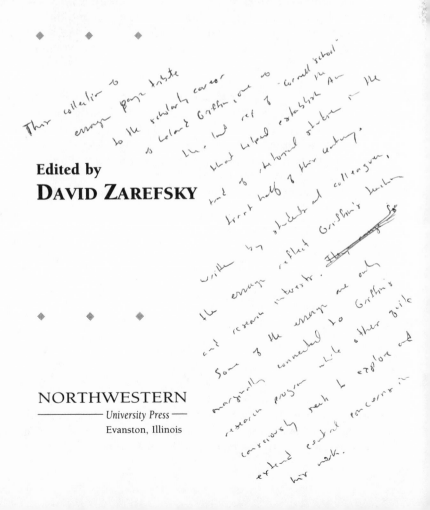

NORTHWESTERN
——— *University Press* ———
Evanston, Illinois

Northwestern University Press
Evanston, Illinois 60208-4210

ISBN 0-8101-1092-X

Library of Congress Cataloging-in-Publication Data

Rhetorical movement : essays in honor of Leland M. Griffin / edited by
  David Zarefsky.
       p.   cm.
    Includes bibliographical references.
    Contents: Leland M. Griffin / Charles J.G. Griffin — The
  beginnings of Greek rhetorical theory / Edward Schiappa — Rhetoric
  in defense of the dispossessed : David Crockett and the Tennessee
  squatters / Royce E. Flood — Nullification in Vermont, 1844 / David
  Waite — Persuasion of the unconscious will : Walt Whitman and the
  rhetoric of indirection / John Lee Jellicorse — Lincoln and Douglas
  respond to the antislavery movement / David Zarefsky and Ann E.
  Burnette — Burkean rites and the Gettysburg address / Thomas F.
  Mader — Manifesting perspectives : rhetoric in the movements of
  modern art / Thomas B. Farrell — The strategy of narrative and
  metaphor in interventionist rhetoric / D. Ray Heisey — The
  construction of appeal in visual images / Sonja K. Foss.
    ISBN 0-8101-1092-X
    1. Rhetoric.   I. Zarefsky, David.   II. Griffin, Leland M., 1920–

P301.R4724   1994
808—dc20   93-41533
                                                                 CIP

CONTENTS

PREFACE

David Zarefsky

The essays in this book were written by students and colleagues of Leland M. Griffin at Northwestern University. Between 1956, when he came to Northwestern, and his retirement in 1989, Griffin taught rhetorical theory and criticism to graduate and undergraduate students and maintained his own research program in these same areas. Although he is best known for his work on the rhetoric of social movements, Griffin emphasized the more general principle of rhetorical movement, the dynamics within texts and historical forces. These essays embody that concern and apply it to topics of Griffin's own interest.

Although he did not publish in the history of rhetorical theory, most graduate students first encountered Lee Griffin in seminars in classical, renaissance, and modern rhetoric. He combined extensive reading of primary texts with application of classical works to current controversies. In particular, he encouraged original, insightful readings of familiar works, as well as studies that focused on movement or evolution within and between texts. The first essay exemplifies these concerns. Edward Schiappa, Griffin's most recent doctoral student, takes a new look at the origins of the concept of rhetoric. His essay is part of a larger effort, encouraged by Griffin and others, to reexamine the Sophists and study them on their own terms rather than from a perspective that presupposes Plato's critique. Schiappa, making extensive use of Protagorean fragments, examines the Sophists as transitional figures between an oral and a written culture. He establishes that what the Sophists practiced was not then classified as rhetoric, and that the term and its underlying theories are of more recent origin than is commonly supposed.

Griffin had a special interest in nineteenth-century American public address, nurtured by his own dissertation research on the anti-Masonic movement. He taught early American discourse for a time following the death of Ernest Wrage, and attracted many students in this field. Four of the essays in this volume focus on antebellum American oratory, and each brings a fresh perspective to the speakers and texts.

Royce E. Flood examines one of the minor figures of the Jacksonian era, Congressman David Crockett of Tennessee. Flood argues that Crockett became a symbol, not a romantic symbol of the frontier as invented by Walt Disney, but a symbol of the dispossessed. His constituents were Tennessee squatters who were threatened by the development and land-reform plans of the rich and powerful. Crockett's rhetorical style was unconventional, Flood suggests, because it was only by violating the conventions of the day that he could gain attention and assure himself a hearing. Flood's study illustrates changes in rhetorical practice as one moves from genteel society to the harsher and more abrasive discourse of the West. Crockett anticipates the populist rhetoric of the late nineteenth century and may be the paradigmatic case of rhetoric of the dispossessed.

David Waite examines a different kind of rhetorical movement— the migration of an argument or appeal from the controversy that originally contained it to quite different circumstances or events. His study concerns the arguments for nullification of federal laws thought unconstitutional. Nullification was championed by South Carolinians who opposed what they thought was an unjust tariff whose proceeds might be used to threaten the peculiar institution of slavery. The nullifiers abandoned their efforts in the face of Clay's compromise tariff of 1833, but under circumstances in which it was never acknowledged that the underlying theory had been defeated. The arguments for states' rights and nullification remained available and were used increasingly by Northerners to justify resistance to fugitive slave legislation. Waite explores an early example of the transposition of the nullification argument by focusing on political debates in Vermont during the 1840s.

Walt Whitman usually is studied as a literary figure, even though the poet himself frequently made clear that his goal was persuasion and not literary art. John Lee Jellicorse remedies this error with an essay examining Whitman as a persuader. Through close reading of Whitman's works, Jellicorse extracts Whitman's underlying rhetorical theory. He calls it a "rhetoric of indirection" and emphasizes its appeal to the unconscious will. Whitman believed that overt acts of persuasion might fail but that literature could succeed as persuasion through subtlety as to its persuasive intent. The individual was governed by a will superior even to the conscious will, and it was this higher will to which literature successfully appealed. Jellicorse's essay is valuable not only in enabling Whitman to be seen in a new and more appropriate light but also in revealing the underlying movement in American rhetorical theory during the antebellum years.

Those same years witnessed a profusion of social movements, born of the perfectionist impulse of the Second Great Awakening. In his essays on movements, Griffin repeatedly emphasized the rhetorical dialectic between movement and countermovement. Those challenged by a movement have options regarding how to respond, and the choices they make help to establish the future direction of the movement itself. David Zarefsky and Ann E. Burnette examine the responses made by Stephen Douglas and Abraham Lincoln to the antislavery movement in Illinois and the nation during the 1850s. Their essay illustrates the use of textual analysis in movement studies. Two "snapshots" are taken, in 1854 and 1858, and two pairs of speeches are compared, to trace the movement in Lincoln's antislavery argument and the constancy of Douglas's response to the antislavery movement. This essay also makes use of the concept of "rhetorical trajectory," which Griffin articulated in his later analysis of the assassination of President Kennedy.

Lee Griffin was one of the first scholars to adapt the writings of Kenneth Burke to the discipline of rhetorical criticism. In an essay published in 1969 he applied Burke's theory of dramatism to the rhetoric of social movement. His seminars in the new rhetoric were, in large part, seminars in the work of Kenneth Burke. He maintained an active correspondence with Burke and on several occasions invited him to the Northwestern University campus for public lectures and meetings with Lee's seminar. One of the assignments in his class on rhetorical criticism was to use Burkean methods in the analysis of a speech text. In this volume, Thomas F. Mader, one of Griffin's many students whose dissertation was influenced by Burke, explicates Lincoln's Gettysburg Address by subjecting it to a Burkean interpretation. Because the method of dramatism emphasizes symbolic action within the text, it is particularly appropriate for revealing rhetorical movement.

Although Griffin's work on movements focused on the social and historical, since the 1970s critics have increasingly recognized that "movement" is a prototype for longitudinal studies of rhetorical action, whether in the form of campaigns, issue management, the history of ideas in use, diffusion studies, or "spin control." Recognizable stages, opportunities, constraints, and choices characterize any effort to persuade over time. In recent years the concept of knowledge itself has been rendered contingent and shown to be the product of social and rhetorical forces. It is not surprising, therefore, that movement studies have examined intellectual trends as well as the social and political. Reflecting this emphasis, Thomas B. Farrell explores the rhetoric of aesthetic movements by examining a sample of artistic manifestos. Farrell is a colleague of Lee Griffin's at Northwestern and shares with him many teaching interests in rhetorical theory and criticism.

The final two essays in this collection are not explicitly tied to the work of Lee Griffin, but they do illustrate a characteristic of his work: encompassing new objects of study and developing methods appropriate to the material. Just as Griffin went beyond the single text to the social movement and beyond traditional analysis to dramatism, so these essays break new ground. In the penultimate study, D. Ray Heisey develops international comparisons in the justifications for military intervention. His specific concern is with narrative and metaphor, but he illustrates both the potential for generic study of war rhetoric and the power gained by subjecting a theory to international comparisons so that it might transcend a particular political culture.

Sonja K. Foss comes to grips with a significant change that has occurred in the rhetorical culture in recent years: increasingly it is visual, not verbal. We know that we are influenced by visual images, but our ability to examine depiction as rhetoric is limited by the absence of usable category systems and methods. Foss responds to this need by offering a framework for examining visual images as persuasion, and through specific case studies she suggests how it might be used.

Taken together, these essays illustrate both the topics and methods that engaged Lee Griffin's attention and the scope and reach of his own interests. From classical rhetoric to contemporary culture, he found wisdom and insight in the phenomenon of human communication. His teaching enriched the lives of generations of Northwestern University students, and his example and inspiration launched many of his graduate students on academic careers. We rejoice in the significance of his career, and we dedicate this book in his honor.

Leland M. Griffin: In Appreciation

Charles J. G. Griffin

Leland M. Griffin was born on April 9, 1920, in Kansas City, Kansas. He was the second of Herbert and Cliffe (Connell) Griffin's three children and the couple's eldest son. In 1924 his parents purchased a home across the river on Victor Street in Kansas City, Missouri. The new house was close to a public library and all three children became regular visitors there. History and imaginative literature were Leland's early preferences, interests no doubt spurred on by the stories told by his grandfather, a Civil War veteran who had come west to homestead after service at Gettysburg and Antietam. An active boy, Leland played trombone, acted in school plays, won a gold medal for poetry, and was elected President of the Emerson Literary Society. In later youth he became an Eagle Scout and in his senior year was chosen editor of his high school newspaper.

In 1937 Griffin graduated from Kansas City's Central High School. He wanted to write professionally and hoped to attend the University of Missouri's School of Journalism in Columbia. But these were Depression years, and expenses at the university (then about $225 per year, including tuition, books, and room and board) posed a substantial barrier to a young man of modest means. So he remained in Kansas City two more years, attending junior college and working to earn the funds necessary to complete his education at the university.

Griffin entered the University of Missouri as a junior in the fall of 1939, but rather quickly became disillusioned with the pace and apparent transience of journalistic writing. He began to look for some other area in which to concentrate his studies. In junior college Griffin had enjoyed a public speaking course under Delyte Morris, who later became president of Southern Illinois University. The memory of that

1

experience prompted him to enroll in a speech criticism class being offered that term through the English Department at Missouri. The instructor, Wilbur Gilman, who had studied under James Winans and Herbert Wichelns at Cornell, was one of a small group of scholars—including Bower Aly, Lee S. Hultzén, and Donovan Rhynsburger—working to establish Speech as an academic discipline at the university. That Griffin at once found a home with this group should not be surprising. In the study of oratory he could combine his interests in history and literature and could research and write under conditions that allowed time for reflection. He became an English/Speech major and even acted in several of Rhynsburger's theatrical productions, including *Missouri Legend* and *Bachelor Beware.* In the latter he co-starred with Dorothy Marion Schlotzhauer, a fellow English/Speech major from Columbia.

Griffin completed his bachelor's degree in 1941 and began that autumn to work on a master's degree in the newly recognized Department of Speech and Dramatic Arts. When the United States entered World War II a short time later, Griffin enlisted in the U.S. Naval Reserve. However, he was permitted to return to his studies until space could be found for him in one of the naval training programs being hastily organized in the aftermath of Pearl Harbor. The delay was of such length that he was able to complete his degree program. Aly directed his thesis, a period study entitled "Public Speaking in Missouri: 1892." Griffin was called to active duty late in 1942. He and Dorothy Schlotzhauer were married on July 4 of the following year. Like many other young couples, the Griffins moved around considerably during the war years: from Olathe, Kansas, to Boston; from Hollywood, Florida, to Twenty-Nine Palms, California. Griffin's last duty station was that of Communications Officer aboard the USS *Loumen* (AKA-30). He was discharged in 1946 at the rank of LT(jg).

Following the war, Griffin taught briefly at the University of Missouri, during which time he became acquainted with Loren Reid, who had joined the faculty during the war. Then in 1947, with Gilman's encouragement, Griffin was off to Cornell to begin work on a doctorate. While there he studied with Herbert Wichelns, Carroll Arnold, and C. K. Thomas in Speech and with Henry Meyers in American Literature. Wichelns, whose pioneering essay "The Literary Criticism of Oratory" (1925) had mapped the route taken by a generation of rhetorical critics, made a particularly strong impression on Griffin. Indeed it was

Wichelns, his advisor, who first suggested that Griffin try his hand at a movement study for a dissertation. Under Wichelns's direction Griffin completed one of the first extended studies in rhetorical movement, "The Rhetorical Structure of the Anti-Masonic Movement," in 1950.

After earning his Ph.D. at Cornell, Griffin went to work for Donald Bryant at Washington University in St. Louis. In 1954 he left Washington University to become Associate Professor and Chairman of the Department of Speech at Boston University. Two years later he joined the faculty of the Department of Public Address (now Communication Studies) at Northwestern University as Associate Professor. He remained at Northwestern until his retirement in 1989, becoming Professor in 1964 and serving conjointly (1958–68) as Professor of Speech at Garrett Theological Seminary in Evanston. The Griffins have three children, all graduates of Northwestern. Dorothy M. Griffin taught for twenty-one years in the English Department at Evanston Township High School before her retirement in 1985. She died in December 1991, following a lengthy battle with cancer.

Professor Griffin's interest in the study of rhetorical movement, which began under Wichelns at Cornell, has continued throughout his years at Northwestern. Following his mentor, he has observed the principle of *Multum, non multa.* The body of his scholarship, while not large, has been distinguished by its imagination, elegance, and influence upon the development of movement studies within the discipline of Speech. From "The Rhetoric of Historical Movements" (1952), which first set forth a theoretical and methodological program for the study of rhetorical movement, through "A Dramatistic Theory of the Rhetoric of Movements" (1969), which grounded movement criticism in the fertile soil of Burkean dramatism, to "Rhetorical Trajectories in the Assassination of President Kennedy" (1984), which explored the powerful consequences that even "imaginary movements" might have, Griffin's work has established much of the basic vocabulary of movement criticism during its first four decades.

At Northwestern Griffin taught primarily in the areas of rhetorical theory and criticism. It was his custom over the years to meet graduate students in his office at 302 Dennis Hall, or, more recently, 1815 Chicago Avenue. Former students will doubtlessly recall his habit of reaching for one of the volumes that line his office walls so that Cicero or DeQuincey might be brought into the hour's conversation. Or how, at other times, he might illuminate an obscure Burkean precept by using it to examine a story in the morning newspaper. Professor Griffin's insight, patience, and gentle humor have been an example and a source of encouragement to many young scholars over the years. While at Northwestern he directed nearly forty doctoral dissertations as well as numerous master's theses.

In the area of professional service, Griffin has thrice served as Associate Editor for the *Quarterly Journal of Speech,* has been both Associate and Consulting Editor for the *Central States Speech Journal,* and was an Associate Editor for the SCA Bicentennial Monograph Series. He has served on the Board of Directors of the Rhetoric Society of America, on selection committees for the Winans/Wichelns and SCA Dissertation Awards, and as a Trustee of the Karl R. Wallace Memorial Award. Over the years, he has chaired or participated on more than two dozen convention programs.

In recognition of his accomplishments as a scholar and teacher, Griffin was awarded the Citation of Merit by the College of Arts and Sciences Alumni Association of the University of Missouri in 1971. In 1982 he was chosen as the first Van Zelst Research Professor of Communication at Northwestern University. The Van Zelst Professorship is awarded annually to both recognize and support significant research in the field of communication studies. Griffin is a member of Phi Kappa Phi, is listed in the *Directory of American Scholars,* and appears in both *Who's Who in America* and *Who's Who in the World.*

Shakespeare, whom Professor Griffin is fond of quoting, once observed that through the poet's pen, "imagination bodies forth the forms of things unknown." In forty years of distinguished scholarship, Griffin's pen has done more than any other to give form and impetus to the study of rhetorical movement. His colleagues, students, and many friends express the hope that he will continue to wield it as creatively in the years to come.

♦   ♦   ♦

THE BEGINNINGS OF GREEK RHETORICAL THEORY

Edward Schiappa

In this essay, the "beginnings of Greek rhetorical theory" refers to the intellectual step of conceptualizing or theorizing about the instrumental use of language. "Self-conscious" rhetoric, understood by George A. Kennedy as oratory embodying conventional expectations of specific "topics, formulae or patterns of discourse," is part of all known cultures and can be traced back as far as 900 B.C.[1] However, not all societies develop "meta-rhetorics"—recognizable conceptual systems or theories of rhetoric. The standard account of the fifth-century B.C. origins of rhetorical theory is the subject of this study.

By "standard account" I mean the historical description of the origins of rhetorical theory that is found in the most prevalent sources on the subject. For the purposes of this study it is fortunate that, with rare exceptions, the reliability of the standard account is not contested in the scholarly literature of classics, philology, or communication studies.[2] A recent study reports that Kennedy's *Classical Rhetoric and Its Christian and Secular Tradition from Ancient to Modern Times* is the most commonly used secondary source in graduate courses on classical rhetorical theory.[3] Combined with his earlier work, *The Art of Persuasion in Greece,* Kennedy's texts have become the standard reference works on early Greek rhetoric for classical scholarship and pedagogy; other standard reference works differ only marginally. Accordingly, my analysis of the standard account focuses primarily on Kennedy's texts.

The basic elements of the standard account are as follows: The overthrow of tyranny in Sicily around 467 B.C. and the resulting establishment of a democracy created a sudden demand for the teaching of rhetoric for citizens' use in the law courts and in the assembly. Two Sicilians, Corax and Tisias, responded to this demand by "inventing"

5

rhetorical theory through the introduction of the first written *Art of Rhetoric*. The primary theoretical contributions of Corax and Tisias were the identification of the parts of forensic speeches and the theory of the "argument from probability." By the end of the fifth century B.C., written technical handbooks known as *technai* were commonly available for people wishing to learn the art of rhetoric. About the same time, a competing approach to the teaching of rhetoric appeared through the teaching practices of the older Sophists—Protagoras, Gorgias, Hippias, and Prodicus—whereby students learned rhetoric primarily through imitating exemplary speeches. The Sophists earned substantial amounts of money as itinerant orators and teachers of rhetoric. However, because their teaching was theoretically modest and philosophically relativistic, and because they emphasized political success above all else, the Sophists motivated Plato and Aristotle to develop more philosophical treatments of rhetoric. Accordingly, three traditions of rhetorical theory are identifiable in the fifth and fourth centuries B.C.: technical, sophistic, and philosophical.

Despite the popularity of the standard account, I believe it is fundamentally flawed on virtually every point. This essay represents part of an ongoing reevaluation and reconstruction of the standard account of early Greek rhetorical theory. Specifically, this essay develops three arguments: (1) There are methodological reasons for reconsidering the beginnings of Greek rhetorical theory. (2) There are textual or substantive reasons for questioning the standard account of the invention of rhetoric by Corax and Tisias—specifically, Kennedy's division of Greek rhetorical theory into technical, sophistic, and philosophical schools is argued to be an inappropriate and misleading schematization, at least with respect to Greece in the fifth century B.C. (3) The beginnings of Greek rhetorical theory are best identified with the sophistic movement of the fifth century B.C. Though the key conceptual term in sophistic theorizing was *logos*, rather than *rhētorikē*, the contributions of Sophists such as Protagoras and Gorgias nonetheless can be recognized as philosophical theories that also represent incipient rhetorical theories.

Taken together, these arguments are intended to suggest nothing less than a new direction for the historical study of early Greek rhetorical theory. By taking the changing technical vocabulary of fifth- and fourth-century thinkers seriously, the resulting picture of the development of rhetorical theory will vary considerably from the standard account. To demonstrate the importance of distinguishing between early theories of *logos* and *rhētorikē*, this essay includes a case against the standard account as well as an initial case for an alternative approach through the examples of Protagoras and Gorgias.

METHODOLOGICAL REASONS FOR RENEWED STUDY

Robert J. Connors's provocative claim that "any scholar who professes to understand classical rhetoric *must* come to terms with [Eric] Havelock's ideas" is based on the belief that Havelock's orality-literacy thesis calls for a dramatic paradigm shift in the interpretation of ancient Greek texts.[4] Prior to about 750 B.C., reading and writing were largely unknown to most Greeks; cultural knowledge and tradition were passed on orally. Language in such a culture must meet the needs of memory, since it is only through repetition and memorization that one generation can pass on to the next what has been learned. The vocabulary of a purely oral culture is, as a result, relatively limited compared to literate cultures. Additionally, the needs of memory affect syntax and composition such that verse, song, and story are the best vehicles to preserve the records of a non-book-oriented culture.

Havelock's thesis suggests that expression and thought differ significantly between oral and literate cultures: "In general the means of communication tends to condition the content of what is communicated."[5] With widespread literacy in Greece came greater freedom to think analytically because formal expression did not have to be crafted with memory as a primary constraint. As Walter Ong points out, "once a formulary expression has crystallized, it had best be kept intact. Without a writing system, breaking up thought—that is, analysis—is a high-risk procedure."[6] Writing facilitates the cognitive ability to objectify people, objects, and events in a way that divorces them from the context of human action. For example, the preliterate Greeks thought of "justice" not as an abstract principle but as a concrete practice involving specific experiences: acting-justly, receiving-justice, and so on.[7] By the time Plato wrote his dialogues, philosophers had advanced the Greek conceptual vocabulary and syntax sufficiently that inquiry could focus discretely on "the knower" and "the known."[8] Once justice became an object of analysis, questions involving intellectual practices such as defining ("What is justice?") were encouraged.[9]

Havelock's orality-literacy thesis is important for the study of early

Greek rhetoric. For example, certain stylistic changes in the surviving orations of the fifth and fourth centuries B.C. are more easily understood if the transition from orality to literacy is kept in mind. Connors's essay "Greek Rhetoric and the Transition from Orality" contends that the highly poetic style of the older Sophists is a reflection of the influence of orality.[10] If the Sophists' discourse seems highly stylized to the modern reader, it is because predominantly oral modes of thinking and speaking are foreign to us. Connors concludes that there is a direct correspondence between the rise of literacy and the decline of the "grand style" of the older Sophists. The change in style has less to do with aesthetics than it has to do with changing syntax, word meanings, and modes of expression.

In addition to enhancing the study of Greek rhetorical practice, the orality-literacy thesis is also useful to the study of early theorizing. Noting that classicists tend to deny that theories or methods guide their research, Havelock argues that four unstated assumptions have influenced most classical scholarship: "Greek culture from the beginning was built on a habit of literacy; Greek prose discourse was commonly composed and read at least as early as the Archaic age; the Greek language is built up out of a set of interchangeable parts; Greek thought-forms give expression to a common fund of basic values and concepts."[11] All four assumptions, Havelock claims, either have been successfully refuted or are under serious question. As a result, most of the history of early Greek philosophy must be rewritten. (The importance of the four unstated assumptions for the study of early rhetorical theory is noted below.) Havelock's point is that the development of philosophical or theoretical thinking is related to the advent of widespread literacy, and that histories of such thinking that do not acknowledge the complex relationship between literacy and philosophical thought may make serious mistakes.

Many comprehensive histories of philosophy, ironically, tend to treat topics unhistorically. Richard Rorty, in an influential article on the historiography of philosophy, has described the genre of works surveying centuries of philosophical thought as "doxography." He complains that such historical accounts treat their topics as "given" or as conceptual constants. Rorty attributes such a tendency to a "natural attitude" on the part of philosophers toward the objects of their analysis: "The idea [is] that 'philosophy' is the name of a natural kind—the name of a discipline which, in all ages and places, has managed to dig down to the same deep, fundamental, questions."[12] The typical format of articles in *The Encyclopedia of Philosophy,* for example, is to compare and contrast different philosophers' approaches, treatments, or theories of "X"—where "X" may be "truth," "ethics," or "justice." Each philosopher is assumed to be addressing the same issue and could, in theory, sit down and compare views of "X" with philosophers of other cultures and ages. As Havelock points out in a critique that parallels Rorty's, such an approach understates important differences between cultures and potentially ignores the role of particular historical contexts. For Havelock, the most significant aspect of the early Greek context is the development of new forms of expression and patterns of reasoning. Anachronistic interjection of a later-developed vocabulary "subtly distorts the story of early Greek thought by presenting it as an intellectual game dealing with problems already given and present to the mind, rather than as a groping after a new language in which the existence of such problems will slowly emerge, as language emancipates itself from the oral-poetic tradition."[13]

Accordingly, historical accounts of early Greek theorizing should focus on the evolution of the conceptual vocabulary and syntax and the related emergence of certain theoretical-philosophical issues. In two provocative studies Havelock has deconstructed the standard accounts of rival pre-Socratic "schools" of philosophical thought.[14] By carefully examining the fragments representing the authentic *ipsissima verba* (original words) of the pre-Socratic philosophers, Havelock documents example after example of long-standing misrepresentations. The major source of distortion is the habit of historians and philosophers to take Aristotle's and Theophrastus's accounts of their predecessors as historically accurate. Once compared to the *ipsissima verba,* the evidence is clear that later doctrines have consistently been read back into earlier thinkers' statements. Certain so-called pre-Socratic schools of thought dissolve under careful scrutiny. Havelock concludes that "much of the story of early Greek philosophy so-called is a story not of *systems of thought* but of a search for a primary language in which any *system* could be expressed."[15]

I believe that many previous studies of early Greek rhetorical theory also have operated under assumptions that the orality-literacy thesis calls into question. The first two assumptions identified by Havelock— that literacy and prose writing were common throughout Greek culture—underlie many claims about the written *technai* of the fifth century B.C. The last two assumptions—concerning the constancy of Greek word meanings and thought patterns—have led to innumerable treatments of Greek history that treat rhetoric as a relatively unproblematic "given." For example, Kennedy's most recent account of Greek rhetorical theory identified three traditions: technical, sophistic, and philosophical.[16] These three "views of rhetoric" are "continuing strands" in the long tradition of rhetoric that stretches "throughout the history of western Europe." Kennedy's treatment of rhetorical theory sometimes parallels the "multiple views of X" approach to philosophy discussed previously. Though much of Kennedy's work is historical and particularistic, if applied too strictly his tripartite schematization is unhistorical and leads to a distorted picture of what transpired in fifth- and fourth-century B.C. Greece. It is my contention that rhetorical theory emerged and evolved during the fifth and fourth centuries in a manner somewhat different from what is traditionally understood.

A fact undercutting any nonevolutionary approach to early Greek rhetorical theory is that the term *rhētorikē* was not coined until the early fourth century B.C.[17] In fact, there were no Greek words or expressions precisely equivalent to the terms "rhetoric" or "art of rhetoric" until the fourth century B.C. The words used during the fifth century B.C. by the older Sophists to describe speech were *logos* and *legein*. The meanings associated with *logos* and *legein* are such that one cannot argue they mean the same thing as was later conveyed by "rhetoric." Accordingly, any thorough historical account of the early development of what is now called rhetorical theory must address the fact that there was a progression from *logos* to *rhētorikē* that took place over a period exceeding a century.

One may well ask, "What difference does it make if the key term was *logos* or *rhētorikē*?" The absence of a word for gravity in prehistoric time, as one critic has observed, does not mean that in prehistoric time such a force did not exist. Thus one could object that the late appearance of *rhētorikē* means little. Nevertheless, I believe that the late appearance of the term must be dealt with in any serious historical account of early rhetorical theory. As intellectual disciplines evolve, so do their conceptual vocabularies. Accordingly, any serious historical description of early Greek rhetorical theory must acknowledge the role of a changing theoretical vocabulary.

An analogy from the history of science can help clarify the significance of an evolving conceptual vocabulary from the standpoint of historical reconstruction. Late in the eighteenth century, the phlogiston theory of combustion was gradually replaced by a new approach to chemistry that included the concept of oxygen. What to us is "oxygen" was to phlogiston theorists "dephlogisticated air." Did oxygen exist prior to the word's coining? Common sense and (some) current metaphysical pieties dictate an affirmative reponse. Indeed, from the standpoint of modern chemists, it does no harm to rationally reconstruct phlogiston theory using the concepts of modern chemical theory in order to understand what the phlogiston scientists were really doing. A mischievous chemist could even call modern oxygen theory "Neophlogiston theory." However, the transition from "phlogiston" to "dephlogisticated air" to "oxygen" is precisely what commands the attention of the historian of chemistry. Phlogiston theory cannot be understood in a historically defensible manner by reducing it to an unrefined theory that (implicitly) included oxygen. Put differently, one cannot fully understand or appreciate the theoretical evolution of chemistry that took place in the late eighteenth century by superimposing a later-developed conceptual vocabulary. From the standpoint of the historian, there are three different topics worthy of study: phlogiston theory in its own right as representative of eighteenth-century science, modern chemical theory in its infancy at the turn of the nineteenth century, and the revolutionary transition of 1772–78 during which oxygen was discovered and phlogiston theory was gradually discredited. As Thomas S. Kuhn puts it, intellectual discoveries typically have three stages: a "prehistory" during which the perception of anomaly grows, a period that Kuhn calls the "proper internal history" of the discovery, and a "posthistory" of assimilation and normalization of the discovery.[18]

With respect to the "discovery" of rhetoric as a conceptualized art, I believe that there are three different topics worthy of study by the historian of early Greek rhetorical theory. (1) In the fifth century B.C., *logos* was the key conceptual term of the older Sophists. Representative texts of this period include the fragments and surviving speeches of the older Sophists and the book now called *Dissoi Logoi*. (2) By the first half of the fourth century B.C., *logos* had been replaced by *logōn technē*, which was sometimes described by Plato as *rhētorikē*. Isocrates' works (which never use the word *rhētorikē*), Plato's dialogues, and the *Rhetoric to Alexander* (which never uses the word *rhētorikē*) best exemplify this transitional stage of theorizing. (3) By the late fourth century B.C. the split between rhetoric and philosophy was more or less successfully reified both conceptually and terminologically in the works of Aristotle and his students.

Each of these periods deserves study in its own right. It is my position that considerable previous scholarship has misunderstood or misrepresented fifth-century thinking by using the later-developed word *rhētorikē* to interpret the texts and fragments of and about the period. Once the methodological necessity of reassessing the standard account of fifth-century Greek rhetorical theory is acknowledged, solid textual or substantive grounds for reconstructing the account become apparent, as the following sections of this essay illustrate.

KENNEDY'S "TECHNICAL RHETORIC" REVISITED

Kennedy's chronicle of fifth-century B.C. technical rhetoric can be distilled into three claims: (1) Technical rhetoric originates with the *technē* of Corax and Tisias of Sicily around 467 B.C. (2) The primary theoretical contributions of Corax and Tisias were the identification of the parts of forensic speeches and the theory of the argument from probability. (3) By the end of the fifth century B.C., people could turn to written technical handbooks to learn rhetoric. There are good reasons to question all three claims.

The story that credits Corax with the invention of rhetoric is widely accepted by historians of early rhetoric. Kennedy's version of the story is as follows:

> In Syracuse in Sicily . . . democracy on the Athenian pattern was introduced suddenly in 467 B.C. Citizens found themselves involved in litigation over the ownership of property or other matters and forced to take up their own cases before the courts. Nowhere in Greece did the profession of lawyer, advocate, or patron at the bar exist. Need to speak in the democratic Syracusan assembly was less pressing, but opportunities for political leadership came to involve the skill of public speaking in a way not previously evident. A few clever Sicilians developed simple techniques (Greek *technē* means "art") for effective presentation and argumentation in the law courts and taught these to others for a price.[19]

Modern scholarship tends to regard the story of Corax and Tisias inventing the art of rhetoric as doubtful only with regard to details.

Standard reference works and textbooks by D. A. G. Hinks, D. L. Clark, George A. Kennedy, Donald C. Bryant, W. K. C. Guthrie, and James J. Murphy all accept the essential validity of the Corax and Tisias legend.[20] Nevertheless, another look at the evidence is warranted.

To begin with, whatever Corax and Tisias may have taught was not under the rubric of *rhētorikē*. Most accounts agree on an early fifth-century (467/66 B.C.) date for Corax's teaching.[21] Yet the earliest recorded use of the word *rhētōr* is in a decree dated sometime during 446/45–442/41, and the earliest surviving use of the word *rhētorikē* is from Plato's *Gorgias*, dated around 385 B.C.[22] If Corax or Tisias had used the word *rhētorikē* as early as 467, surely it would have surfaced again prior to the fourth century B.C.

If Corax and Tisias did not literally invent *rhētorikē*, then what was the nature of their theoretical innovation? Unfortunately, a survey of the available ancient evidence demonstrates that most accounts are notoriously derivative.

The earliest extant reference to Corax or Tisias is in Plato's *Phaedrus*, published sometime around 365 B.C. The first reference in the text appears in a section in which Socrates is summarizing the contributions of books on rhetoric: "Shall we leave Gorgias and Tisias undisturbed, who saw that probabilities [*ta eikota*] are more to be esteemed than truths, who make small things seem great and great things small by the power of their words, and new things old and old things the reverse, and who invented conciseness of speech and measureless length on all subjects?"[23] As history the foregoing passage is highly suspect, having little in common with the authenticated teachings of Gorgias and attributing far more to Tisias than is plausible.[24] The only reference to a doctrine of Tisias that is repeated by any other source is that of "probabilities," which is treated in more depth a little later in the same dialogue. Socrates says that Tisias considers probability (*to eikos*) to mean "that which most people believe" (273b1). Tisias's "clever discovery of [this] technique" (273b3) is said to lead to the position that what is more believable is more valued by rhetors than what is true—a position Plato critiques at length.

Does the concept of "probabilities" represent an authentic contribution to rhetorical theory by Corax or Tisias? It is difficult to consider Plato's testimony in the *Phaedrus* as firm evidence that such was the case. Plato makes no mention of Corax at all, and soon after his mention of Tisias's "discovery" he hints that "Tisias" may be a pseudonym: "a wonderfully hidden art it seems to be which Tisias has brought to light, or some other, whoever he may be and whatever country he is proud to call his own!"[25] Pseudo-Tisias's "discovery" is described as part of a *logōn technē* (266d6)—an expression found in the fourth century B.C. but not in the fifth. The passage (267a6–b2) that first mentions Tisias is, in fact, a direct reference to Isocrates' claim that speech can "represent the great as lowly or invest the little with grandeur, to recount the things of old in a new manner or set forth events of recent date in an old fashion."[26] Could the object of Plato's attack on appeals to *eikos* have been Isocrates' teachings? Probably so, since in the *Helen* in the midst of an attack on rival "useless" philosophers—including, it is now generally agreed, Plato—Isocrates makes the explicit claim that "likely conjecture [*epi-eikos doxazein*] about useful things is far preferable to exact knowledge [*epistasthai*] of the useless" (¶5). This and other passages give us reason to believe that the targets of Plato's arguments against *eikos* are Isocrates and other fourth-century rivals, not long-dead teachers.[27] Plato's attack on the position that what is more believable is more valuable to rhetors than what is true need not have been against any particular doctrine or theory. The attack simply represented another level of criticism Plato had for any philosophy that sacrificed truth for expediency. No doubt to Plato Isocrates convicted himself of promoting what was "likely" to the crowds over "truth": "It is evident that those who desire to command the attention of their hearers must abstain from admonition and advice and must say the kinds of things which they see are most pleasing to the crowd" (*To Nicocles* ¶49).

The somewhat specialized sense of "argument from probability" described by Plato is different than the sense of *eikos* found in fifth-century B.C. sources. In Herodotus, Thucydides, Aeschylus, and Sophocles, for example, *eikos* means "likely," "fitting," "meet," "right," or "reasonable."[28] The technical conceptualization of the term, signaled by the neuter singular construction (*to eikos*), cannot be found prior to Plato's writings.[29] Even in Antiphon's *Tetralogies,* in which arguments over what is likely or probable play a central role, one does not find *eikos* used in the way attributed to Corax or Tisias by Plato. Furthermore, the notion that Tisias favored probability over facts is obviously a Platonic invention, since prior to Plato's dialogues there is no evidence of this particular epistemological or logical dichotomy. The earliest clear use of the concept of "argument from probability" outside of Plato and Aristotle postdates their writings.[30]

The final reason to doubt the historical accuracy of Plato's account is his implicit claim that Tisias's discovery is found in a book (*Phaedrus* 226d6). Yet the earliest surviving prose text is that of Herodotus, who wrote in the last third of the fifth century B.C.[31] Again, Plato's description seems to fit fourth-century writings such as the *Rhetoric to Alexander* better than anything known from the fifth century. In sum, nothing found in Plato can be used as a reliable indication of the contributions of Corax or Tisias.

The most commonly cited authority for the story that Corax and Tisias invented rhetoric as an art is Aristotle's *Synagōgē*, indirectly referred to by Cicero and Quintilian. Before considering the testimony of Cicero and Quintilian, Aristotle's surviving references to the Corax and Tisias story must be considered.

There are two extant references by Aristotle to Corax and Tisias. The first is in the *Rhetoric* in a section describing the fallacious use of argument from probability:

> The *Art* of Corax is made up of this topic; for example, if a weak man were charged with assault, he should be acquitted as not being a likely suspect for the charge; for it is not probable [that a weak man would attack another]. And if he is a likely suspect, for example, if he is strong, [he should also be acquitted]; for it is not likely [that he would start the fight] for the very reason that it was going to seem probable. And similarly in other cases; for necessarily, a person is either a likely suspect or not a likely suspect for a charge. Both alternatives seem probable, but one really is probable, the other so not generally, only in the circumstances mentioned. And this is "to make the weaker [seem] the better cause." Thus, people were rightly angry at the declaration of Protagoras; for it is a lie and not true but a fallacious probability and a part of no art except rhetoric and eristic.[32]

It is difficult to ascertain how much history can be reliably taken from this passage. As mentioned previously, the odds of Corax having published a book constituting a *technē* are slim. Unlike Plato, Aristotle does not attribute a book to Corax, only a *technē*. It is possible that what is referred to here is not a book but a set of precepts or examples passed down orally.[33] The likelihood is increased by the fact that the strong man versus weak man example was common during the fourth century B.C. and is the sort of easily remembered lesson an oral tradition of teaching would produce. There are peculiarities in the attribution, however, that require consideration.

To begin with, it is strange that Corax is never mentioned by Plato or any other fifth- or fourth-century writers. In an insightful treatment of Aristotle's and his student Theophrastus's historical summaries of pre-Socratic philosophers, Havelock has noted that figures we now take for granted, such as Anaximander and Anaximenes, had never been mentioned previous to Aristotle.[34] Havelock's point is not that such people did not exist, but that Aristotle and Theophrastus demonstrate a penchant for rewriting history, a criticism already thoroughly documented by Harold Cherniss.[35] Aristotle consistently sought to identify his predecessors on each subject he wrote about and to contrast his philosophical system as superior or at least more complete. Havelock suggests that Aristotle sometimes invented anticipations of his own philosophy by stretching what was known about his predecessors. Is it possible that the attribution of a theory of *eikos* to Corax is an instance of such stretching? There are two reasons for suggesting that it might be. First, Corax is linked to Tisias in a lost writing of Aristotle mentioned by Cicero (*Brutus* ¶46). It is likely that the reference to Tisias is taken from Aristotle's teacher, Plato. Unfortunately, as shown above, Plato's historical picture of Tisias is probably apocryphal. If Aristotle's description of Corax is based on the assumed commonality of doctrine between Corax and Tisias, and if there is reason to doubt the ascription of a theoretical doctrine of *eikos* to Tisias, then there is cause to suspect that Aristotle's use of Corax parallels his unhistorical treatment of other pre-Socratics. The second reason to harbor such a suspicion is the same passage's treatment of Protagoras. After describing the spurious appeal to probability, Aristotle claims it is what Protagoras meant by making the weaker *logos* the stronger. However, such a rendering is clearly false. Protagoras's weaker/stronger statement is best understood as companion to his two-*logoi* thesis. Influenced by Heraclitus's "unity of opposites" thesis, Protagoras claimed that concerning every "thing" (*pragmata*, also "event") there are two *logoi* in opposition. The same thing can be experienced in opposite ways: the same food can taste sweet to one person and sour to another, the same wind can feel cool to one person and warm to another, and the same law can appear just to one person and unjust to another. What Protagoras meant by making one *logos* stronger than its opposite was the substitution of a preferred (but weaker) *logos* for a less preferable (but temporarily dominant) logos of the same experience.[36] As noted by Classen, Aristotle's descriptions of sophistic doctrines were always in contrast with his own systems, which Aristotle presents as superior (in modern terms) epistemologically, ontologically, and ethically.[37] Aristotle's treatment of Protagoras in the present case is historically implausible and typifies the kind of distortion cited by Cherniss and Havelock.

The careful development of logical theory, including the categorization (based on epistemological criteria) of genuine and spurious arguments from probability, originated certainly no sooner than Aristotle. It is highly probable, therefore, that Aristotle's description of Corax's *technē* is at least anachronistic. It is plausible that the reference to a theory of *eikos* is based on no more than an orally transmitted anecdote concerning the strong man versus weak man defense. It is even possible, as is suggested below, that the entire Corax and Tisias story is a convenient myth.

The other extant reference to Corax and Tisias by Aristotle is found in a famous passage concluding *Sophistical Refutations*. Noting that his current study might be seen as less than adequate, Aristotle points out that some discoveries are older than others, so it is natural that some arts are more developed than others:

> This is in fact what has happened in regard to rhetorical speeches [*rhētorikous logous*] and to practically all the other arts; for those who discovered the beginnings of them advanced them in all only a little way, whereas the celebrities of today are the heirs (so to speak) of a long succession of men who have advanced them bit by bit, and so have developed them to their present form; *Tisias after the first* [contributors] [*Teisias men meta tous prōtous*], Thrasymachus after Tisias, Theodorus then after them, while several people have made their several contributions to it. Therefore it is not to be wondered at that the art has attained considerable dimensions.[38]

The passage demonstrates Aristotle's interest in creating a lineage for contemporary rhetorical teaching. His effort here parallels his efforts in physics and metaphysics to establish a direct line of successors that begins with "first philosophers" and ends with his own grand synthesis. An additional motivation for this particular bit of history is admitted by Aristotle: he has had less time to develop the particular art he is writing about than those who currently teach rhetoric. In fact, the passage continues by attacking the recitation methods of current teachers of "contentious arguments." Accordingly, once again it is likely that Aristotle is writing less as an historian than as an advocate for a current school of thought. The people Aristotle mentions may have made contributions to what would later be called the art of rhetoric. The evidence concerning Thrasymachus and Theodorus is scanty but suggestive.[39] What the contributions of Tisias and the first contributors may have been, unfortunately, remains an open question.

Cicero twice makes mention of the invention of rhetoric by Sicilians. The first mention is in *On Invention,* in which he states that "Aristotle collected the early books on rhetoric, even going back as far as Tisias, well known as the originator and inventor of the art."[40] Cicero wrote *On Invention* in his youth, and it may consist primarily of notes from lectures he attended.[41] Accordingly, it is difficult to know if Cicero had read the *Synagōgē* himself at this point or if the information was derived from a teacher's reading of Plato's *Phaedrus.* The reference in *On Invention* certainly does not provide the information necessary to make an assessment of the historical Tisias's contribution to rhetorical theory.

Cicero's other mention of the invention of rhetoric is in the *Brutus:* "Thus Aristotle says that in Sicily, after the expulsion of tyrants, when after a long interval restitution of private property was sought by legal means, Corax and Tisias the Sicilians, with the acuteness and controversial habit of their people, first put together some theoretical precepts; that before them, while many had taken pains to speak with care and with orderly arrangement, no one had followed a definite method or art" (¶46).

The story provides more detail than other references in Cicero and Quintilian and appears to be a more credible account. Unfortunately, the story may be an imaginative fiction by either Aristotle or Cicero. Commenting on Cicero's *Brutus* ¶46–48, A. E. Douglas claims that Aristotle's *Synagōgē* was "on the historical side highly tendentious."[42] Hypothesizing that the *Synagōgē* may have been written by one of Aristotle's students, Douglas suggests that it may reflect more concern for fourth-century controversies than with accurately portraying the early history of rhetoric.[43] Of course, even if Cicero is representing

Aristotle faithfully, the historical accuracy of Aristotle's account has been shown to be in doubt.

There is no guarantee that Cicero is representing Aristotle faithfully. As Kennedy notes, Cicero may have had a political agenda in mind in writing the *Brutus*. Cicero despairs of the current political situation and "it has even been plausibly suggested that one of Cicero's objectives was to incite Brutus to rid Rome of Caesar."[44] Cicero cites Aristotle's account in order to provide evidence for the claim found immediately before the Corax and Tisias story: "For the ambition to speak well does not arise when men are engaged in establishing government, nor occupied with the conduct of war, nor shackled and chained by the authority of kings" (¶45). Cicero's alterations of Aristotle's story, however, are probably minor. The more significant change may have been the substitution of a forensic setting for the birth of rhetoric rather than a deliberate one (as found in other versions), since in Cicero's time it was the courts that "were the arena for the structure and maintenance of Roman values" and hence "served as a forum for public articulation of political positions."[45]

Even if Cicero did not alter Aristotle's story in order to provide an analogy to his own political-rhetorical scene, it is entirely possible that Aristotle's version of events was motivated by the desire to make the same point that Cicero wanted to make: "Upon peace and tranquility eloquence attends as their ally, it is, one may say, the offspring of well-established civic order" (*Brutus* ¶45).

Quintilian's claim that Corax and Tisias were "the earliest writers of textbooks"[46] on rhetoric is apparently derived from Cicero, so it does not offer independent corroboration of the Corax and Tisias story. Furthermore, the claim that Corax or Tisias wrote a textbook is highly dubious, for reasons cited above.

The remaining ancient authorities who refer to Corax and Tisias have been preserved in the introductions to rhetoric and the prefaces to commentaries on Hermogenes, which were written after the third century A.D.[47] These are referred to as the *Prolegomena* and were collected in the 1830s in Christianus Walz's *Rhetores Graeci*, reedited by Hugo Rabe a century later.[48] The following representative passage narrates three origins of the art of rhetoric—one among the gods, one among heroes, and one among mortals:

> We must look into the following matters with regard
> to the third major point which needs investigating: how

rhetoric came to men. After the already mentioned
divine heroes, we are justified in demonstrating its in-
born rational nature. The Syracusans were accordingly
the first men to display it. Sicily . . . was ruled as a
tyranny by Gelon and Hieron, very savage tyrants, who
strengthened the force of their tyranny against the Syracusans to the point where the Syracusans rejected them
and escaped from this cruel slavery. It is said that the
tyrants indulged their savagery to the extent of forbid-
ding the Syracusans to utter any sound at all, but to
signify what was appropriate by means of their feet,
hands, and eyes whenever one of them was in need. It
was in this way, they say, that dance-pantomime had
its beginnings. Because the Syracusans had been cut
off from speech (*logos*), they contrived to explain their
business with gestures. Because, then the Syracusans
were ruled so harshly and savagely and because they
prayed to Zeus the deliverer to free them from this
cruel slavery, Zeus, acting as both savior and deliverer,
liberated the Syracusans from tyranny by destroying
the tyrants. Then, since the citizenry (*dēmos*) among
the Syracusans feared that they might in some way fall
upon a similar tyrant, they no longer entrusted their
government to a tyrant. The people (*dēmos*) themselves
wanted to have absolute control over all things.[49]

The preceding passage is from what is generally regarded as the
oldest and purest account of the Corax and Tisias legend.[50] It has been
conjectured that the passage was originally derived from the writings
of the fourth-century B.C. historian Timaeus, but the attribution is both
unlikely and uninformative.[51] It is uninformative because the highly
mythologized retelling of the fall of the Syracusan tyrants suggests that
any subsequent claims about a Syracusan invention of rhetoric must
be considered a historical legend. And it is unlikely because the extant
text is filled with historically impossible claims such as the one that
Corax defined rhetoric as *peithous demiourgos*—the producer of belief.
The practice of definition originates with Plato and cannot be documented in the fifth century B.C. Furthermore, as Hermann Mutschmann
argued decades ago, the definition of rhetoric as *peithous demiourgos*
first appeared in Plato's *Gorgias* (453a2) and "has nothing to do" with
Corax and Tisias.[52]

An additional passage from the *Prolegomena* preserves the legend that rhetoric originated from the disputes after the fall of the Syracusan tyranny:

> And thereupon, democracy came once again to the Syracusans. And this man Korax came to persuade the crowd and to be heard. . . . He observed how the people had produced an unsteady and disorderly state of affairs, and he thought that it was speech by which the course of human events was brought to order. He then contemplated turning the people toward and away from the proper course of action through speech. Coming into the assembly, where all the people had gathered together, he began first to appease the troublesome and turbulent element among them with obsequious and flattering words, and he called such things "introductions." After this, he began to soothe and silence the people and to speak as though telling a story, and after these things to summarize and call to mind concisely what had gone before and to bring before their eyes at a glance what had previously been said.[53]

The unreliability of the story is underscored by the fact that two traditions exist about the nature of Corax's teaching: one, represented by the above passage, suggests his teaching was geared for the assembly; another suggests it was used only in the law courts.[54] Interestingly, Corax is not described as teaching rhetoric or even *logos* (the word translated as "speech" above). His primary contribution is the introduction of names for parts of a speech, a contribution credited also to Theodorus and Protagoras.[55] Furthermore, the Sophist Antiphon is said by Hermogenes to be "the absolute inventor and originator of the political genre."[56]

Obviously it is impossible to ascertain who first codified the traditional terminology for the parts of a classical oration. The evidence concerning Corax and Tisias is notoriously inconsistent, describing as few as three and as many as seven parts of speech. Furthermore, it is possible that the whole legend is ideologically inspired and that Corax did no more or less than become a successful *rhētōr* (politician and speaker) after the fall of the tyranny. An alternative hypothesis concerning the different parts of speech is possible, one that would preserve the originality of Corax's contribution without making obviously anachronistic assumptions about the invention of rhetoric. It is possible that what is commonly referred to as the early sophistic rules for speaking before the law courts and the assembly were just that—regulations governing speaking procedure on par with the water clocks of the time. Such a possibility has been anticipated by Havelock, who has suggested that Plato's *Protagoras* and other fifth-century writings imply that the Sophists first promulgated norms for the conduct of political discourse.[57] Given that Protagoras was selected by Pericles to write the laws of the new colony of Thurii in 444 B.C., it is entirely possible that the early *technai* ascribed to Corax and the older Sophists were manuals for learning the speaking procedure of the courts and the assembly. The basic structuring of the parts of speech attributed to Corax and Tisias would have been useful for both the audience and the speaker as analytical and organizational guides. Such a possibility gains further credence when it is recalled that the court system in Greece evolved during roughly the same time as the older Sophists. Homicide courts may have an older history, but the popular law courts in which so many fortunes were won or lost flourished in the fifth century B.C. along with the older Sophists.[58]

What, then, can reasonably be taken from the various accounts of Corax and Tisias? At the very least, several traditional legends can be rejected. To begin with, whatever Corax and Tisias did was not under the rubric of rhetoric. A developed theory of *eikos* that contrasted the concept of probability over certain truth can also be ruled out as anachronistic. It is possible that the long-standing traditional link between *eikos* and Corax and Tisias is an error resulting from Plato's name games in the *Phaedrus*. The most that can be confidently ascribed to Corax and Tisias concerning *eikos* is an oral tradition of the usefulness of arguing what seems reasonable, as exemplified in the strong man versus weak man anecdote. It is impossible to ascertain what contributions Corax and Tisias may have made concerning the introduction of the parts of speech, but it is possible that Corax introduced a procedure for speaking before the newly created democracy that was later codified into a method or *technē*.

The various *technai* attributed to fifth-century Sophists are without authority. There may have been collections of speeches dubbed "manuals" of rhetoric in the fourth century B.C., but no fifth-century Sophist wrote a treatise on *rhētorikē* per se. Historically, no "Art of Rhetoric" is attributed to Protagoras, Hippias, Prodicus, or Critias. The "Arts" attributed to Gorgias, Thrasymachus, and Antiphon are probably the result of the publication of exemplary speeches. Kennedy asserts that "the existence of Aristotle's summary [the *Synagōgē Technōn*] seems to have rendered the survival of the original handbooks superfluous."[59] A more likely explanation is that there were no theoretical "Arts of Rhetoric" written in the fifth century B.C.

In short, there are reasons to doubt the applicability of Kennedy's category of technical rhetoric to the activities of the fifth century B.C., and in particular there are good reasons to challenge the standard origin myths concerning rhetorical theory. Accordingly, the search for the beginnings of Greek rhetorical theory must turn to fifth-century Athens and what is commonly known as the "sophistic movement."

"SOPHISTIC RHETORIC" RECONSIDERED

Kennedy characterizes sophistic rhetoric as the teaching of rhetoric through example and imitation.[60] In the genre of sophistic rhetoric, Kennedy places such fifth-century figures as Protagoras, Antiphon, and Gorgias as well as figures from the fourth century B.C. through the first century A.D. The method of imitation is considered morally neutral by Kennedy; it can be used for good or ill. In Kennedy's conceptualization, sophistic rhetoric is not as powerful as either technical or philosophical rhetoric.

Kennedy's treatment of fifth-century sophistic rhetoric is important to examine because it is clearly during the fifth century B.C. that theorizing about the practice of persuasive speaking has its beginnings. Though the term *rhētorikē* does not appear until the early fourth century B.C., its intellectual antecedents are readily identifiable in the fifth. Unfortunately, fourth-century notions of *rhētorikē* are all too often assumed to be equally present and active in the fifth century B.C., creating a category error that has seriously distorted our understanding of the early theorizing about *logos*. Specifically, most treatments of fifth-century theorizing make distinctions between philosophy and rhetoric that were not clearly drawn until the late fourth century B.C. and, as a result, underestimate (what would now be called) the philosophical content of sophistic theorizing.

Kennedy describes the Sophists as "self-appointed professors of how to succeed in the civic life of the Greek states." Though a few of the leading Sophists can "rightly be thought of as philosophers," most were "little more than teachers of devices of argument or emphasis."[61]

Kennedy's treatment of the older Sophists, like most (if not all) other standard accounts, is based upon the assumption that the teaching of rhetoric is the most fundamental defining characteristic of being a Sophist: "Sophistry was in large part a *product* of rhetoric, which was by far the older and in the end the more vital [art]."[62] The most obvious problem with such an assumption is that since the word *rhētorikē* was not coined until early in the fourth century B.C., the sense of such statements as "sophistry was in large part a product of rhetoric" must be clarified. All too often, Platonic or other pejorative senses of "rhetoric" are assumed, rather than proven, to describe aptly what the Sophists were about. The absence of a clear concept of *rhētorikē* or even *logōn technē* in the fifth century B.C. requires a careful reconsideration of what is asserted in statements defining or describing the Sophists with the term "rhetoric."

A few examples can illustrate the point. Douglas J. Stewart asserts that rhetoric was the "chief preoccupation of all sophists." "Prevailing opinion" is that the "real interests" of all Sophists were rhetorical and hence "their reported views and writings on special questions in science, history, or politics are normally taken as mere methodological devices and stances bound up with their prime goal of teaching their pupils cultural and political adroitness."[63] Stewart's position crudely prejudges the worth of sophistic teaching, and is based on the assumption that anything that resulted from the study of rhetoric (which he does not define) cannot be of real intellectual value. Not only is such a position grossly unfair to the subject of rhetoric, it is an unsound way to begin a study of an older Sophist.

Stewart is far from atypical. C. J. Classen, former president of the International Society for the History of Rhetoric, has made a similar statement regarding sophistic fragments about language: "The linguistic studies of the sophists were carried out not for *philosophical* reasons, not to examine the means by which a statement can be made, but for *rhetorical* purposes: to persuade people successfully, *even at the expense of truth*; and it was more or less *accidental* when some of these investigations produced philosophically important results."[64] Similarly, Kennedy asserts that in the tracts of Sophists such as Gorgias "the subject matter was apparently of only incidental importance—a fact which awakened the opposition of Socrates. The technique was the thing: the sophist is purely rhetorician."[65] Such statements go out of their way to deny the Sophists theoretical significance by attributing to them merely rhetorical motivations. Precisely what "rhetorical" means and how it applies to Sophists but not "real" philosophers is never explained. Or, sometimes those associated with rhetoric are simply assumed to be base. Bruce A. Kimball's recent book represents an example of this tendency: "The sophists thus attended more to devising persuasive techniques than to finding true arguments, and this amoralism exacerbated the disintegration of the ethical tradition and led to their condemnation."[66]

Space does not permit a comprehensive rehabilitation of the dominant view of the older Sophists. For a thorough treatment of how the Sophists have been misunderstood throughout much of history, the reader is directed to the works of G. B. Kerferd.[67] For the purposes of this essay I will simply assert the existence of a counterview that portrays the Sophists as quite different from what Plato described. According to the revised view, the Sophists were not fundamentally different from the persons now referred to as "philosophers."[68] From the standpoint of method of inquiry, subject matters pursued, and even specific doctrines espoused, what the pre-Socratic philosophers, Socrates, the Sophists, and Plato had in common "was of greater importance than what separated them."[69] All were philosophers in the sense that they all represented an intellectualist movement that broke from traditional modes of discourse and thinking. "If they were called 'philosophers,' it was not for their doctrines as such, but for the kind of vocabulary and syntax which they used and the unfamiliar psychic energies that they represented. Sophists, pre-Socratics, and Socrates had one fatal characteristic in common; they were trying to discover and to practise abstract thinking."[70]

The most significant difference between those the ancient sources call "Sophists" and those called "philosophers" seems to be the economic and social class with which each group is identified. As Martin Ostwald has documented in detail, most writers from the fifth and early fourth centuries B.C. were conservative members of the upper classes. Their writings display a remarkably consistent bias against Athenian democracy in general and against the middle class from which most democratic leaders came (after Pericles) in particular.[71] Accordingly, since the Sophists were often from middle classes (or, worse yet from an Athenian standpoint, foreigners) they are seldom treated kindly in the literature of their time. Regardless of the reasons for traditional biases against the Sophists, the important points are that the standard view of the Sophists is being radically revised and that part of that revision must include a reconsideration of what is meant by "sophistic rhetoric."

As mentioned previously, any thorough account of the early development of what is now called "rhetorical theory" must address the fact that there was a progression from *logos* to *logōn technē* to *rhētorikē* that took place over a period exceeding a century. As is further documented below, the key conceptual term with which the fifth-century older Sophists were concerned was *logos*. By the end of the fifth century B.C., the phrase *logōn technē* had emerged to describe sophistic teaching. The phrase could equally well describe any kind of conceptual or philosophical teaching, and it is possible that Plato originally coined the word *rhētorikē* in order to distinguish between his type of teaching and that of his rivals.[72] During most of the fourth century the terms *logōn technē* or *logōn paideia* were used by such writers as Isocrates and the author of the *Rhetoric to Alexander,* but not the term *rhētorikē*. The first half of the fourth century can be understood as a transitional stage during which the difference between "rhetorical" and "philosophical" training was very much a matter of controversy, as the sometimes heated rivalry between Isocrates and Plato readily attests. It was not until the influential teachings of Aristotle that the split between rhetoric and philosophy was more or less successfully reified.

In the remainder of this essay I want to focus on the first, or *logos,* stage of the progression from *logos* to *logōn technē* to *rhētorikē*, since it represents the authentic beginning of Greek rhetorical theory. The following discussion is intended to highlight two facts about sophistic theorizing about *logos:* (1) The Sophists are best understood as representatives of the intellectualist "philosophical" movement spawned, in part, by rationalism enabled by growing literacy. (2) The older Sophists were serious individual thinkers, and efforts to characterize their doctrines concerning discourse should avoid overly simplistic schematizations. This treatment will underscore the need to revise the standard view of sophistic rhetoric found in such sources as Kennedy.

PROTAGORAS AND GORGIAS

The term *logos* was one of the most overworked words of ancient Greek and is difficult to translate into English. Summarizing the predominant senses of *logos* found in the fifth century B.C., G. B. Kerferd has written:

There are three main areas of its application or use, all related by an underlying conceptual unity. These are first of all the area of language and linguistic formulation, hence speech, discourse, description, statement, arguments (as expressed in words) and so on; secondly the area of thought and mental processes, hence thinking, reasoning, accounting for, explanation (cf. *orthos logos*), etc.; thirdly, the area of the world, that *about* which we are able to speak and to think, hence structural principles, formulae, natural laws and so on, provided that in each case they are regarded as actually present in and exhibited in the world-process.[73]

The *logos* of sixth- and fifth-century thinkers is best understood as a rationalistic rival to traditional *mythos*—the religious worldview preserved in epic poetry: "Philosophy proper arose as a commentary upon and correction of the cosmic imagery of Homer and the cosmic architecture of Hesiod's *Theogony*."[74] The epic poets in general and Homer in particular enjoyed a sort of institutional status in Greek society. The poetry of the time performed the functions now assigned to a variety of educational practices: religious instruction, moral training, history texts, and reference manuals.[75] Because the vast majority of the population did not read regularly, poetry as preserved communication served as Greek culture's collective stored memory. Accordingly, poetry enjoyed a monopoly over education in general and citizenship training in particular.[76]

Havelock has documented in detail the role of those we now call pre-Socratic philosophers in advancing abstract analysis over the mythic-poetic tradition.[77] The evidence is clear that the older Sophists performed the same role in the fifth century B.C. as Plato did in the fourth. In Plato's *Protagoras*, Socrates and Protagoras engage in an analysis of a passage by the poet Simonides (338e–348a). Commentators have viewed Socrates' outrageous (mis)interpretation of the passage as evidence of Plato's distrust of poetry and poetic interpretation.[78] As Taylor notes, the section also provides clues about Protagoras: "It seems likely that he saw the importance of literary criticism rather in developing the critical faculty and the exact use of language than in promoting the understanding and appreciation of poetry as an end in itself."[79] In his analysis, Protagoras points out a contradiction in Simonides' poem and claims that it is important to be able to evaluate poetry and give a *logos* when questioned (339a). Even allowing for some degree of distortion by Plato, it is clear that Protagoras has made a crucial analytical leap from mere repetition of the culture's repository of wisdom to its critical analysis. His analysis was meta-poetic in the sense that poetry had become an *object* of study rather than being the medium through which the world was understood (as it was for the nonliterate).

Aristotle also provides evidence of Protagoras's critical approach to poetry. In *Sophistic Refutations* (173b17) and in the *Rhetoric* (1407b6), Aristotle reports that Protagoras was concerned with the proper gender of words, and in the *Poetics* claims that Protagoras criticized the opening of Homer's *Iliad* for using the mode of "command" rather than "request" (1465b15). Ammonius quotes Protagoras critically analyzing another passage in the *Iliad* (DK 80 A30). The *Gnomologium Vaticanum* records the following anecdote: "When a maker of verses cursed Protagoras because he would not approve of his poems, his answer was 'My good sir, I am better off enduring your abuse than enduring your poems.'"[80]

In short, there is strong evidence that Protagoras broke from the poetic tradition by making poetry a subject of critical analysis. Other pre-Socratics had criticized Homer and Hesiod, but Protagoras's method of analysis was different and original. When Heraclitus criticized the poets for failing to recognize that day and night are One, it was a matter of his opinion (*doxa*) against theirs.[81] After Parmenides describes the nature of "what-is," it is defended as being the result of divine revelation. In both instances *logos* is understood as rationalized *mythos*, and is set against a traditional *mythos*. With Protagoras *mythos* becomes an object of analysis, a text or *logos* that can be analyzed, criticized, and altered. Protagoras's analysis of epic poetry is the earliest recorded instance of textual criticism, one that apparently started a practice that was continued by other Sophists at least through Isocrates' time.[82]

Viewed as a whole, the extant fragments of Protagoras form a coherent view of discourse, humanity, and the world.[83] A summary of his more important fragments can demonstrate, albeit in cursory fashion, how his theorizing represented an advance over mythic explanations of the world and contributed to the further development of rhetorical theory and practice. His most famous aphorism is "Of all things the measure is Humanity: Of that which is, that it is the case, of that which is not, that it is not the case."[84] This aphorism was allegedly the opening line of a book that was motivated, in part, as a critique of Eleatic monism as espoused by Parmenides.[85] Protagoras's point seems to have been that humans are the judge of what is or is not the case—not the gods or heroes of epic poetry, and not the divinely inspired philosophical poets like Parmenides. It is commonly accepted that Protagoras helped provide the theoretical justification for Periclean democracy. Although the precise relationship between Pericles and Protagoras is far from certain, it is clearly the case that both Parmenides's and Protagoras's philosophical positions had strong ideological implications.[86] Accordingly, it is accurate to say that Protagoras's particular rationalization of the *mythos* is in keeping with the trends of Athenian democracy.

Protagoras's two-*logoi* fragment states that two opposing *logoi* are true concerning every experience. The thesis is an extension of contemporary theorizing about the nature of "things." By the fifth century B.C., the predominant rationalistic (non-mythical) method for understanding nature was through various theories of opposites.[87] Human health was understood by many fifth-century physicians as being an appropriate balance of opposites, such as dry and wet, hot and cold.[88] During the fifth century B.C. theories of opposites grew more sophisticated as the available analytical vocabulary and syntax evolved, and Protagoras's two-*logoi* statement contributed to that evolution. The two-*logoi* statement has proven difficult to interpret because the meaning of *logoi* mentioned is unclear. Did Protagoras simply mean that two competing speeches are possible about every "thing," or did he mean that each "thing" could be experienced in contrary fashion such that two opposing accounts could both be true? The answer must be "both." The philological evidence from the fifth century B.C. suggests that *logos* covered equally the notions of objective states, courses of action, or ways of life, as well as speeches about the states and actions.[89] Accordingly, Protagoras's statement must be interpreted as a claim about the world as well as a claim about discourse.

The Protagorean fragment most conducive to interpretation as an incipient theory of rhetoric is his alleged "promise" recorded by Aristotle to "make the weaker argument stronger" (*Rhetoric* 1402a23). Traditionally, the statement has been interpreted as representing sophistry at its worst, as reflected in Lane Cooper's translation "making the worse appear the better cause."[90] Accordingly, those who reduce sophistic teaching to "mere" rhetoric tend to refer to Protagoras's promise as evidence of the unethical nature of their lessons. Such an interpretation of the fragment does much violence to the actual Greek and ignores much of what is known about the historical Protagoras. As mentioned earlier in this essay, the superior interpretation is to read the promise in tandem with the two-*logoi* fragment. What Protagoras meant by making one *logos* stronger than its opposite was the substitution of a preferred (but weaker) *logos* for a less preferable (but temporarily dominant) *logos* of the same experience.[91] Again, *logos* carries a dual reference: to the end condition a speaker seeks to change (from the weaker to the stronger) and to the means of producing such a change.

Over time the sense of *logos* as an end condition would fade as increasing attention was given to *logos* as a means of effecting change. Nevertheless, it can be stated with confidence that Protagoras's theorizing about *logos* heralds an important beginning of the development of rhetorical theory. Based strictly on his methods and doctrines, it is difficult to distinguish between Protagoras and his predecessors. Both broke from the poetic-mythic tradition and both sought a rationalistic account of the world and how to change it. Philosophical and sophistic rhetoric have more in common than Kennedy's tripartite scheme acknowledges.

Protagoras's doctrines by no means exhaust fifth-century theorizing about *logos*. A second example of an incipient rhetorical theory of the fifth century B.C. is that of Gorgias's approach to *logos*. The prevailing opinion concerning Gorgias is that he was not a particularly serious thinker, that his rhetorical style was excessively ornate, and that the portrayal found in Plato's dialogue of the same name is generally accurate. In the past thirty years an alternative picture of Gorgias has begun to emerge that treats him as a serious thinker with legitimately philosophical interests. The difference between the two views can be attributed in large measure to the relationship one assumes between Gorgias and rhetoric. Kennedy, reflecting the attitude that rhetorical interests logically precede the content of the Sophists' teachings, suggests that the new "philosophical approach to Gorgias . . . probably exaggerates his intellectual sophistication and credits him with an uncharacteristic power of conceptualization."[92]

This essay sides with the position that Gorgias, like Protagoras, was a serious thinker who shared an interest in advancing *logos* over *mythos*. Like Protagoras, Gorgias's training, acknowledged interests, and early writings suggest that the difference between Gorgias and "real" philosophers is more illusory than real.

Gorgias is said to have been the student of the philosopher Em-

pedocles (DK 82 A2, 3, 14), who in turn is said to have been a follower
of Parmenides (DK 31 A7). Plato and Theophrastus report that Gorgias
subscribed to Empedoclean theories concerning the sun, optics, and
color (DK 82 B4, 5, cf. A17, B31). Such interests clearly identify Gorgias
with the new rationalism considered characteristic of the philosophers
of his time. Charles H. Kahn has written two seminal works concerning
the Greek verb *eimi,* "to be."[93] Kahn's extensive survey of the ancient
Greek literature revealed that there were certain technical constructions
of the verb "to be" that occurred very rarely in pre-Platonic writings.
According to Kahn, at least one of the technical uses, the negative form
of *eimi,* was employed exclusively by philosophers.[94] Significantly, both
Protagoras's and Gorgias's extant fragments employ such a negative
form of *eimi.* Protagoras uses the negative construction of *eimi* twice
in his "man as measure" statement, and Gorgias authored an entire
address under the title "On Not-Being."

The argument advanced in Gorgias's "On Not-Being" has long
been the subject of controversy. Gorgias's argument was threefold:
"(1) nothing is, (2) even if it is, it cannot be known to human beings,
(3) even if it is and is knowable, it cannot be indicated and made
meaningful to another person."[95] Most commentators agree that the
argument was prompted by the extreme monism embodied in Parmenides' work "On Being," and that Gorgias was attempting to refute
Parmenides' position by reducing it to absurdity. However, there is
little agreement over whether the argument should be considered philosophical or merely rhetorical. As has been suggested previously, the
dichotomy is anachronistic. As has been amply documented by Kerferd,
the address was concerned with theoretical controversies that were at
the heart of the fifth-century intellectual movement.[96] Gorgias raised
issues that would now be referred to as having to do with predication,
meaning, and reference—issues that later became of vital importance
to Plato. Accordingly, it makes little sense to dismiss the seriousness
of Gorgias's addresses on the premise that a "mere" rhetorician would
not have held serious theoretical positions.

Like Protagoras, Gorgias held an implicit theory of *logos* that can
be usefully understood as an incipient rhetorical theory. Gorgias's
theory of *logos* has been carefully analyzed by Charles P. Segal and is
only briefly summarized here. According to Segal, the key to Gorgias's
theory is a literal analogy between drugs and *logoi.* As a doctor's drugs
affect the diseases and the life of the body, *logoi* alter the psyche and

the emotions: "The processes of the psyche are thus treated as having a quasi-physical reality and, perhaps more significant, as being susceptible to the same kind of control and manipulation by a rational agent as the body by the drugs of the doctor."[97] The force of *logos* works directly on the psyche, having an immediate ability to change it from one state to another. Gorgias's conception of *logos* and the psyche has more in common with Democritus's materialism than with Plato's idealism. For that reason, it, like other fifth-century writings concerning *logos,* rarely has been understood or appreciated. Viewed in its proper context, Gorgias's theory can be respected as an early effort towards theorizing about subjects that remain difficult more than two thousand years later.

CONCLUSION

This essay has offered a case for the renewed historical study of the beginnings of Greek rhetorical theory. Paralleling Havelock's re-examination of the standard account of early Greek philosophy, this essay suggests that a careful reading of important fifth- and fourth-century texts calls into question much of the standard account of early Greek rhetorical theorizing. In particular, the Corax and Tisias origin myth was found to be suspect on almost every point: Whatever Corax and Tisias may have taught was not under the rubric of rhetoric, it was probably not in the form of a book or *technē,* it is unlikely that they advanced a theory of argument from probability, and they may or may not have offered an original division of forensic discourse. It is also extremely unlikely that written technical handbooks on rhetoric were common in the late fifth century B.C., as is held by the standard account. In more general terms, Kennedy's tripartite division of early Greek rhetorical theory as technical, sophistic, and philosophical was shown to be misleading. Most of the characteristics of the technical tradition are found in the fourth century B.C. rather than the fifth. Furthermore, the sophistic and philosophical traditions are differentiated by Kennedy and others on grounds that cannot be supported by the available *ipsissima verba.* The philosophical significance of the Sophists' theorizing has been underestimated by importing later-developed conceptions of the nature, scope, and value of rhetorical theory. Once the methods and doctrines of Sophists such as Protagoras and Gorgias are evaluated on their own terms, it becomes clear that philosophical and sophistic theories of rhetoric have more in common than Kennedy's tripartite scheme acknowledges.

If the origins of Greek rhetorical theory are worth recovering, either as history or as an aid to contemporary theorizing, then they are worth recovering on their own terms.[98] A new story of the emergence and development of Greek rhetorical theory requires considerable revision of the standard histories of fifth- and fourth-century rhetoric. Though much of this essay has been aimed at deconstructing the standard account, it is hoped that it also contributes to the formulation of a new account, one that recognizes the importance of Havelock's orality thesis, the intellectual depth of sophistic theorizing, and the importance of recognizing *logos* as the precursor to *rhētorikē* and as the key conceptual term of fifth-century rhetorical theory.[99]

RHETORIC IN DEFENSE OF THE DISPOSSESSED: DAVID CROCKETT AND THE TENNESSEE SQUATTERS

Royce E. Flood

Some thirty-five years ago, thanks to the influence of television and film, a new folk hero burst into the consciousness of American youngsters. In backyards throughout the country coonskin-capped children reenacted the exploits of their champion, while for weeks the hit parade was topped by a catchy, if not particularly inspired, ballad describing the adventures of "Davy, Davy Crockett, King of the Wild Frontier." A rather obscure frontiersman/politician from Tennessee had become all the rage.

Yet in retrospect, this admiration for Crockett is not especially surprising, for it simply mirrored the fondness with which he was regarded by the poor voters of his West Tennessee congressional district who saw in him their sole advocate. As Stiffler has commented, Crockett was "one of the few individuals who dared to support the rights of West Tennesseans against the Nashville basin and East Tennessee regions."[1] As a result, the West Tennesseans twice elected him to the state legislature and three times sent him to the House in Washington. Even on those occasions when Crockett lost a congressional election (also three in number), the votes that defeated him came from the most urbanized part of the district; the poor never wavered in their support of their spokesman.

It might be interesting to inquire, however, if this admiration for Crockett was shared by educated individuals of his own time or by historians and writers of our day. The answer is, decidedly not! To these persons, Crockett represented much that was least desirable in our social and political system. A sampling of their opinions will make the point quite clearly.

34

One of Crockett's fellow congressmen, William Grayson of South Carolina, described him as "a dull, heavy, almost stupid man, in appearance. I never heard him utter a word that savoured of wit or sense."[2] Even more succinct was a middle-class listener at one of Crockett's stump speeches, where the frontiersman was berating President Andrew Jackson: "Surely," the auditor was heard to mumble, half to himself, "the man is crazy."[3]

Modern writers have done little better by Crockett. Richard Hofstadter (probably the only modern historian to approach an understanding of the frontiersman) describes him as "provincial and . . . unreliable."[4] Others are far harsher. Robert Remini advances the opinion that "as for Crockett, there was no way to account for the antics of that strange loon."[5] Vernon Parrington describes him as "vain, ignorant Davy Crockett! A simple minded frontiersman . . . pretty much of a sloven . . . a true frontier wastrel . . . a game-hog . . . a hard, unlovely fact."[6] Even our own field of communication has dealt unkindly with Crockett. Robert Gunderson, an ardent admirer of Andrew Jackson, saw Crockett as a demagogue, a dupe, and a ghostwritten fake.[7]

What can account for this tremendous hostility toward one who for others reigned as a hero without peer? The answer lies in Crockett's political activities, for much of his career was spent defending a particularly unloved group of the dispossessed—the poor squatters in his West Tennessee congressional district—and that defense frequently took the form of rhetorical extremes.

The dispossessed, like the poor with whom they are often equated, have always been with us. "Give me your tired, your poor," wrote Emma Lazarus, "your huddled masses yearning to breathe free, the wretched refuse of your teeming shore."[8] Unfortunately, for many of Crockett's day this poem's promise remained unfulfilled; numerous immigrants continued a wretched existence even after reaching this land for, like nearly every other organized society in human history, our country has included dispossessed elements—those individuals and groups who are in the society but not of it. Often nearly invisible to their more fortunate neighbors, such persons eke out a living doing what no one else will undertake and living where no one else wishes to dwell. And if others wish to enter their occupations or inhabit their land, the dispossessed must move on to even less desirable life-styles. Lacking the educational background, political clout, economic wherewithal, or social position to move up in class, they have constituted a multigenerational undergroup on whose backs the rest of society has built. And on the West Tennessee frontier in the 1820s and 1830s the dispossessed were most commonly observed among the landless squatters who clung to the mean patches of ground on which they illegally dwelled, trying desperately to wrest a living from the inhospitable land.

Why, however, would merely defending such a group bring down upon Crockett's head the abuses cited above? The answer lies in the attitudes of his contemporaries toward the dispossessed in general, modern attitudes toward his constituents in particular and, most important, strong reaction of all parties toward the type of rhetoric in which he couched his defense.

The prevailing view one hundred fifty years ago was not favorable to those who seemed unable to make it in society. Given the democratic spirit of the age, the vast amounts of land available in the West, and the feeling that it was possible to rise in the world if one but put one's mind and body to the task, few individuals were willing to sympathize with those at the bottom of the social ladder. Bremner, in his history of poverty in the United States, makes the point most clearly: "Poverty was unnecessary. When there was work for all, no man who was willing to do his share need want. Indigence was simply the punishment meted out to the improvident by their own lack of industry and efficiency. . . . Poverty was the obvious consequence of sloth and sinfulness."[9] With such an attitude prominent in the thought of the age, it becomes clear that any advocate such as Crockett who requested public aid for the dispossessed would himself become a highly unpopular figure among the well-to-do.

But given the more sympathetic attitudes held by moderns toward the less fortunate, it is perhaps surprising that our age has not shown greater awareness of the squatters' plight. Two factors may account for this. First, they were not, to be blunt, a particularly lovely or lovable people. Ignorant, apathetic toward education, possessing few marks of culture, and frequently suspicious of outsiders, they simply were not the kind of persons an educated academic would find appealing. Second, the squatters possessed no distinctive demographic feature that would cause them to stand out for consideration. They were white, largely Anglo/Celtic, of relatively lengthy habitation on these shores and, as far as religion touched their lives, Protestant. In short, they were not the type of group whose advocacy is in any way chic.

In spite of the foregoing reasons, however, it is clear from an analysis of writers old and new that the major source of their hostility was the nature of Crockett's rhetoric in defense of his constituents. He frequently gave way to hyperbole and excess and he took positions that appalled those who valued reasoned discourse and held in esteem the role of education and culture in society. Given the nature of Crockett's rhetoric, which often mirrored the beliefs of his people, it became virtually impossible for educated individuals—particularly academic practitioners of history—to sympathize with him; he represented all that was anathema to them.

It will be the purpose of this paper to examine the rhetoric David Crockett practiced in defense of his squatter constituents and to discover in it those elements that repulsed and offended the educated elite of his day and ours. In order to set the stage for this analysis it will be profitable to examine the nature of land tenure in old Tennessee (which was at the heart of the squatters' difficulties); to describe the squatters themselves; and finally to examine Crockett's early life, in which may be discerned those elements of existence that made him so eager to defend the dispossessed of his district.

The frontier squatters of West Tennessee during the 1820s and 1830s were truly among the dispossessed—not only in a figurative sense, but frequently in a literal sense as well. Many of them had been driven from the land on which they lived—but did not own—and forced to move to much poorer, less desirable quarters. This forced migration was created by two main factors: first, the confusion surrounding land titles in Tennessee, and second, the activities of land speculators, many of whom were in positions of political power within the state. Both of these factors, in turn, could be traced to events that occurred east of the Appalachians in much earlier times.

The original charter of Carolina, granted in 1663, extended that settlement to the "South Sea," and thus the colony of North Carolina claimed territory as far as the Mississippi.[10] During the latter stages of the American Revolution, the Old North State, desiring to increase the size of her continental line, legislated a bounty of 200 acres in the west for each new recruit, each man wounded in action, and all heirs of deceased soldiers. The grants were awarded in the form of redeemable certificates known as warrants.

While the purpose of this act may have been noble, the result was to prove a disaster. The most insidious part of the legislation was the provision for grants to soldiers' heirs. The heirs, and thus the warrants, seemed to multiply without ceasing. In the end, if curbs had not been applied, the whole of Tennessee would not have been sufficient to satisfy the claims. In addition, this act proved a windfall for land speculators. Many returning soldiers had no desire to cross the mountains to the west; others were unable to do so. Most were short of money and happy to trade their warrants for cash.

At the close of the Revolution in 1783, the speculators who controlled the Carolina state legislature opened the transmontane region to survey and entry (registering of claims) for a brief period, permitting the accumulation of vast acreages by themselves and their friends. In 1789, as a condition for joining the new federal union, North Carolina stipulated that all existing land claims should be honored. When, seven years later, Tennessee achieved statehood, she found herself struggling with the burdens the land question placed on her. The Old North State continued to meddle in the affairs of its neighbor and insisted on the right to issue titles to land in Tennessee under the warrant system. The situation was too chaotic to continue. Under an 1806 compromise Tennessee was granted title to all land in the eastern two-thirds of the state; out of this the North Carolina warrants had to be satisfied. In addition, one section of each township had to be set aside for the support of education. The western part of the state was retained by Washington and labeled the Congressional Reservation.

This agreement might have worked were it not for the prodigious number of outstanding warrants and the activities of the speculators. Within four years, claiming that all good lands had been appropriated, North Carolina began sending her surveyors into the Congressional Reservation. Tennessee's own speculators so manipulated ownership of the eastern lands that practically nothing was left for the schools. In addition, the North Carolina Assembly ceded all ownerless warrants to the state university and that institution began to enforce its claims on Tennessee, adding to the confusion of the situation and the distress of the inhabitants. In a final attempt to solve the crisis, the Tennessee legislature charged its congressional delegation with the task of obtaining the Congressional Reservation, with the express understanding that the land would be used for benefit of education within the state. With Andrew Jackson in the White House and a powerful contingent in Congress headed by James K. Polk, the Tennesseans had every hope of success.

While this attempt to gain control of the remaining vacant land did have some potential public benefit to recommend it—funding for education is usually considered a social good—there were also many less altruistic aspects of the proposed cession. The Tennessee legislature was controlled by members from the more settled eastern and central parts of the state, many of whom, as indicated above, were land speculators. It seems fairly clear that many of the squatters' suspicions about the legislature, which Crockett was later to voice forcefully, were well founded: many prominent Tennesseeans did desire to speculate in the newly available land, and they were likely to put a high price on it (which the poor could not afford), sell it in large parcels (more conducive to their planter life-style than to the requirements of small farmers), and use the proceeds for the state university rather than for the grammar schools of the west. In short, the proposed cession threatened the squatter class with great harm while promising them few if any benefits in compensation.

But who, exactly, were these squatters? In order to answer that question, it is necessary to examine the three groups that made up West Tennessee society during the pioneer period.

The settling of the American frontier in the 1820s was accomplished by three groups of individuals: pioneer farmers, town dwellers, and squatters.[11] The first and probably largest group constituted what is brought to mind by the term "frontier settler." Some of these individuals were well down the socioeconomic scale, but by far "the largest element of the population was the middle class."[12] They were distinguished by their ownership of the land on which they lived, having acquired it either by direct purchase or by possession of a North Carolina warrant. The tract settlers chose was cleared by their own family, occasionally with the help of a few slaves, and it generally produced not only sufficient food for the group but enough to exchange for manufactured goods at the nearest settlement. Farmers might possess a small amount of cash, but this was usually depleted by the requirements of the settling process; more often than not, they lived within a joint barter and money economy.

The second group was made up of service-oriented or professional individuals—shopkeepers, teachers, clergy, and lawyers—who formed the small communities that began to appear in the midst of the forest. They were no less pioneers than their farmer neighbors, but, of a more settled nature, they disliked the isolation of the frontier farm and preferred the greater safety and convenience of town life. Generally better educated than the settler and dealing more often in a money economy, these individuals brought a touch of civilization to the wilderness as they imported needed manufactured goods or brought the influence of the classroom, the church, or the courtroom to their fellow pioneers.

Finally, there were the squatters. Exactly what proportion of the population they formed is difficult to say, since no authority will venture a percentage figure. Philbrick considers that they were "certainly a very considerable fraction of early Westerners,"[13] and Abernathy even goes so far as to assert that by Crockett's time they "evidently had grown to outnumber the owners."[14] Whatever the precise figure, it is obvious that they were numerous enough to exert a considerable influence upon the political character of the district.

The squatters were of several types. Some were completely improvident individuals, who "without initiative either to move or rise, became the substratum of the social structure and progenitors of the tenant class and poor whites."[15] Others, in spite of hard work, remained poor, persons "of worth whose handicap was penury."[16] Still others were former warrant-holding settlers who had been deprived of their land because their grants were of relatively recent date. Several of these unfortunates, Crockett attested, "had been driven from improvement to improvement, and from home to home, till, in despair . . . they had settled on land that nobody would claim—on scraps and refuse fragments of the soil."[17]

Of whatever type, the squatters all faced the same fears: that a warrant holder would arrive and claim even their poor homestead, or that the state legislature would acquire the land and force them to pay for it. In either case they would have to move on. Even on their claims, the marginal land barely produced enough for subsistence, and the squatters were forced to grub a living as best they could. Often ignorant as well as illiterate, and suspicious of the forces of civilization that constantly pushed them about, the squatters formed the basis of the lowest free class of West Tennessee.

As the preceding description makes clear, the western squatters faced an unfriendly world with few allies or advocates. Obviously, the more educated town dwellers would have little sympathy for the squatters' plight. Too impoverished to take advantage of the services or professions offered by the middle class, and frequently hostile to that class's aspirations—such as urban growth and education—the squatters were more often viewed as enemies or as a blight on society than as a beneficial addition to the local community. Even the settlers were often less than friendly to the surrounding squatters. As individuals who possessed their own land and were thus anxious to see rights of private property protected, and perhaps their own holding extended, they could not have been happy to see large sections of the vacant land occupied by those who had neither paid for it nor had any real legal claim to it.

In this largely hostile environment, the West Tennessee squatters had only one true friend and advocate in political circles—their congressman, David Crockett. How Crockett came to be the great—and only—defender of the squatter class will be revealed most clearly through a brief biographical sketch.

David Crockett's ancestors were Scotch–Irish who emigrated to this country around the middle of the eighteenth century and eventually settled in the mountains of East Tennessee.[18] It was here that Crockett was born in August 1786 at his family's cabin on Limestone Creek, a tributary of the Nolichucky River, near Greeneville, Tennessee.

Grinding poverty "was the birthright of the pioneer and . . . Crockett inherited his full share of it."[19] In a futile attempt to make a decent living the family was constantly moving. They tried farming near Greeneville and failed. Crockett's father went into partnership to build a mill, but the new structure was carried away by a sudden flood. The family next settled on a farm of some three hundred acres only to see it sold the following year for debts of over four hundred dollars. Finally they moved to Morristown, Tennessee, where Crockett's father opened a tavern on the main route from Knoxville to Abingdon, Virginia. This appears to have been a modest success and remained open for a number of years.

The conditions of the frontier required that boys mature at an early age. The need to produce a living was so severe that even the youngest were expected to do their part. Thus it is not surprising to find young David being hired out at the age of twelve to help drive a herd of cattle four hundred miles into Virginia. Returning home, Crockett had a serious difference of opinion with his father, which caused another, hasty, departure. He helped drive another herd north and then supported himself for two and a half years by working as a laborer and teamster and finally by apprenticing himself to a hatter.

Eventually Crockett returned to Tennessee and became reconciled with his father, working six months to pay off one of the older man's debts. He then went to work for a Quaker named Kennedy, one of whose schoolmaster sons undertook to provide Crockett with a bit of education. As the frontiersman described it in his *Autobiography,* "In this time [I] learned to read a little in my primer, to write my own name, and to cipher some in the first three rules in figures."[20] This was all the formal schooling David Crockett ever received. By now in his late teens, Crockett was at the age when, among frontier youth, marriage was common. After two or three unsuccessful attempts at romance, he finally received a positive response to a proposal and in 1804 was married to a beautiful young Irish girl, Mary "Polly" Finley. Young Crockett's fortune, however, was far from made, as the Finleys were even poorer than he. As he expressed it, "Having gotten my wife I thought I was completely made up and needed nothing more in the whole world, but I soon found that this was all a mistake. For now having a wife, I wanted everything else and worse than all I had nothing to give for it" (*Life,* 35). During the next five years the family doubled in size as two sons were born, John Wesley in 1807 and William in 1809. In spite of hard work, however, prosperity would not come and concluding "I was better at increasing my family than my fortune," Crockett began the peripatetic life that had characterized both his father and grandfather (*Life,* 36). Over the next two years the family moved twice to farms in the central section of Tennessee, ending up at a homestead near the Alabama border.

It was from this location that Crockett departed on his only real experience with military service, participating in a frontier expedition under the command of Andrew Jackson against a coalition of Indian tribes. Crockett experienced two or three actions which he records in his *Autobiography,* observed the manner in which the professional military both mistrusted and mistreated the short-term volunteer, and acquired both an admiration for and a suspicion of Andrew Jackson.[21]

Returning to his home after military service, Crockett suffered a devastating loss. His wife died of complications shortly after the birth of their third child, Margaret. By the fall of 1815, then, David Crockett was left a widower on a poor farm with three small children to raise. And yet soon afterward his fortunes began to improve. He married the widow of a soldier killed in the Creek war, a woman who not only had two small children but a sizable farm and a fortune of several hundred dollars.

Shortly thereafter the family moved further west in Tennessee to the area near Lawrenceburg, and Crockett's rise in the world began. He became a local justice, was chosen a colonel of the state militia, and was eventually elected to two terms in the state legislature, from which position he engineered his rise to Congress.

During his first term, as the Tennessee delegation sought the granting of the vacant lands to the state, Crockett loyally supported the Jacksonian position; but, as he later revealed, he fully expected—correctly—that Polk's bill would fail, upon which he was ready with his own measure, requesting that the land be made available for sale at the price of twelve and one-half cents an acre, with the squatters who currently resided on the land having the first right of purchase. Crockett rather naively believed that his support of the delegation's bill would result in their support, in turn, of his. It was in the context of the debates over these two measures that many of Crockett's arguments in favor of his constituents were presented.

The foregoing account should make clear that Crockett was actually of the settler, not squatter, class of western pioneer. And yet his struggles for financial integrity, his constant movement from property to property, and his seeming inability to make a true success of enterprises to which he put his hand placed him in the lower ranks of the settler class and give evidence that in attitude and behavior he was close to the poor squatters he came so strongly to defend. Indeed, the only real difference between Crockett and those he represented was that throughout his life he was fortunate enough to be able to own the property on which he lived. By luck or sheer accident he was never faced with the arrival of a North Carolina warrant holder to drive him from his home. And yet in spite of this significant distinction, his life was close enough in many of its drearier and darker aspects to those of the squatters that he fully understood their predicament; when he spoke so movingly in Congress on their behalf it is not difficult to understand that he spoke several words for them and at least one for himself.

Having examined the nature of the dispossessed group and those features in Crockett's life that made him their supporter, we can now focus on the speeches he gave in defense of his constituents. This paper will consider both the attitudes that underlay Crockett's rhetorical positions and the techniques or elements in his speaking that so offended those better placed in society. An analysis of Crockett's addresses reveals three primary elements: an antipathy to the world of the intellect, a conviction that his people were equal to any in society, and a fear that his people's plight was the result of a conspiracy against them by the rest of society. Among the most prominent of the speaker's techniques were frequent appeals to pathos and the use of radical or offensive language.

A position often taken by defenders of the dispossessed—and one Crockett frequently expressed—was opposition to matters of the intellect and especially to higher education. In his seminal work on anti-intellectualism in American life, Richard Hofstadter has pointed out how extensive this attitude has been during popular movements in American history.[22] Thus it is not surprising to find Crockett allying himself with those who argued that education made a distinction among the classes and that its costs should never be borne by the poor, who were seldom if ever able to reap advantage from the institutions thus financed.

Crockett's antipathy to higher education can be seen in several arguments he presented during his campaigning in the west and in his speeches in the House. First, Crockett argued that higher education was not necessary to make one a good citizen or even a good leader of society. The uneducated could understand the law and could lead the nation's military forces. In support of these arguments he advanced as evidence his own and General Jackson's careers. Concerning his own time as a justice of the peace in his native Tennessee, Crockett wrote in his autobiography, "My judgments were never appealed from, and if they had been, they would have stuck like wax, as I gave my decisions on the principles of common justice and honesty between man and man, and relied on natural born sense, and not on law learning to guide me; for I had never read a page in a law book in all my life" (*Life*, 69). In questioning the value of the United States Military Academy, Crockett argued in this fashion: "Thousands of poor men . . . had also gone out to fight their country's battles, but none of them had ever been at West Point, and none of them had any sons at West Point. A man could fight the battles of his country, and lead his country's armies, without being educated at West Point. Jackson never went to West Point school."[23] Thus the common citizen could use common sense and did not require education in order to conduct the country's business.

Second, the matter of education particularly concerned Crockett because the avowed purpose of awarding the vacant lands to the state legislature of Tennessee was to sell those lands for the advancement of education—particularly higher education—in the state. When to this was added the enforcement of warrants within the Volunteer State by the University of North Carolina, it becomes clear that not only Crockett but also the vast majority of his constituents held deep suspicions about the worth of higher education. Crockett argued that his people seldom would be able to take advantage of higher educational opportunities. As he put it, "If we can only get a common school, or as college graduates sometimes deridingly call it, a B.A. school, convenient enough to send our big boys in the winter and our little ones all the year, we think ourselves fortunate, especially if we can raise enough coonskins and one little thing or other to pay up the teacher at the end of every quarter."[24]

Crockett continued by observing, "The children of my people never saw the inside of a college in their lives and never are likely to do so."[25] This was especially true of the military academy, for, as he argued, "It could be of little use to the poor any how; for if a poor boy could by chance get appointed, he could not get there, the expense would be too great; and if he could get there, it would be at the risk of his ruin, as the chance would be that he would have to go home on his own means."[26] Thus, because Crockett and his constituents perceived higher education as an institution that sought the dispossession of the poor from their lands and of which the poor could never take advantage, such places of learning were felt to be highly undesirable.

Finally, as regards education, Crockett perceived it as an agent that drove a palpable wedge between the well-to-do and the people of his class. This position is strongly implied in the foregoing quotations, but Crockett on occasion made it explicit in arguing for the granting of the Tennessee lands to his constituents. "The benefits of education are not to be dispensed with an equal hand. This college system went into practice to draw a line of demarcation between the two classes of society. It separated the children of the rich from the children of the poor."[27] The case against West Point, which Crockett argued several times during his congressional career, was particularly strong, since that institution was supported by tax money—much of which came from his own constituents. In a speech of February 1830 Crockett made these observations:

> The institution was kept up for the education of the sons of the noble and wealthy, and of members of Congress, people of influence, and not for the children of the poor. . . . It was not proper that the money of the government should be expended in educating the children of the noble and wealthy; that money was raised from the poor man's pocket as well as the rich. Every poor man, who buys a bushel of salt to salt his pork, or a pound of sugar for his children, or a piece of cloth for his coat, pays his portion of the taxes out of which this West Point Academy was maintained for the education of rich men's sons for nothing, twenty-eight dollars a month besides.[28]

Thus in addition to being unnecessary and inaccessible to his people, higher education was viewed as an actual class distinctor, creating an invisible but essential line between the children of the classes.

Crockett's views on the nature of education, as well as his contempt for Andrew Jackson, may be summed up by a story he told during his tour of the Northeast during 1834. Jackson had recently been awarded an honorary LLD degree by Harvard, and when Crockett was visiting in Boston he was invited to visit the same institution. He recorded: "I would not go, for I did not know but they might stick an LLD degree on me before they let me go; and I had no idea of changing a member of the House of Representatives of the United States for what stands for Lazy Lounging Dunce, which I am sure my constituents would have translated my new title to be" (*Life,* 132). Concerning Jackson, Crockett remarked, "One dignitary was enough from Tennessee" (*Life,* 132). Thus, Crockett argued the undesirability of the world of the intellect and of higher education—places where his people seldom, if ever, could go.

Crockett presented a picture of his constituents that painted them as among the most decent, honorable, and noble individuals on the globe; they were truly—to use the ancient phrase—the "salt of the earth." Crockett began by attributing to them a whole series of positive qualities. They were, while poor, not improvident. They were hard-working, industrious individuals who had suffered from misfortunes throughout their lives. Crockett described them as "an honest, industrious, hardy, persevering, kind-hearted people,"[29] and as evidence of these assertions he recorded that they were "the hearty sons of the soil . . . men who had broken the cane and opened . . . the wilderness."[30] Thus initially, Crockett's constituents were deserving of sympathy because they were striving against poverty. Next, they were deserving because they had been mistreated by the forces of society. Many of them, Crockett affirmed, had "seen their little farms, which had afforded bread for their children, taken from them by warrants held in hands more fortunate than their own."[31] Even then, his constituents were deserving for they did not complain but, as he put it, "They have submitted, and submitted without a murmur. But in the midst of their humble submission they have not ceased to look up to Congress as children would to a parent, for assistance and protection."[32]

Moreover, these individuals were patriotic, for they had fought against British and Indians. Crockett reminded his listeners, "When your country was invaded, and the flag of its honor insulted, they shouldered their guns and fought in its defense; and, not to pay myself a compliment, I had the honor to fight, side by side, with them."[33] From his military experience Crockett had formed a very high opinion of their value in contrast to the members of the regular army. He had discovered "who fought the bravest, the regulars or the volunteers and militia."[34] The granting of the vacant lands to the poor would even increase this devotion, for, as Crockett asked rhetorically,

> Why does a man pride in his country? Why does he fight to defend it? It is, sir, because in so doing he fights for his home—for the spot upon which all his affections are fixed—and which stands identified with ten thousand enduring recollections. . . . To make of your citizen a land holder, you chain down his affections to your soil, and give him a pride and elevation of character, which fires his heart with patriotism, and nerves his arm with strength.[35]

This was especially true of his constituents, who were of inestimable value in a free republic: "In times of peace they are the bone and sinew of the land. They are a strength and bulwark in war; in the hour of danger they are the first to breast the onset of an enemy."[36]

The most significant aspect of these positive descriptions was that they seemed to render the subjects worthy of far better treatment than they had received. If people were decent and hardworking, if they made every effort to be an asset to their community, and if they had suffered through no fault of their own, then surely they were worthy of sympathy from the powerful interests that ran the country and might reasonably expect fair and decent treatment from their leaders. Thus, in presenting such an affirming picture of his constituents, Crockett was subtly demanding of his fellow legislators, "How dare you not aid such deserving fellow citizens?"

The very fact that many members of Congress seemed unwilling to render such aid helped to reinforce the third major element of Crockett's oratory: conspiracy. Conspiracy as a form of argument has been the subject of significant study over the past several decades. Richard Hofstadter has pointed out how this attitude has shaped significant social and political controversies of our era.[37] In summarizing Hofstadter's findings, Larson indicates that conspiracy frequently is used when three factors exist: the persons involved have something to lose, they see themselves as likely to lose it, and they see themselves as powerless to prevent this loss.[38] Clearly, all three of these conditions apply in the case of poor squatters: they were settled on land they did not own, there was a strong likelihood that they would be evicted from that land, and there seemed to be nothing to prevent that disaster from occurring. Thus, if Hofstadter and Larson are correct, the perfect conditions existed for a conspiracy argument to arise—and arise it did, for Crockett frequently claimed that a conspiracy of the rich and powerful vested interests of society lay behind the misery of his people.

Crockett argued that the land-hungry power structure of Tennessee and the state's delegation in Congress were engaged in an unholy alliance to deprive his people of what little they possessed. Even as he defended Polk's bill during his first congressional term, Crockett voiced his fears as to what would happen once the state legislature got its hands on the Congressional Reservation: they would "set up a swindling apparatus,"[39] and to prevent the squatters from obtaining the land "the legislature will fix their own price on it."[40] Thus Crockett saw in the attitudes of his colleagues evidence of a conspiracy to defraud his constituents.

Once the frontiersman had introduced his own bill to sell the land in small parcels at a low price, with the squatters getting the first right of purchase, he experienced even more hostility from those around him; as a result he became convinced that the main reason his measure failed to pass was a secret agreement among the Jacksonian members of the Tennessee delegation to prevent a successful conclusion to his efforts. The extent of Crockett's feeling on this matter may be garnered from a letter he wrote in mid-January 1829 to the editor of the major newspaper in his district, the *Jackson Tennessee Gazette,* reluctantly informing his constituents of the failure of the Tennessee land bill. The letter reads in part,

> I am sorry to inform you that on yesterday the Ten-
> nessee land bill was laid on the table, by a large ma-
> jority. . . . I have every reason to believe I could have
> passed my amendment if our own Delegation had not
> have opposed me. . . . I am really sorry to inform you
> that there was no opposition to my amendment, except
> the members of our own state. I was opposed by Messrs.
> Polk, Bell, Blair, Lea, Mitchell, and Isaacs, all come out
> with long speeches against me. You must know I was
> overpowered.[41]

Clearly, then, Crockett was attempting to justify his defense of the land bill and to argue that he did his best for the measure; it failed because there was a conspiracy on the part of the other Tennessee delegates, acting on instructions from President Andrew Jackson, to oppose him.

These attitudes carried over into Crockett's personal relations with the other members of his delegation. Within two months of the above-quoted letter, Crockett received notice that a missive highly critical of his efforts had been received and published by the *Jackson Gazette.* Crockett eventually discovered that this letter had been written by one of his colleagues, Representative Prior Lea, and Crockett in return published a lengthy letter of outrage, attempting to prove the extent of the conspiracy against him. A short section of the letter will fully indicate its tone:

> The manner in which you have attempted to destroy
> me is worthy of remark. You and myself were in daily
> habits of intimacy. . . . This confidence I must have en-
> joyed for near four weeks after you have forfeited every
> claim to it, by sending forth to the world . . . charges
> against me which, if you believe them true, should have
> closed your friendly intercourse with me, at a much
> earlier period. But was it so? No sir—to the very last
> hour that your attempt to ruin me was sealed in secrecy,
> you seem to meet me friendly—to converse with me
> as a friend!!!—affording in your conduct not the
> *slightest index to the feelings of your heart.* Sir, you

> complain that my feelings were alienated from my col-
> leagues;—and well they might have been so, had they
> all been like you—had their countenances been lighted
> with affected smiles of friendship, while their hearts
> burned with secret flames of ambition.[42]

Thus not only in the collective, but also in the individual sense, Crockett felt oppressed by a conspiracy of his colleagues to destroy him.

Late in his career, Crockett became more vehement in his denunciation of Jackson and the Jacksonians. He frequently voiced his opinion about the conspiracy that had been set in motion against him. His letters, his congressional orations, and his speeches in the Northeast are full of remarks indicating how he alone among the delegation from Tennessee remained independent and free of party control. Thus, along with other defenders of the dispossessed, Crockett felt himself the victim of a conspiracy because of the stands he took and felt it necessary to denounce that conspiracy on numerous occasions.

A final question that emerges under the heading of the conspiracy argument is one of cause and function: Why did Crockett, his constituents, and so many others among the dispossessed assert the presence of a conspiracy to keep them down? Clearly, the belief that "everyone is out to get us" is frequently seen among members of the lowest social groups. For such persons this belief serves a useful ego-defense function, protecting them from the unpleasant truth about their limited value to society.[43] Were it not for the conspiracy argument, it might be necessary for the dispossessed to admit that their failure to achieve a loftier social position was the result of their own inadequacies; this admission of their inferiority to others around them would, of course, be devastating to their egos. If, on the other hand, people are able to assert that their place in the world is not really the result of their own inadequacies but stems from the deliberate efforts of others to hold them in an inferior status, then any blame falls not on the disadvantaged themselves but on those who conspire to keep them down; after all, who can be held responsible for their own persecution by social, political, economic, and educational institutions? Thus, frequently, conspiracy claims are a desperate attempt by the poor and downtrodden to justify their failure to rise. Nevertheless, such claims must not be dismissed out of hand, for there may be from time to time considerable truth in the positions taken by speakers like Crockett— for, as Goodnight and Poulakos tellingly remind us, "Since not all conspiracy discourse . . . .necessarily remains the sole concern of a few . . . adherents, a theory of conspiracy discourse must account for the possibility that those upholding an unpopular . . . view may be participating in the restructuring of social consensus."[44]

Therefore, as Crockett addressed his colleagues and his constituents, his discourse was shaped in large part by three underlying attitudes: antipathy to education, the worthiness of his people, and the fear of conspiracy. In addition to these attitudes, however, Crockett also displayed in his addresses several rhetorical techniques; in particular, he made frequent appeals to pathos and used radical and offensive language.

Crockett made frequent use of pathos in order to acquire from his hearers sympathetic feelings toward those he was defending. Previously quoted passages from Crockett's arguments in Congress on his land bill have provided ample examples of the language he employed; words such as "hardy," "humble," "honest," and "kind-hearted" appear consistently in his discourses. His people were brave and patriotic in time of war; they were industrious in time of peace. Yes, Crockett knew his constituents well, "having shared the hospitality of their cottages."[45]

Perhaps the best example of Crockett's appeal to pathos is found in the concluding paragraph of his arguments before Congress on the land bill. In a dramatic peroration he uttered this highly moving picture of his constituents.

> I have seen the last blanket of a poor but honest and industrious family sold under the hammer of the sheriff . . . I saw the little furniture they had saved from better days or earned by long and honorable toil torn from them. . . . Exactions like these were made on men whose whole worldly estate consisted of some 20 or 30 acres of the worst land. Sir, it is for such men that I plead. I ask in my place as their advocate and representative that you will make them a donation of that little property. Let it be their own while they bedew it with the sweat of their faces; let them at least have the consolation of knowing that they may leave it to their own children and not have it squandered on the sons of a stranger.[46]

Thus, in his position as virtually the sole advocate for the poor squatters of his congressional district, Crockett spoke from the heart, voicing highly emotional pleas to his colleagues in Congress.

As speakers for unpopular causes sometimes do, Crockett frequently employed offensive or radical language that upset the staid parliamentarians of his day. He was particularly inventive when referring to President Andrew Jackson, his principal opponent. In Cincinnati, Ohio, having compared the chief executive's tyrannies to those of George III, Crockett concluded by labeling the president "King Andrew the First."[47] Jackson was also comparable to another ancient tyrant, Julius Caesar, Crockett informed an audience in Louisville, because he was now "holding the sword of the nation in one hand, and seizing in the other the purse of the people, bidding defiance to Congress, to the laws, and to the nation" (*Tour,* 186).

In his addresses to the New England Whigs, where he could be sure of a favorable response, Crockett gave even fuller play to his language. He could at times be clever, as in Boston where he observed the frigate *Constitution* fitted with a new figurehead in the form of a bust of Jackson. The frontiersman quipped that this placed Jackson "just where he had placed himself, that is, in front of the Constitution" (*Tour,* 64). More often, however, Crockett was merely nasty. Philadelphians were informed, for example, that all of the country's recent problems had been created merely "to gratify the ambition of one superannuated old man" (*Tour,* 25). Time and time again Jackson was labeled a tyrant or a despot or referred to insultingly as that "old fellow."

Not just Jackson himself, but Jackson's friends and supporters also came in for abuse. The president's problem was that he had surrounded himself with a group of inept, self-promoting opportunists who were bidding fair to wreck the nation: "He got round him a set of advisors who cared nothing for the honour and dignity of the government, but had their own low, interested views to accomplish, and cared not how they accomplished them" (*Tour,* 106). These persons were "sycophants and timeservers," and "a set of the greatest scrubs on earth" (*Tour,* 172). Chief among them was Vice-president Martin Van Buren, Jackson's hand-picked successor. At a Whig party dinner in Elizabethtown, Kentucky, Crockett gave Van Buren the full treatment; the vice-president was "a political Judas" who, "like a real Gopher, works more *under* than above ground" and who had been "smuggled into the vice-presidency, in the seat of Jackson's breeches" even though as a youngster he had been a "little, lying, tale-telling boy" (*Tour,* 190–91).

Crockett reached the height (or depth) of abusive language, however, during his election campaigns for the House. The Tennessee frontier of the 1820s and 1830s was a rough locality in any case, and Crockett certainly did nothing to raise the level of political argument currently in vogue. An outstanding example of such language is contained in a letter Crockett had published in the local newspaper after becoming aware of an anonymous criticism of him being circulated around the district. Crockett wrote:

> My patience would not permit me to answer at any considerable length, the production of so *base a scoundrel,* as the author of the letter alluded to, evidently is. I know not who he is, nor do I believe he has the *courage* to avow himself the author of his *vile calumny.* I should not notice it, if I were not convinced beyond the reach of very rational doubt, that like a *midnight assassin,* he was aiming a secret stab at my reputation and standing in society.

After quoting from the attack on him, Crockett concluded by lashing out:

> Who, to read the foregoing, can fail to shudder for the *corruption* of a heart so *base,* so deranged by malignity, as to embody so many wicked falsehoods; and that, too, without provocation? . . . The kindness of my feelings towards the human family in general, would prompt me to give it some softer name, if I were not so fully convinced that the author of this WICKED LIE, is some *contemptible wretch,* who seeks to gratify a *secret* feeling of revenge. . . . I consider him a *poltroon,* a *scoundrel,* and a *puppy.*[48]

While some of the above examples may appear as much amusing as offensive, it is clear that Crockett was not amused by the actions of his adversaries nor, clearly, were they provoked to laughter by his descriptions of them. In fact, much of Crockett's terminology here contained dangerous overtones; the words which he used, such as "poltroon" and especially "puppy," were the exact terms used among southern gentry to call out an opponent for an affair of honor. It is indeed surprising, considering the violence endemic in his society, that Crockett was not in fact challenged to a duel as a result of his intemperance.[49]

In attempting to bring his message to the public and to be assured of a hearing, then, Crockett clearly and extensively employed radical language. In reality, however, this technique worked to ensure an even less favorable reaction from those around him, who

felt affronted or offended by what he had to say and—especially—
the way he said it.

The nature of Crockett's defense of his squatter constituents raises
some intriguing questions: Was Crockett alone or unique in his position
as a rhetorical advocate for a disliked, dispossessed group? If other
such advocates can be found, did they employ techniques similar to
those Crockett used? If this is the case, did those techniques redound
to their disadvantage, as was true for Crockett? And, if the reaction
was not similarly hostile, can features be found in the dispossessed
group or in the advocate that would account for a different reaction?

Whatever answers may be discovered to the foregoing questions,
it is clear that Crockett spoke for the poorest of his constituents—
those who had neither money nor land but only the vague hope that
they might eventually be able to establish a home, free of the fear that
once again they would be driven out. In spite of his failure to achieve
his ultimate objective, we can see in the life and career of David Crockett
the features that make him the noblest and most altruistic of all
rhetoricians—the advocate for the voiceless, the defender of the
dispossessed.

◆   ◆   ◆

NULLIFICATION IN VERMONT, 1844

David Waite

[handwritten margin note: Hartford convention / Fed opposition to war of 1812]

In October 1844, the executive address of the governor of Vermont was read to the General Assembly of the state by the governor's secretary. The wildly and widely applauded speech climaxed in a ringing declaration that if Texas were admitted to the Union, "it would be the duty of Vermont to declare her unalterable determination to have no connexion [*sic*] with the new union."[1] This threat echoed the theories of nullification embraced by the South Carolinians a decade earlier. The nullifiers argued that if a state found a federal act unconstitutional, then that state had the power to render the act null and void. If the conflict reached an impasse, then the state had the right to secede from the Union. *[handwritten margin note: grounds in religion / national myth > ?]*

Such arguments were made possible by appealing to an evolving concept of American destiny or mission. In the turbulent decades after 1789, a beckoning vision of American destiny became embedded in the nation's rhetoric. The concept of an American mission grew out of the search for a usable past, one that would provide a national identity. Dispossessed of their European roots by emigration and revolution, Americans attempted to cloak their national past in ornate apocalyptic metaphor. They proclaimed that they were God's new chosen people, that God had led the nation out of bondage and extended his special favor and protection over them, the New Israel. Of his chosen people, moreover, God required much. Like the Jews, Americans were chosen for a divine mission: to be the repository of the world's hope and the agency for the world's salvation. Given such millennial responsibility, Americans were simultaneously hopeful and pessimistic.[2] *[handwritten margin note: Jeremiad]*

This belief—that Americans were ordained by God to fulfill a divine mission—provided the reformer and the politician with an ultimate

55

order for grounding both the moral and the expedient in God's divine purpose. Americans could not be God's agents or an example to the world unless they were pure themselves. First the individual would be saved, then the country, and then the world. Thus moral perfectibility was a consequence of the view of Americans as the chosen people. Inevitably, Americans forged this myth into weapons for their attack on the evils of slavery or for their defense of the status quo.

In *Forerunners of Black Power,* Ernest Bormann isolates two major types of abolitionist speakers who drew upon various elements of the American myth: first, the more hopeful evangelists who founded their arguments on the religious principles embodied in the ideal of America as humanity's last, best hope; and second, the pessimistic radical agitators who rejected large portions of the American ideological past and institutional present. While the evangelists emphasized the power of moral principle to purify the Union, the agitators argued that the Union was beyond salvation.[3] Both sides evoked their understanding of the principles of divine mission to bolster their position.

The existence of rhetorical conflict often breeds attempts to transcend it, especially by moderate, mainline elements or politicians. In antebellum New England, however, the most striking appeals of the evangelists and agitators did not have a moderate ring. Nullification, including threats to secede from the Union, was instead used to unite antislavery New Englanders.

Ironically, nullification principles originated in arguments used by the southern slaveholders to defend slavery. In 1832 and 1833, South Carolinians precipitated the crisis that stands as the prominent example of nullification. Demanding the repeal of the protective tariffs, the South Carolina legislature passed an ordinance nullifying the operation of the tariffs of 1828 and 1832 in their state. President Andrew Jackson ended the crisis with offers of the carrot of a compromise tariff coupled with the stick of military action. Although South Carolina did not secede, the underlying principle of nullification remained intact, ready to be resurrected by New Englanders in their battle against the "slavocracy."

This essay examines how the Vermont Whigs embraced nullification as the centerpiece of their antislavery rhetoric by appealing to their variant themes of American mission. Specifically, it analyzes how the Whigs combined, balanced, and confused the appeals of the radicals with the appeals of the evangelicals in order to retain political power in Vermont between 1840 and 1853.

The Whigs weathered political crises by manipulating three inter-twined themes in Vermont's Union sentiment: the hand of God in the American mission, the nature of Union as polity, and the legitimate means of persuasion. To explore these three themes and their relationship to nullification, a dramatistic or Burkean vocabulary will be employed. A Burkean lexicon echoes the voices of the articulate politicians who combined partisan politics with religion and social reform. The key Burkean concepts are "constitution," "constitution-behind-the-constitution," and "constitution-for-the-nonce." The hand of God in the American mission (Unionism) was both a constitution and a constitution-behind-the-constitution that the Vermont Whigs modified into their political platforms (constitutions-for-the-nonce).

Chronologically, this analysis divides into three parts: from 1835 to 1844, the antislavery movement gained political ground in Vermont, forcing the Vermont Whigs to act; in 1844 and 1845, William Slade and the Vermont Whigs quashed the antislavery Liberty Party; and after 1845, the Vermont Whigs abandoned much of their antislavery rhetoric.

I.

Isolated from the realities of slavery, most Vermonters were united in opposition to the South's peculiar institution and the early triumph of the antislavery movement seemed inevitable. The several Vermont constitutions and the state's earliest memorials contained strong antislavery feelings. In this both Vermont Whigs and Vermont Democrats concurred. A typical Whig declaration came from the Reverend George Campbell, who said that slavery was the root of all the national ills, "a national evil . . . of monstrous magnitude." The Vermont Democrats, led by such prominent editors as J. T. Marston of the Montpelier *Vermont Patriot*, echoed the Whig utterances. Marston argued that all persons "should frown upon a principle, at once so repugnant to the spirit of our institutions and all our ideas of the relations between man and man and man and his Creator."[4] To most Vermonters, the evils of slavery tainted a free society.

Still, many Vermonters were hostile to the strident abolitionists who stumped the state in the 1830s, and many of the earliest abolitionist speakers were physically assaulted. Brandon reformer Orson Murray, who was a Garrisonian abolitionist, temperance reformer, and antimason, was mobbed in Bennington, Woodstock, and Burlington for his abolitionist views. Abolitionist Samuel May, a Unitarian minister from Brooklyn, Connecticut, was mobbed five times in Vermont during 1835, and at Rutland and Montpelier his speeches were silenced by mob violence.[5]

Despite early resistance, the radical agitators, or "ultras," made headway in Vermont and in 1837 they began testing political candidates' soundness on the slavery issue. Although a question-and-answer strategy decided at least one close election, partisan politics and the ephemeral nature of political pledges brought the strategy of endorsing candidates to naught. By 1838, abolitionists like Quaker reformer Rowland T. Robinson argued that the antislavery movement had reached a strategic fork in its campaign. The crusade was faced with the choices of strategy that confront all political movements when persuasion fails or momentum slows: they had to continue what had apparently failed or switch to political action.[6] To the dismay of the Vermont politicians, the antislavery movement chose the second alternative and founded the one-issue Liberty Party.

For both Whigs and Democrats, the Liberty Party presented a problem. Under the Vermont Constitution, the governor was elected yearly by an absolute majority of the electorate. A plurality would throw the election into the General Assembly, where each town had one vote. In the General Assembly, the small hill towns (traditionally Democrat) could outvote the few large cities and towns (traditionally Whig). Consequently, the small Liberty Party could throw the gubernatorial election into an unpredictable political arena. Small wonder that the Whigs developed strategies to spike the guns of the Liberty Party.

The first strategy that Whigs hit upon was to run prominent antislavery Whigs for the governorship. Consequently, William Slade dominated the Vermont Whigs' antislavery arguments from 1840 to 1845. Slade's checkered political career helps to demonstrate just how desperate the Vermont Whigs were. Party loyalty was not one of Slade's strong points—he was a Democratic-Republican turned Antimason turned Whig. (In 1848, either from expediency or on principle, Slade would abandon the Whigs and bolt to the newly formed Free Soil Party.) His political allies feared his inconstancy; moreover, Slade was uneasy in the harness, unorthodox, and erratic. He attacked his fellow Whig, the highly respected Senator Phellps, as a drunkard; Phellps replied in kind and a mud-slinging match spattered on for years, much to the detriment of both men. If Slade's allies feared that he was unreliable, his enemies found him treacherous. An anonymous letter charged that Slade would willingly sacrifice anyone, friend or foe, who stood in his way.[7]

Despite his erratic nature, Slade was in many ways typical of the prominent Vermont Whigs. He combined interests in politics, social reform, and religion. In addition to various political offices, Slade was a member of the Vermont Missionary Society and the Vermont Antislavery Society. Although he sometimes blundered, Slade was a canny politician and a brilliant debater with the ability to combine morality and expediency. Although the positions were distinct, Slade equivocated on the terms "antislavery" and "abolition." He was consistently antislavery, and sometimes struck the more radical abolitionist note. Whatever his political abilities, however, his value to the Whigs was his strong antislavery record.

Slade made his antislavery reputation in the national political arena. From the start of the decade until Vermont's declining population erased his district, he was a representative in Congress. Despite the controversial nature of abolition, or "immediatism," Slade became the darling of the Northern abolitionists by reading their antislavery petitions on the floor of the House. When Congress refused to receive the petitions, Slade pressed for abolition of slavery in the District of Columbia. When Congress passed gag laws, Slade responded on January 18 and 20, 1840, by delivering the first call for immediate abolition ever heard on the floor of Congress. Vermont historian David Ludlum called this Slade's "most important abolition address."[8] Slade's strategy was to combine the antislavery impulse with some other fundamental value—in this case, freedom of speech and the right of petition. He repeated the same strategy in 1844.

Even as Slade spoke, the Liberty Party had become a troublesome element in the Vermont state elections. In the 1842 election, the third party received only slightly more than 3,000 votes, but since neither of the regular candidates received a majority of the popular vote the election was decided in the legislature.

Unable to control the Liberty Party, the Whigs seemed to succumb to the lure of political abolition. As their next candidate for the governorship, they nominated former Congressman John Mattocks, a thoroughgoing abolitionist. Mattocks confided to Theodore Weld, the prominent reformer, that he "would vote for any anti-slavery measure no matter how ultra it was . . . 'no abolition was too ultra for me.'"[9] Despite Mattocks's candidacy, the election of 1843 ended up in the General Assembly again. The Liberty Party candidate, Charles Williams (who would be the Whig governor less than ten years later), had received 3,700 votes, but Mattocks was elected by the assembly.

After his election Mattocks used the governorship as a pulpit for his antislavery beliefs. In his executive address he lamented the existence of slavery in the Union: "[It] should be the cause of deep humiliation to the moralist, the patriot, and the christian." On the annexation of Texas, Mattocks stressed the conspiracy theory: annexation was another slaveholder attempt to control the national government. If this were to happen, Mattocks argued, then "woe betide our unhappy country"; "who can hope the wrath of Heaven can be longer restrained?"[10]

The partisan (but observant) Democratic editor of the *Vermont Gazette* put Mattocks's executive address into perspective: the Whigs were spending a lot of time and effort wooing the antislavery forces, but Whig platforms were constitutions-for-the-nonce—declarations of principles to get votes. Once the votes were cast, the principles would be abandoned. Tongue in cheek, the editor suggested that Mattocks's speech should have contained the following passage: "To prevent those benighted abolitionists from voting against me again, I beg your patience while I devote one third of this my most noted speech to you men most noted for wisdom, in letting those naughty abolitionists know how much they will lose if they don't vote for me to be Governor next year."[11] Whatever Mattocks believed, the cynical Democrats saw the governor's abolitionist message as a political corrective.

Mattocks's year in office was marked by several nonpartisan antislavery resolutions. He recommended a bill that prohibited all officers of the state from "arresting or detaining in jail, any person who is claimed as a fugitive slave." This popular bill passed the Vermont House by a vote of 168 to 5. The General Assembly adopted a number of antislavery resolutions of a strong abolitionist stamp by equally large majorities. For example, the Vermont House and Senate resolved: "We desire the speedy abolition of slavery throughout the whole land; . . . we will use all just and lawful means within our power to accomplish that end."[12] An overwhelming majority of the Vermont legislature was fundamentally opposed to slavery.

In 1844, as the annexation of Texas seemed more certain, the antislavery crusade made increasing inroads in Vermont. On the Whig side the issue was annexation. At a political rally in the town of Lunenburg, the Whigs resolved that annexation was a "measure tending to the dissolution of the confederacy." The meeting declared that they would not be "bound by a broken constitution." When the Whigs deplored the admission of Texas, they implictly directed their appeals toward the preservation of the Union and the Constitution as they stood in 1840. The Whigs' constitution-for-the-nonce created division out of communion. Specifically, the Whig State Convention resolved that the admission of Texas would be "a virtual dissolution of the Union." Moreover, the dissolution would abolish the old Constitution and "break up the foundation of our federal Union."[13] Paradoxically, the admission of Texas (communion) would destroy the old political compact and be a fall from Eden.

The Democrats were as concerned as the Whigs about the annexation issue, but they were not sure how to handle it. Because the governor and the General Assembly had little influence, many Democrats labeled annexation as a phony issue and prayed that "it will be hard work to make much political capital out of this question." Others wrote that annexation "would tend to speed the abolition of slavery." Still others argued that annexation would create free states out of slave states by draining slaves from the older slave states. In such a political climate, many other issues were drawn into the antislavery debates. When the Democratic editors of the Danville *North Star* toted out the old national bank issue, for example, they gave it a new antislavery facade: they predicted that a national bank would "retard . . . emancipation half a century."[14]

To counter a desperate Liberty Party effort, the Whigs used the stock arguments that Slade had developed in Congress. Slade and the Whigs deplored the extension of slavery and declared that annexation was a constitutional issue. The bulk of these attacks were directed at the Democrats' reluctance to embrace antislavery. To distance themselves from the Liberty Party, the Whigs built on Slade's reputation and dusted off the traditional charge leveled at one-issue parties: the political abolitionists would "leave unregarded, and undecided at the ballot box, many great important issues which must be acted upon before slavery can be abolished."[15] Moreover, the Whig editors argued that no one could do more than they were doing. Consequently, the

Liberty Party undermined the antislavery cause: "[It works] efficiently only for evil and is at once the tool and jest of the slave party." Further, the Liberty Party attacks on the Whigs were "ungenerous and unfair" and "most bitter and vindictive."[16]

In the September election the Whigs scored a decisive victory. Slade received 28,000 votes, the Democratic candidate received almost 21,000, and, despite their intensive campaign, the Liberty Party's candidate finished a distant third with 5,600 votes. Vermont historian Wilbur H. Siebert calls it a "crushing defeat."[17] As a result, the Liberty Party lecture campaigns ceased; the new emphasis was on town and county organization.[18]

Even after the overwhelming vote of confidence, the Whig position was far from enviable. As long as the third party survived, the Whigs were trapped between the more moderate Democratic Party, which was laboring to defuse the issues of slavery, and the more radical Liberty Party, which was trying to make antislavery a test for political office. The Whig victory had been a staggering blow for the Liberty Party, but the Whigs had to be certain that the corpse would not be resurrected. Consequently, the new governor continued to usurp the Liberty Party platform. His election victory was the first nail in the Liberty Party's coffin; his executive address was the second.

II.

On Friday, October 11, Slade's executive address was read to the General Assembly.[19] Containing an exhaustive discussion of annexation, his address was the longest and most important governor's message of the decade. To ensure that the Liberty Party's wound was mortal, Slade explored three major aspects of Unionism's entanglement with slavery. He used three arguments that he had developed in Congress and in his gubernatorial campaign: he appealed to the evangelists by invoking the image of God in the American mission; he appealed to the antislavery radicals by declaring that if Texas was admitted to the Union, "it would be the duty of Vermont to . . . have no connexion with the new union" (27); and he transcended the apparent contradiction by discussing the legitimate means of persuasion.

Slade's executive address was given in a context of Unionism, a narrative ultimate order that designated America as a new promised land, that anointed Americans as the new chosen people, and that subordinated the individual to the purpose of a supreme founding father. Slade opened his executive address with a nod to the appeals of the evangelists. In the Vermont variations on the emerging national legend, Vermont politicians witnessed the hand of God intervening to shape and alter events all around them. Annually, the governors of Vermont thanked God for the blessings bestowed upon the state and the nation in the last year. Following this tradition, Slade praised God for this bounty. Woven throughout the address were tributes to the "great Author of our being" for the "great domain," and "garden, rank with luxuriance," the "teeming riches," and the other signs of "His peculiar favor" (13–14). Such public acknowledgments of God's favor were petitions for his continued munificence.

The governor and many Vermonters also believed that they could earn God's favor by acting as his agents on earth. Responsible "ultimately to Him who will Judge," Slade contended, Vermonters were required to fulfill God's divine purpose: "It is thus, in the right use of the means for national improvement which God has given us, that He will bless us—will make us a great and good nation, and enable us to accomplish the ends of His Providence in giving us a national existence" (24). In another passage Slade makes it clear that government has the obligation to use God's gifts to fulfill his divine plan: "The beneficent action of government . . . ought to be felt . . . in the drawing forth from the earth . . . teeming riches, to make them subservient to the purposes of their gift, in the wisdom and goodness of their Great Author" (13).

Such appeals to the hand of God in American history were the stock in trade of Vermont politicians. By 1844 a well-developed body of Union sentiment existed. As Benjamin Labaree, president of Middlebury College, argued, "We have all indulged in the pleasing idea that our country is destined to exert a commanding influence on the nations of the earth. It has been the theme of the orator, the statesman, and the poet."[20] With this much of the Union theology, many Americans agreed. God had established his new chosen people (the New Israel) in a new world (the New Eden), provided them with great blessings and, in return, demanded that they fulfill his divine mission. When they attempted to define the exact nature of the national mission, however, Americans were sharply divided. This led to a search for a national mission consistent with the will of God.

The first major explanation of the Union's destiny was the evangelical-militant ideal of a New Israel.[21] The evangelical component of

New Israel appealed to Vermonters because it allowed a state whose population was declining through emigration to reclaim its place in the world. Whig Congressman, scholar, and diplomat George Perkins Marsh explained that Vermonters should not discourage emigration; instead, they should glory in their sacrifice: "If then we cannot be the legislators of our common country, let it be your care that we are not unworthy to be its teachers, and though we cannot give it law, let us not cease to give it light."[22] In the spiritual realm, a purified nation could legitimately convert the world.

The redemption of the world was to come in three stages: Vermont would be purified, then Vermonters would aid in the redemption of the nation, and finally the nation would save the world. The Vermont Domestic Missionary Society, of which Slade was a member, described such a campaign of world salvation: "Efficient labors for the religious improvements of Vermont will be felt in their influence upon our whole country and upon the world. Vermont is exerting and *will* exert no small degree of influence, by the emigration of her sons, upon the forming character of the West. And we ever love to contemplate the connection which may exist between the salvation of the United States and the salvation of the world. A glorious destiny seems to be marked out for this nation if we will make it ours."[23] In Vermont Union sentiment, the creation of a moral example and its export through migration became a means of spiritual regeneration.

In its temporal manifestations, the ideal of New Israel was less popular among the Vermont Whigs. The idea that the Union should physically expand to dominate North, Central, and even South America seemed to most Vermonters an excuse for the proposed annexation of new slave states. Consequently, most Vermont Whigs combined the spiritual ideal of America as redeemer nation with a second major theme of America as the New Eden.[24] America was both the great experiment in self-government and the last, best hope of mankind. The example of a nation conducting a successful experiment in liberty would transform the world.

To combine the ideal of New Israel with the ideal of New Eden while avoiding what would become labeled "manifest destiny," Slade described an America that had been ordained by God as a model for the world. If that nation could demonstrate that people were capable of self-government, then the example of stability and order would spread the cause of republicanism throughout the world. In his executive ad-

dress the governor suggested, "It is . . . in the order of Providence . . .
that this nation should be a model of virtue, intelligence and good government for the world" (18). This ideal of Union as republican experiment contradicted the most militant ideals of manifest destiny. A nation
based on the capacity for self-government could not stoop to conquer
those who were less exalted without undermining the purity of its example. In other words, conquest and rule represented the corrupting
influence of coercion.

   Although this ideal of Union might be moral and rhetorical proof
against the conquest of new slave states, Slade felt that another set of
arguments was needed to justify Vermont's resistance to the annexation
of Texas. That second set of arguments hinged on the nature of the
Union as political compact.

   Slade's second major theme was borrowed from the arguments of
the radical agitators. Since the founding of the republic, Americans
had debated the nature of the national Union. Broadly, there were two
major views of the Union. One view held that the Union that was
embodied in the Constitution had risen organically, that the union
antedated both the states and the Constitution. Eventually, this view
became a brief for Union absolute; the Union could never be dissolved.
The other view was Union as polity. Union was formed as a contract
or compact; it sprang from the deliberate actions of the nation's founders and the states. In this view, the national Constitution was a written
contract and the general tenets of contract law applied. Any abridgment
or change not contemplated in the original contract was subject to the
agreement of every member of the partnership. In the case of Union,
the partners were the states. Consequently, all states had to consent
to any change. Of course, such arguments sired the bedeviling doctrines
of nullification and secession. Without some arbiter among states or
between state and federal government, the only recourse was revolution
and civil war. In 1833, for example, Daniel Webster argued that nullification and secession sprang from the same premises and were equally
destructive of the Union.[25] If Slade could avoid the term "nullification,"
the pattern or form of argument that supported nullification was available to the antislavery forces in Vermont.

   Slade based his argument for Vermont's resistance to annexation
on the view of Union as contract. In his executive address, Slade stressed
the contractual foundation of the Union. The "confederacy," as he
called it, was "a compact into which [Vermont] has entered" (25). The

admission of Texas without the consent of all the states of the Union was "as though a majority of members of an ordinary partnership were to attempt to force a member into the concern without the common consent" (26). South Carolina had stood upon the same theory of contract in 1832 and had won a compromise tariff. In 1844 Slade was playing the same argument for different stakes.

As Calhoun had, Slade stressed the illegality and immorality of coercion. The federal government lacked the power to coerce any state into compliance. Slade declared that if the question of annexation was "submitted to Vermont . . . we would deliberate upon it; but the question whether we will submit to be forced into it . . . is not to be debated for a moment" (27). This idea of a voluntary compact was rooted in the major tenets of Unionism. If a common citizen was capable of self-government, then force would be unnecessary; personal interests would be submitted to the will of the majority voluntarily.

Conversely, the use of force would be self-defeating. An unequivocal advocacy of the principle occurred on the eve of the Civil War. Vermont editor and Congressman E. P. Walton argued, for example, that if the Union were dissolved, then the main purpose of the Union—an experiment in self-government—was defeated, and forcing a state to remain could not change that. Walton argued, "As our government originated, so it must be maintained, by the voluntary and unrestrained will of the people. If it cannot be maintained, then our system is radically wrong and destined to failure."[26] In 1844, as in 1860, the use of force to compel a state to remain in the Union undermined the reason for the Union's existence.

In principle, Union by force was an empty husk devoid of moral or spiritual power. Slade linked annexion with Union by force. Annexation was an "insufferable invasion of our rights." The attempt to force Vermont into a "new union" was the equivalent of invasion, and if Vermonters acquiesced it would be like "submission to a foreign yoke" (27). Slade went beyond annexation as destruction of principle. He argued that a Union by force was no Union. The very process of annexing a new state without the consent of all the partners created a "new confederacy" that destroyed the "old," exercising a power "equivalent to suicide" (25). Although his argument sounded like a justification of secession, Slade did not lead Vermont out of the Union. The force of Slade's argument was that the slaveholders and not the antislavery forces were the real threat to the Union. Slavery aside, the violation of the compact was reason to resist the slave power.

To the question of polity, Slade linked a second question which he labeled "constitutional" (26): the purpose of annexation. Annexation, Slade suggested, was an attempt to rescue slavery, "to infuse into it fresh life and vigor, and to prolong and perpetuate its power" (27). In a campaign speech at the Whig State Convention, Slade had stressed that extension of slavery was the only reason for annexation: "I come now to the *purpose* of the annexation movement. From its commencement to this hour, it has obeyed a single impulse—that of a determination to obey the slave power."[27]

Although morality was deeply entwined in his argument, the motives that Slade adduced to explain why the South championed annexation were political ones. Directed at a distant enemy—a different economic and cultural system—Slade's arguments were appeals to political xenophobia. The question he argued was "not one of mere philanthropy [morality], but has other bearings [expediency]. Slavery is an element of political power; and how long, and to what extent, it shall be suffered to control the politics and mold the destiny of this nation, is a question whose consideration cannot be postponed indefinitely" (28). Slade labeled the argument "political" to allude to the theories of slaveholder conspiracy.

Slavery was a vast Southern political conspiracy that was bent on extending slavery, on dominating the federal government, and on subverting the nation's true purpose. In a particularly vivid series of passages, Slade personified slavery and charted its triumphant progress. At each step, the moderates were forced to give ground as slavery demanded more and more: "Slavery has planted itself in new fields—has struggled for ascendency, and maintained it; and has finally come to the ground that it must be fostered, and cherished, and extended" (28). Slade's choice of language made it clear that moderates were being driven into a corner. The evil of slavery must be either stopped or "fostered" and "cherished."

When he labeled the argument "constitutional," Slade was faced with a document that seemed to protect slavery. The radical abolitionists rejected the Constitution and appealed to the ideal of Unionism or the constitution-behind-the-constitution. Slade took a different route. He denied that the Union had been formed to perpetuate or

protect slavery. Slavery was not an inextricable compromise of the
Constitution. In his 1840 congressional address, Slade's argument was
based on an appeal to consistency: both Constitution (Union) and the
antislavery impulse were manifestations of God's will. Moreover, Slade
assumed that the Constitution was good and slavery was evil. An
assumption that slavery was inextricably embedded in the Constitution
would place two manifestations of God's will (Union and antislavery
impulse) in opposition. Further, redemption would come, in Slade's
view, through persuasion. Slade argued that if the constitutional compromise forbade the discussion of slavery then something was vitally
wrong: "*Before* the Union we might have spoken with great effect.
Without the Union, we might now put forth our moral power. . . . But
the Union has been formed, and we must be silent."[28] Only an inconsistent God in a perverse universe would create such a situation.

In his executive address of 1844, Slade modified his argument.
God's agents on earth were the nation's founders. To transcend constitutional justifications of slavery, Slade appealed to their expectations:
"If the purpose of the Fathers had been carried out, slavery [would
have] gradually yield[ed] and given place to the institutions of freedom"
(28). Such an expectation was based on the inevitable triumph (syn-
onymous with God's will) of freedom: "The onward progress of freedom, under its high impulses, is rapidly changing the balance of power
and leaving slavery to perish" (27). In a just world, freedom and liberty
would inevitably triumph over sin and error.

The abolitionists founded their rejection of the Union on such
arguments. Slavery was wrong and could only be saved from destruction
by political action. If Union and the Constitution protected slavery,
then Union and the Constitution were wrong. Both Slade and the
abolitionists agreed on that. The abolitionists concluded that the ideal
of the Union could only be preserved if the physical Union were
destroyed. Slade used a construction that paralleled the abolitionist
argument. Although he "greatly" valued the Union and "would preserve
it," he suggested that attempts to contravene the intent of the founders
and God's "onward progress of freedom" were as destructive to the
experiment as dissolution of the Union (27).

Despite an apparently abolitionist appeal, there were several differences between how the abolitionists and Slade approached antislavery. The essence of Slade's antislavery tactics was to reverse the
argument. He transcended the conflict between the various portions

of Union sentiment by arguing that two such valuable things could not be in opposition. Since all parts sprang from God, the principles had to be consistent. The Constitution and Union were not flawed; only the machinations of the slaveholders (slavocracy or slave conspiracy) brought two fundamental principles of freedom and Union into opposition.

When called upon to explain his position, Slade took the approach that the extension of slavery was possible only through a "violation of the Constitution." In the campaign preceding his election and during his executive address, Slade isolated "the addition of slave states from territory not within our original limits" as the sole cause of the present conflict.[29] Consequently, the unconstitutional actions of the enemy perverted God's purpose.

To meet the vast Southern conspiracy, Slade brought his state to the brink of nullification and disunion. He declared that if Texas were admitted, Vermont would "have no connexion with the new union" (27). Rhetorically, however, Slade refused to countenance either annexation or nullification. Whigs did not advocate disunion, for if they had advocated disunion (or nullification) openly they would have legitimized the position of the Garrisonians and the Southern disunionists. Slade carefully distinguished Vermont's resistance from disunion or nullification: "To carry out this determination would not dissolve the union, but to refuse to submit to its dissolution,—not to nullify, but to resist nullification" (27). Although his argument could be construed as a threat of disunion, Slade avoided either extreme. Instead, he shifted the blame to those who were supporting annexation.

The conditional sentence "If Texas is admitted to the Union, then the Union will be dissolved" can be interpreted in three ways: first, as a threat of disunion or nullification; second, as mechanical causation—if Texas is admitted to the Union, then disunion will somehow follow inevitably; and third, as a prediciton that the nature of the Union would be irrevocably altered by annexation.

The Democratic press interpreted Slade's position in the first way. The editors of the Danville *North Star* called Slade's executive address "egotistical," "dictatorial," and "rank *Nullification*." The editor of the *Vermont Gazette* charged that, if Texas were annexed, Slade would "call out the forces of Vermont to divide the Union." Many Whigs met the Democratic fusillade head on. When Maine Democrats suggested that

Vermont could be forced to remain in the Union, the editor of the *Rutland Herald* responded with chauvinistic references to the fighting prowess of the Green Mountain Boys. Obviously, however, Union was not held in high regard when the chief magistrate of the state was able to declare that the Union was "virtually dissolved."[30]

On the other hand, the Whigs were leaving themselves an out. The second and third hypotheses suggest that something of the lawyer's brief was creeping into the Whig attacks on annexation. The Whigs were saying precisely what they wanted to say, nothing more and nothing less. In this context, Slade's calls for immediate emancipation on the floor of Congress and in his 1844 campaign are suggestive. In both cases, Slade did not advocate disunion or nullification overtly. The Whigs never declared that Vermont would secede or dissolve the Union. They were exceedingly careful also to place the blame for disunion on the actions of the South, the slaveholders, and slavocracy.

Whenever he approached the issue of disunion, Slade used two parallel constructions. If the South posed a threat to the Union, Slade's construction was that if a certain action is taken, then the South will dissolve the Union. If disunion talk originated in Vermont, Slade's construction was that if a certain action is taken, then the Union will be automatically dissolved. In 1840, Slade had argued that if slavery was protected by the Constitution, "then it was a Union placed on a *mine,* to be shattered into a thousand fragments by its inevitable explosion." The suppression of free speech would "dissolve the Union": "You might as well expect the stopping of Aetna's crater would not produce an earthquake, as that a dissolution of the Union would not follow such a suppression."[31]

Grammatically, therefore, Vermonters' actions could never destroy the Union. Disunion was the inevitable result of some impersonal historical force set in motion by another's action. Consequently, the Southern politicians and their allies, the slavocracy, were always the unregenerate foe.

Having appealed to both the radical agitators and the evangelists, Slade used the third portion of his speech to smooth over any contradictions. Having just prepared his audience for dissolution, he warned them that they should avoid both "indifference" and "over-heated and headlong zeal." To reach the "seat of the evil," Vermonters were required to make a "calm, steady, patient, persevering effort" (28–29).

Slade's emphasis on the length of the struggle was based on a popular Vermont rhetorical theory. In the Vermonters' struggles against sin and error, time was of little consequence. By necessity, truth would inevitably triumph over error. Observing the world through Platonic glasses, John Wheeler, president of the University of Vermont, told an audience in Andover, Massachusetts, "Moral truths are in their nature imperative. They need but to be seen, for the feeling of obligation to exist."[32] Vermonters had merely to confront sin with virtue and God's will would inevitably triumph.

If the inevitable triumph of truth is incorporated into a rhetorical system, then a strategy can be used to avoid what James Andrews calls the morality-expediency conflict. In the morality-expediency dichotomy, the introduction of moral principles into a debate decreases the potential for compromise because the world is reduced to two warring sections—sin and virtue.[33] However, if the triumph of truth is both gradual and inevitable, then the potential for compromise is not diminished. Although no compromise on ends is possible (the evil must be destroyed), compromise on means is possible, and the moralist can grant the enemy time in which to repent and reform.

When the reformer loses patience or becomes convinced that the enemy is unregenerate, the compromise on means will end. The reformer will press for legislation or form a political movement. At this point, the politician can still confound the reformer by converting the inevitable triumph of truth into a moral imperative. Ironically, the primacy of moral suasion was a stock argument of the abolitionists. During the congressional debates over the gag laws and the right of petition, for example, the Vermont Antislavery Society created a strong argument for the "right of free discussion" as the "vital principle of popular institutions."[34] Slade and the abolitionists gained sympathy by arguing that abolition was a free speech issue. What made the gag laws so galling to all reformers (not just abolitionists) was that the abridgment of free speech blocked the operation of God's truth on the souls of the unregenerate.

Of course, the defense of free speech was a double-edged sword. Appeals to the First Amendment rallied support not for the abolitionist positions on slavery but for the principle of moral suasion. It was enough for the politician to allow free speech to operate. Consequently, the Vermont politicians from both parties continued to argue that moral suasion or the influence of God's truth was the only legitimate means of influence long after the abolitionists had abandoned moral suasion for political action. Legal suasion or coercion was morally wrong, impractical, and at variance with the basic tenets of Union doctrine.

Slade declared that morality and moral influence were paramount to legislation: "The most efficient laws are those which govern, not by the power of the sword, but by the silent influence of virtuous and enlightened principle" (14). Moreover, his extended discussion of what had to be done to convert the South contained all the premises that underlay the doctrine of moral suasion. Slade called for "gradually changing the character of state and national legislation, while no great interest of the country shall be left forgotten, uncared for, or neglected" (28–29). In deference to Southern "jealousy" of the North, Slade counseled that the Vermonters' efforts to end slavery should advance with moderation and forbearance (28–29). The emphasis on gradualism and the stress on forbearance and moderation were derived from the concept of moral suasion.

As long as he defended the ideal of moral suasion, Slade could strike a moral balance between the Whigs' two paramount enemies— the slaveholders and the Liberty Party. His attacks on slavery and slaveholders were direct; his attacks on the political abolitionists were indirect, but his intentions were unmistakable. Slade blamed the rise of political abolition on the "pretensions and encroachments of the slave power." As a result, Slade argued, the abolitionists were drawing "every other question of morals or politics within their vortex" (28). As the vortex metaphor suggests, Slade perceived the movement of abolition as around and down. By embracing abolitionist doctrine, Slade hoped to quash Vermont's antislavery Liberty Party.

On the antislavery issue, Slade and the Whigs played both sides. Vis-à-vis the federal government and the national political parties, the Whigs represented the antislavery ultras, attacking the Southern slaveholders as a political conspiracy bent on subverting liberty and destroying the Union. Vis-à-vis the Vermont antislavery crusade and the one-issue parties, the Whigs were defenders of the old order, calling for moderation and patience.

The political battles over annexation sputtered on into 1845, but the results were inconclusive and anticlimactic. On the issue of slavery, the Democratic editors repeatedly charged that the Whigs' rhetoric was indicative "more of love for office than love for the slave." Their arguments included jibes at Vermont's continued presence in the Union and appeals to love of the Union. Further, the Democrats continued to argue that because antislavery was a moral issue only moral suasion would work: "Moral suasion, and not political action will secure so desirable an end. Political hostility to slavery . . . can avail but little in overthrowing the system."[35]

With this both Whigs and Democrats could agree. So long as the Whigs could defend the ideal of moral suasion they were safe. The system would break down only if the enemy demonstrated their unregenerate nature beyond question. In part the Vermonters' tolerance of the increasingly vehement attacks on slavery sprang from the increasing evidence of Southern intransigence. The best evidence of the unregenerate nature of the enemy came from attempts to extend slavery. Time and time again, Slade and the Vermont Whigs stressed the rhetorical principle that Vermonters could not afford to strike the first blow. Just as the enemy had to fire the first shot at Lexington, so the slaveholders had to fire the first volley by attempting to extend slavery. Only the unregenerate nature of a foe who attacked, together with the slaveholders' attacks on the Constitution and the principles of Unionism that were ordained by God, could justify counterattack. Once the attack was made, however, the counterattack could and should be unrestrained.[36]

When the legislature convened again in October 1845, annexation had taken place and Vermont had not withdrawn from the Union. In his second executive address, Slade was more subdued than he had been in 1844. Slade declared that the only bond of Union was "the apprehended evils of actual separation." There was no "confidence of affection" existing in the "injustice and usurpation" that surrounded the new Union.[37] Whatever Slade's original intention, his disunionist outburst became no more than a cathartic rumbling of discontent and frustration.

On the other hand, Slade had accomplished much. He had demonstrated that a one-issue antislavery party could not convert moral and religious indignation into victory at the polls. Using the tenets of Unionism to divide friend from foe, he had stolen the Liberty Party's thunder and reestablished Whig hegemony in Vermont. Once the Liberty Party had been destroyed, the Whigs felt little need to proceed further, and after 1845 they began to quietly abandon major portions of the antislavery ground they had won.

III.

In retrospect, William Slade's two terms as governor marked a minor watershed in Vermont politics. Never again would a governor of the state advocate anything close to a dissolution of the Union. In the next five years the Whigs shifted their political constitution once more and abandoned the extremes of antislavery. Into the breach left by the demise of the old Liberty Party stepped the Free Soil Party.

One indication of the Whig recessional on antislavery was Slade's move to the new party. Despite his popularity, Slade was no longer at home in the Whig Party councils after 1846. He bolted his old affiliation and laid down the guidelines for the new Free Soil Party in a series of published letters. Slade called upon the North to unite in opposition to the slave power: "In such a crisis as this, we *must* dismiss our prejudices; for if we would maintain our rights, there must be union."[38] Of course he was not necessarily speaking of the union of the states but a union of northern political interests, a defensive reaction to the old Southern slave conspiracy.

In a letter read before the 1848 Buffalo Free Soil Convention, Slade addressed the dual issues of slavery and disunion once again. Although he modified his wording, the arguments were very similar to the ones that he had used in 1844. Slade foresaw no dangers of disunion in the actions of the Free Soilers; instead, they offered the hope of preserving the Union intact: "I think it necessary to the preservation and perpetuity of the Union." Slade concluded that if slavery were extended, "this nation will die, if freedom is essential to its life, and the providence of a just God has anything to do with its preservation."[39] The destruction of the Union would proceed from the actions of the South or the will of God; Northerners would be guiltless provided their intentions were pure.

In the gubernatorial election of 1848, however, the advantage went to the Whigs. The Whig candidate, Carlos Coolidge, fell short of a majority by over 6,000 votes but was easily elected by the legislature. The other two parties finished in nearly a dead heat. The Free Soilers finished second; ex–Liberty Party candidate William Shafter, who had never received more than 7,000 votes in his previous attempts at the governorship, received 15,000. The Regular Democrat, former Congressman Paul Dillingham, finished with just under 14,000 votes, a drop of 5,000 from 1847.

Clearly the Free Soilers influenced the outcome of the election, even if they could not elect their own candidate. More importantly, they showed that Vermonters were incresingly demanding strong anti-slavery platforms. This is where historian David Ludlum leaves the issue, arguing that by 1848 war was inevitable: "There could be no turning back now; slavery must go or Christianity be repudiated."[40] Rhetorically this was not true. In 1848 disunion and war were still two separate issues, and disunion would not automatically lead to civil war. To many Vermonters, the use of coercion even to perpetuate the Union was unthinkable, and even after 1848 the Whigs successfully took a very moderate antislavery line.

For many Vermonters, the last great battle between slavery and freedom was the battle over the Great Compromise of 1850. Moderates, including Northern Whigs such as Henry Clay and Northern Democrats such as Stephen Douglas, joined in an attempt to stop the widening division between North and South. The territorial compromises included the admission of California as a free state. The price for these concessions included stricter fugitive slave laws. The initial response in Vermont was vehement opposition. To Vermonters, antislavery and political power seemed to be the only tests of the acceptability of the Compromise. Even the highly respected Daniel Webster came under attack. The editor of the *Vermont Patriot* declared that Webster had "sold himself to the slave power." Throughout the summer of 1850, the majority of Vermont editorial opinion opposed the Great Compromise. Although it came from the national Whig administration, Regular Democrats supported it and the Whigs and Free Democrats denounced it. The Whig Committee on Resolutions for the State Convention declared that the Compromise was "another stride from the path of honor, of safety, and of liberty itself." The Democratic editor of the *Burlington Courier* asserted that Compromise was worse than disunion: "Religion and humanity are a price too dear to pay even for Union."[41]

With such strong antislavery and antiadministration rhetoric, the Whigs weathered another antislavery storm and maintained political power. In the September elections, former Chief Justice and former Liberty Party candidate Charles K. Williams received an impressive majority of the popular vote in a three-candidate field. Despite this overwhelming show of popular support and despite his Liberty Party connections, the sixty-eight-year-old Whig was unwilling to add any new antislavery kudos to the Whig record.

In 1851, for example, Williams declared that the principle of majority rule was so vital that Vermonters would uphold it even when their interests were threatened. Renouncing the principles that Slade had espoused, Williams argued that even "if our wishes be disregarded, and a policy still more fatal to our interests be pursued, we shall endeavor to seek redress in the Union, and not out of it."[42] Majoritarianism reigned supreme now.

The Vermont Whigs based their antislavery recessional on the Compromise of 1850. In 1851, the columns of the *Green Mountain Freeman* contained a concise assessment of Whig editorial opinion. At a minimum, nine of thirteen Whig journals supported the Great Compromise explicitly or tacitly. The *Bellows Falls Gazette*'s editor claimed that an "immense majority of the Whig party" and a "majority of the people are triumphantly sustaining the peace measures of the late Congress."[43] Rhetorically, the Compromise allowed the Whigs to straddle the antislavery issue.

For the next three years the Whigs kept things quiet. During this time, the fortunes of the political abolitionists had been linked to the Free Soilers. As the Vermont Whigs transformed their party into an antimovement, the political abolitionists had been looking for the crisis that would tie the sagging fortunes of their single issue to either Whig or Democratic constitutions-for-the-nonce. When the administration Democrats introduced the Kansas-Nebraska bill onto the floor of Congress in 1854, the long-awaited crisis came.

Between 1840 and 1854, Vermonters created a host of elaborate and competitive constitutions. Each variation was a corrective and produced a countercorrective. As a countermovement, the Whigs ensnared the Liberty Party by sounding as radical as the abolitionists. No one in the Liberty Party could match the antislavery credentials of William Slade or even John Mattocks. For the campaign of 1844, Slade borrowed the theory of nullification from the South Carolinians and gave it an antislavery twist. Slade and the Whigs seemed to rank the ideal of Union above the reality of Union. Even after his impressive victory, Slade repeated the warning. In his executive address in 1844, he prepared Vermonters for the sacrifice of the Union on the altar of liberty. To escape the moral corruption of slavery in 1844, the Vermont Whigs seemed prepared to destroy the Union and thus keep the nation's moral example intact.

Once the Liberty Party was defeated, however, the doctrine of moral suasion allowed the Vermont Whigs to abandon much of their anti-slavery platform—at least as long as the South did not reveal its unregenerate nature. Moreover, the passage of the Great Compromise of 1850 provided the Vermont Whigs with an opportunity to quiet the antislavery agitation by using the Compromise as a corrective to their earlier platforms. However, the proposed destruction of the Compromise by the South confirmed Vermonters' suspicions that the South was unregenerate, and, confronted with evidence of the South's moral intransigence, the Whigs became increasingly frustrated with moral suasion. In the end, the massive complex of corrective constitutions-for-the-nonce collapsed when Vermonters became convinced that legal suasion or coercion might be the only answer. By 1854, moreover, Vermont politicans were less willing to see the Union destroyed. The Whigs buried their old party label, coalesced with the remaining Free Soilers, and founded the Vermont Republicans, a new antiadministration party dedicated to antislavery and Union. Yet, for fourteen years, the Whigs had manipulated the themes of Unionism to maintain power.

[Handwritten annotations at top of page:]
→ meticulous inventions

continues the artful natural vein ... idea that flies — note

1. Is this an effort to reconstruct the implicit rhetorical theory of historical figure — thereby helping us appreciate the nature of theory/practice at particular time __ or __ an effort to contribute to cont theory?

◆ ◆ ◆

PERSUASION OF THE UNCONSCIOUS WILL: WALT WHITMAN AND THE RHETORIC OF INDIRECTION

John Lee Jellicorse

"NO DOUBT THE LITERARY, PROFESSIONAL, FELLOWS MAY TAKE HOLD OF US IF WE LAST, BUT I CONFESS I SHRINK FROM IT WITH HORROR."
—WALT WHITMAN, 1889[1]

Taking "A Backward Glance O'er Traveled Roads" in 1888, Walt Whitman (1819–92) consigned his lifelong "*sortie*," *Leaves of Grass,* to the future, concluding, ". . . whether to prove triumphant, and conquer its field of aim and escape and construction, nothing less than a hundred years from now can fully answer."[2] In March 1992 a major conference was held to evaluate Whitman's legacy. Convened on a university campus, the Walt Whitman Centennial Conference featured presentations by "twenty of the world's eminent Whitman critics, biographers, and textual scholars."[3] With few exceptions, those who gathered to assess his work, including all twenty of the presenting scholars, were from the academic literary establishment. Although there was a program on "The Influential Whitman," the influence discussed was Whitman's literary influence.[4] Far different this gathering from those political and ethical society activists, reformers, lawyers, physicians, artisans, and others who, during Whitman's lifetime and long after his death, gathered, often as a formal "Walt Whitman Fellowship," to honor the "new birth" they had experienced from association with Whitman and/or his *Leaves of Grass.*[5] A hundred years after his final sortie, the "death bed" 1891–92 edition of *Leaves of Grass,* what Whitman feared has taken place. He has been taken hold of by "the literary, professional, fellows."

WHITMAN AND LITERARY CRITICISM

"CRITICISM IS A NECESSARY TEST—THE PASSAGE OF FIRE: WE HAVE GOT TO MEET IT—
THERE IS NO ESCAPE. I DO SAY WITH REGARD TO MYSELF THAT I MUST BE JUDGED
ELEMENTALLY—THAT THE [MATTHEW] ARNOLDS, THE DISCIPLES OF BOOKS AS BOOKS,
THE SECOND AND THIRD HAND MEN, THE SCHOLARS PURE AND SIMPLE, THE LOVERS OF
ART FOR ART'S SAKE, CANNOT UNDERSTAND ME—CANNOT TAKE ME IN—I ELUDE THEIR
CIRCUMSCRIPTIONS."
—WALT WHITMAN, 1888[6]

Consistently throughout his career, Whitman denied literary intent.
"'I do not value literature as a profession,'" he proclaimed. "'I feel about
literature what Grant did about war. He hated war. I hate literature. . . . it is a means to an end, that is all there is to it: I never attribute
any other significance to it.'"[7] This oft-repeated derogation of "literary
literature" and academic and professional literary scholars was based
on fear that literary criticism misinterpreted his works and thwarted
his efforts to reach his audience. Increasingly in his lifetime, and
dominantly in the twentieth century, the approach to Whitman's work
is to apply a priori literary theories to his "poetry" while dismissing
his nonliterary motives. His antiliterary stance is interpreted as a defensive "pose" adopted to rationalize lack of literary acceptance in his
own era or as a conspiracy on the part of the "poet's" early misguided
admirers and followers. The results of such efforts, as Whitman said,
"'to confirm a round world by square tests,'"[8] have been exceedingly
strained because the process denies and ultimately refutes clear evidence that Whitman was more concerned about his message than about
his poetics: "'I don't value the poetry in what I have written so much
as the teaching; the poetry is only a horse for the other to ride.'"[9]

WHITMAN AND RHETORIC

"THE GREAT FUNCTION OF THE CRITIC IS TO SAY BRIGHT THINGS—SPARKLE,
EFFERVESCE: PROBABLY THREE-QUARTERS, PERHAPS EVEN MORE, OF THEM DO NOT
TAKE THE TROUBLE TO EXAMINE WHAT THEY START OUT TO CRITICIZE—TO JUDGE A
MAN FROM HIS OWN STANDPOINT, TO EVEN FIND OUT WHAT THAT STANDPOINT IS."
—WALT WHITMAN, 1889[10]

If Whitman's works were not intended to be literature, what
were they? If they were means, not ends, what results were sought?
How well did his "horse" carry its burden? These are rhetorical
rather than literary questions, and Whitman provides a model case

study for the relationship between rhetorical intent and effect. From 1855 until his death in 1892, he continued to revise a single work, *Leaves of Grass,* as his primary rhetorical weapon. In private journals and diaries, and sometimes in conversation with friends, later published, he stated clearly and precisely his rhetorical intentions for *Leaves of Grass* as a whole or for new works to be added as annexes or integrated into the body of the book. After the delivery of a message—through a new edition of *Leaves of Grass,* or in a lecture, individual poem, or prose work—he would then add entries to his journals or diaries analyzing how successful the effort had been in achieving its objectives. Frequently, moreover, he would also explain a work after its presentation and attempt to guide the potential audience member as to the appropriate response. To disguise his purposes while maintaining the potency of his message, these post-delivery explications were often published anonymously or under the name of a friend.

Because rhetoric is sometimes approached as rhetorical criticism, a sister art of literary criticism, it too can shoehorn phenomena into a priori categories. Applying Aristotelian or Burkean criticism to Whitman can be just as distorting as applying inappropriate literary criteria.[11] If Whitman is to be understood from his own standpoint, the first task is accurately to describe—not evaluate—his endeavors. The purpose of this essay, therefore, is to take Whitman seriously as a rhetorician and to explicate his concept of persuasion, his rhetorical "standpoint." This will be done by (1) analyzing his rhetorical purposes against the background of the theories of persuasion available to him, (2) detailing how he evolved a rhetorical theory appropriate to his purposes, (3) providing an overview of the basic assumptions inherent in his rhetorical theory, and (4) noting briefly the relationship of his rhetorical concepts to twentieth-century theories. A sustained critique of his rhetoric is left to others. Here the effort is simply to take the trouble to find out what Whitman intended, and why.

WHITMAN'S RHETORICAL PURPOSES

THE WHOLE DRIFT OF MY BOOKS IS TO FORM A RACE OF FULLER ATHLETIC, YET UNKNOWN CHARACTERS, MEN AND WOMEN FOR THE UNITED STATES TO COME. I DO NOT WISH TO AMUSE OR FURNISH SO CALLED POETRY. . . .
—WALT WHITMAN, 1869[12]

After 1855, Whitman's primary purpose as a persuader was nothing less than to initiate a new society, which he called the Religious Democracy. The Religious Democracy was to result from the creation of physically and morally perfected individuals, and his specific purpose in his interaction with audiences, through whatever media, was to influence individuals to undertake the physical and moral perfection that would evoke the new order. As a means to accomplish his goals, he attempted to create a model life as well as a model rhetorical literature that would extend his influence beyond the range of his own physical presence and personal magnetism. Coexistent with this public program was also a major ulterior purpose, one that grew stronger with his increasing age. It was his need to attract attention, respect, and love for himself. "'This is the precious return: personal love: the precious return,'" he said a few years before his death as he gloried in the positive, appropriate responses to his work by men and women beyond his personal world.[13]

Whitman's rhetorical purposes were the efforts of a practical persuader. His was the task not of speculating about the future Religious Democracy but of initiating it. With the exception of the 1855 Preface to *Leaves of Grass* (later redacted into poetry) and a few explicatory essays, Whitman's published efforts were devoted primarily to the practice rather than the theory of persuasion. From his essays, third-person reviews, prefaces, recorded conversations, and manuscripts, however, it is possible to explicate the principles that governed his attempts to persuade. In the discussion that follows, aspects of Whitman's rhetorical theory are presented in abstraction from their application in his poetry and prose. His concepts of persuasion are outlined in relation to their historical background, to the contemporary theories and doctrines from which they were adapted, and to Whitman's rhetorical goals.

In many of his statements of purpose, Whitman announced his primary goal and his rhetorical methods together. His intention was twofold: to create great persons directly through his own personal influence and to create a great literature that would convert others and nourish the copious race of the new Religious Democracy. A typical statement is that in "Poetry To-Day in America":

> With the poems of a first-class land are twined, as
> weft with warp, its types of personal character, of in-

dividuality, peculiar, native, its own physiognomy, man's and woman's, its own shapes, forms, and manners, fully justified under the eternal laws of all forms, all manners, all times. The hour has come for democracy in America to inaugurate itself in the two directions specified—autochthonic poems and personalities— born expressers of itself, its spirit alone, to radiate in subtle ways, not only in art, but the practical and familiar, in the transactions between employers and employ'd persons, in business and wages, and sternly in the army and navy, and revolutionizing them. I find nowhere a scope profound enough, and radical and objective enough, either for aggregates or individuals.[14]

Whitman's theory of persuasion, therefore, can be discussed in terms of a general theory, the body of principles that informs all of his practices; his concept of the manner in which perfected persons will serve as ideal persuaders, carrying the message to others; and his concept of the autochthonic media of persuasion that are to be the permanent embodiment of the doctrines of the Religious Democracy, creating converts and maintaining the faith.

THE UNDERSTANDING-IMAGINATION DICHOTOMY

IF YOU ENGAGE HIS *HEART*, YOU HAVE A FAIR CHANCE FOR IMPOSING UPON HIS
UNDERSTANDING AND DETERMINING HIS *WILL*.
—LORD CHESTERFIELD[15]

Prior to about 1847, Whitman appears to have accepted conventional theoretical assumptions about the nature of rhetoric. His dual career as a writer of light fiction and a political journalist, pursued through his twenties and well into his thirties, reveals little that is inconsistent with the contemporary practice of didactic fiction or argumentative journalism. His comments on persuasion and composition reveal him to be in general agreement with a rationalistic approach to argumentation.[16] Moreover, his desire to use literature to establish the Religious Democracy was a serious attempt to apply the accepted poetic theory of his age: an age of didacticism. The pragmatic orientation had dominated the literature of the eighteenth century, from the legalistic education preached in Henry Fielding's *Amelia* to the subtle attempt to "engage our moral feelings" in Oliver Goldsmith's "The Deserted Village."[17] Throughout the nineteenth century in Great Britain and

America, literature was considered less a medium of entertainment than a means for moral improvement. "I believe his grand books influenced more persons for better lives than even his personal presence and Christ-like magnetism," wrote Kate Sanborn, not of Whitman, but of Edward Everett Hale.[18]

In the notebooks containing the manuscripts that became *Leaves of Grass*, there are indications of Whitman's mature theories for what he considered a new form of rhetorical literature.[19] These theories are based on appeals to nonrational and subrational human perception.[20] The key to his concepts of persuasion, as to the poetics of the Romantics and the philosophy of the Transcendentalists, was the rejection of empirical epistemology and rationalistic rhetoric.

One of the cruxes of Western philosophy has always been the duality of the rational versus the irrational, reason versus emotion, or intellect versus faith. With the introduction during the Middle Ages of the Judeo-Christian concept of the will, the basic philosophical and religious dualism became that of faith versus reason and the related issue of the will versus the intellect. At the beginning of the Renaissance the scholastics were still divided on the issue of will versus intellect, but out of their speculations had developed faculty psychology, or mental philosophy as it was then called. In the Renaissance and through the nineteenth century, epistemological speculation revolved around identifying the mental faculties, explaining their function, and postulating their relationships.[21] The most prevalent scheme included three primary faculties: the understanding, the emotions, and the will. The understanding (often symbolized as the "head") was the faculty engaging sense perception, empirical knowledge, and rational (i.e., good or comprehensible) motives and desires. The emotions (symbolized as the "heart") engaged not only irrational feelings but also nonrational spiritual intuition. The will, highest of the faculties, was the volitional element, that which determined behavior. In many philosophical schemes the will replaced the emotions as the faculty of religious intuition and faith. According to this simple psychology, behavior is determined by the interaction of the understanding, the emotions, and the will.[22]

The various movements in the history of Western philosophy, rhetoric, and poetics are characterized by differing emphases on the elements of the trinity of head, heart, and will.[23] During the seventeenth and eighteenth centuries emphasis was primarily on the head, the understanding. The empiricists, represented by Hobbes, Locke, and Hume, believed that the mind is a tabula rasa and that knowledge is produced by the influence of sense perception on the understanding. The rationalists, represented by Descartes, Spinoza, and Leibniz, believed that knowledge can exist innate within the understanding (or reason) and that the understanding is adequate to explain its own function and to attain knowledge. Both empiricists and rationalists believed that persons can control their passions by the operation of reason, but most admitted the power of the emotions in influencing the will and thus determining behavior.[24] They conceded that knowledge achieved through the understanding or generated by the reason is insufficient to influence the will. In their normative statements they declared that both the understanding and the emotions should function to determine behavior: either the intellectual faculty controls the passions in their influencing of the will, or it motivates the emotions which in turn influence the will.[25]

The new intellectual movements of the late eighteenth and early nineteenth centuries were reactions against the empiricists and, to a lesser degree, the rationalists.[26] Although empiricists and rationalists had acknowledged that some desire or emotion must serve as the trigger of the will, they had denied a priori religious and mystical knowledge and had reduced God and the universe to a system of mechanisms. Many empiricists, in addition, had dismissed poetry as trivial or unimportant.[27] Kant and the German Idealists reacted by expanding the rationalists' concepts and by postulating a "Pure" or "Speculative Reason" that deals with a noumenal order rather than the phenomenal order. These noumena, or "ideas," transcend experience; and, while they cannot be "proven" or "understood" by the mind, they are nevertheless realities. Thus German Idealism restored verity to such grand ideas as God, Freedom, Morality, and Immortality.[28]

At the beginning of the nineteenth century, the English and American philosophical reaction to empiricism and rationalism was dominated by Idealism and Neoplatonism, the latter in fashion because of the verity which the Platonic concept of ideas gave to a priori religious and philosophical truths. On both religious and poetic premises, Romanticism and Transcendentalism—a heady American homebrew of Romanticism, German Idealism, and pietism—were also reactions to empiricism and rationalism.[29] Although there was great diversity among the Romantics and Transcendentalists, the unifying characteristics of the movements were derogation of the understanding; postulation of the ultimately unknowable character of reality; emphasis on the primacy of a creative, intuitive, emotional, and religious faculty which they called the "imagination," or, simply, "the soul"; and a return to the classical rhetoricians' emphasis on vis oratoris.[30] Unwilling to accept the empiricists' insistence on the tabula rasa and suspicious of the rationalists' belief in the sufficiency of reasoning, the Romantics insisted upon a projective human soul that does not take its shape from phenomena but which orders and shapes reality by projection of the noumenal reality of the soul.[31] The Romantics divided and subdivided the faculties and used a variety of often contradictory terms in discussing the faculties—"reason," for example, ranging in meaning from a pejorative label for the understanding to "Reason" as the highest union of will and soul. Underneath all of the various theories, however, was the assertion of the primacy of intuitive, emotional, and mystic determinants of behavior. For the Romantics, the imagination was not only the poetic faculty but also the soul itself.[32]

The dichotomy between intellect, understanding, and empirical and analytical reasoning on one side versus emotion, intuition, mysticism, and imagination on the other also had an impact on rhetorical theory and practice during the late eighteenth and early nineteenth centuries. Rhetoricians introduced a "teleology of 'ends'" by classifying discourses according to the faculty to which they were primarily addressed.[33] The major rhetoricians, however, followed the empiricists and rationalists in their arguments that "conviction" of the "understanding" (the use of arguments) is necessary as an adjunct to "persuasion" of the "imagination" (the use of emotional appeals).[34] Steeped in traditions of rationalism and argumentation, rhetoricians such as Campbell, Blair, and Whately assigned more importance to the rational determinants of behavior than did the Romantics or the Transcendentalists. Although influencing intellectuals, academics, and the modern tradition of argumentation and persuasion, the rhetoricians' attempts appear to have had only modest influence on many contemporary poets, artists, orators, and preachers.[35] "Reason" and "Reasoning," "Logic" and "Logical," "Intellect" and "Intellectual" became pejorative terms, while "Imagination," "Intuition," "Feeling," and "Eloquence" increasingly became the concepts that characterized the theories and practices of poets and rhetors.[36]

To understand Whitman's theory of rhetoric it is necessary not only to know the general antirationalistic movement of his era, but also to explain some of the fundamental assumptions of that movement. First, the arts were considered to be effective, albeit indirect, instruments of persuasion. Was not art—especially poetry—the direct product of the imagination, and was not the imagination the highest faculty, the center of volition? Logical and empirical arguments did not appeal to the whole person, but the Romantics believed that through their poetry they could engage all of the faculties, be they of the understanding, the emotions, or the will.[37]

Poets in the pragmatic tradition had always elevated the social, religious, and political power of the poet as an influence in society, and a second assumption produced by the antirationalistic spirit of Whitman's age was an increased emphasis on the social utility of the poet.[38] The poets' power to influence the imagination created for them the role of "unacknowledged legislators of the world"; the poet regained stature in comparison with the scientist.[39] In poetics and rhetoric the emphasis on subjectiveness, intuition, feeling, and spiritual insight also led naturally to the emphasis on personal influence as the primary means of persuasion.[40] In rhetoric the "great man" theory of the orator was both preached and practiced,[41] and in poetics the poet rather than the audience, subject, or poetic technique became the criterion by which a work was evaluated. Poetry, believed the Romantics, can be judged only in relation to its maker, rather than in relation to nature as in mimetic theories or in relation to the audience as in pragmatic theories.[42]

A third significant assumption produced by the antirationalistic spirit was that poetry was considered not as the technique or form of a work but as the product of a human faculty.[43] The dualism was not poetry versus prose, but "brain" versus "heart," science versus poetry.[44] Thus, by the early Victorian period, the association of poetry with intuition, with metaphysics, and with morality and moral duty became also an association with religion. Religion stood with the imagination and poetry in opposition to rationalism and science.[45] The association of poetry with religion was to have a profound effect on Whitman, who, in the white-hot heat of his effort to create the Religious Democracy, called *Leaves of Grass* a "New Bible" and inserted appropriate margin numbers to mark its chapters and verses.[46]

Whitman absorbed antirationalism and an awareness of the understanding-imagination distinction from a variety of sources. The

Romantic and Victorian concepts of the intuitive, religious, poetic imagination were widely accepted among both radical and conservative groups in the United States. W. A. Jones and Evert A. Duyckinck were especially active in promoting the theory that "the highest poetry is religious" and that "the imagination is the most religious of our faculties, and consequently the grandest." They accepted the Romantic concept that the imagination is superior to the understanding in religious instruction because it inculcates its lessons "without seeming to teach at all."[47]

Whitman was also exposed to the understanding-imagination distinction in his study of classical oratory and philosophy. For example, he contrasted Plato and Aristotle on the criterion of intuition versus intellect:

> Plato treated philosophy as an *art*—Aristotle as a *science*. That is, Plato was [made up of] intuitions, and was calm, full of enjoyment, admiration, beauty, the pictorial—was large, flowing, relied on the feelings, and made swift and imperious conclusions, often he was a mystic, can only be understood from the same platform with himself.
>
> But Aristotle was rather intellect, purer from the rest, keen, convinced by proof and argument, inquiring into all things from a devouring need of knowledge in itself. Aristotle represents mediums between extremes; also experimental philosophy. (It seems to be the substratum on which are based modern literature, education, and very largely modern character.)[48]

Whitman was aware of the contemporary rhetoricians' distinctions between conviction and persuasion, writing—for example—in one of his early editorials: "Mankind will resist being driven on a road, which they would travel willingly, when persuaded by gentleness, and convinced by reason."[49] He was aware of the faculty psychology of the day, and he made notes on the power of the orator to use "the memory, the fancy, the judgment, the passions."[50] Whitman was also influenced by the antirationalism of Emerson, the Transcendentalists, and the Romantics,[51] and he recognized the value of German Idealism as an answer to the empiricists. "Long before, the speculations of Locke and the other materialists, had reached the formula that 'there is nothing in the understanding which has not arrived there through the senses,'" Whitman wrote. "Leibnitz had replied, 'Yes, there is the understanding itself.' Kant's entire speculations are but a splendid amplification of this reply."[52]

Whitman's antirationalism was most influenced, however, by his pietism. The "inner light"—the mystical spirit of God within a person's soul—was always his ideal of inspiration, and when forced to compare his religion with others he claimed to be "perceptibly Quaker."[53] He glorified Elias Hicks, the great Quaker preacher, because his powerful oratory was "not argumentative or intellectual" but appealed to the "moral mystical portion of human nature."[54]

THE CONSCIOUS AND UNCONSCIOUS WILLS

HE IS BUT A POOR LAWGIVER WHO LEGISLATES ONLY FOR THE REASON AND UNDERSTANDING, WITHOUT REMEMBERING THAT MEN ARE ALSO ENDOWED WITH THE FACULTIES OF IMAGINATION. "LET ME MAKE THE BALLADS OF A NATION AND I WILL MAKE ITS LAWS," WAS A DECLARATION SUGGESTED BY THE FACT THAT THE REASONS OF MEN ARE INFERIOR TO AND UNDER THE CONTROL OF THEIR IMAGINATIONS. —WALT WHITMAN, 1848[55]

Whitman's rhetorical theory is based on his adaptation of the understanding-imagination distinction. Occasionally he used conventional terminology such as "intellect" versus "soul" and "brain" versus "heart," or he subdivided the "faculties" into various consciences such as "the emotional, courageous, intellectual, esthetic, &c."[56] Most typically, however, he considered the "soul" as the "will" ("Great—unspeakably great—is the Will! the free Soul of man!"), and grouped rational factors as the "conscious will" and the emotional, intuitive, spiritual factors as the "unconscious will":

> Wise men say there are two sets of wills to nations and to persons—one set that acts and works from explainable motives—from teaching, intelligence, judgment, circumstance, caprice, emulation, greed, &c.—and then another set, perhaps deep, hidden, unsuspected, yet often more potent than the first, refusing to be argued with, rising as it were out of abysses, resistlessly urging on speakers, doers, communities, unwitting to themselves—the poet to his fieriest words—the race to pursue its loftiest ideal. Indeed, the paradox of a nation's life and career, with all its wondrous contradictions, can probably only be explain'd from these two wills, sometimes conflicting, each operating in its sphere, com-

bining in races or in persons, and producing strangest results.[57]

Whitman's concept of the two wills provided him with an explanation of human behavior. In the individual in whom one will is predominant, the other is likely to be retarded. There are "cases, often seen, where, with an extra development and acuteness of the intellectual faculties, there is a mark'd absence of the spiritual, affectional, and sometimes, though more rarely, the highest aesthetic and moral elements of cognition."[58] It also provided him with an explanation of the origin of the opposed philosophies of materialism (product of the conscious will) and spiritualism (product of the unconscious will).[59] And it furnished him with a theory of motivation: to achieve spiritual results the persuader must appeal to the unconscious will, which "knows without proof, and is beyond materialism."[60] Thus, to understand Whitman's theory of persuasion, it is necessary to understand his concept of the two wills and how they function to determine behavior.

The conscious will deals with matters of the intellect such as "facts, statistics, materialism,"[61] and with "logical" and "explainable motives" such as greed or emulation; it operates through the laws of logic and understanding.[62] It includes the "esthetic" faculty as well as "the desire for knowledge" and the "psychological" point of view.[63] The conscious will comprehends verbal appeals and is teachable, but appeals by "Statements, Argumentation, [and] Art" can achieve results that are only "temporary."[64] Believing that the conscious will can be appealed to by conventional methods of argumentation, Whitman never abandoned his own use of such methods. He wrote very little about the conventional modes of argument, however, and developed few unique strategies in his own practice of argumentation. Throughout his career his concepts of argumentation did not change significantly from those he had learned and used as a young newspaper editor and public speaker.[65]

The unconscious will is the center of insight, intuition, and spiritual truth. "Very late, but unerringly, comes to every capable student the perception that it is not in beauty, it is not in art, it is not even in science, that the profoundest laws of the case have their eternal sway and outcropping," wrote Whitman.[66] The unconscious will is the equivalent of the faculty of the passions or emotions, for "what is humanity in its faith, love, heroism, poetry, even morals, but *emotion*?"[67] In addition, it deals with spiritual motives, the relation of a person and his or her soul, and it cannot be taught. Its meanings cannot "be defined to the intellectual part, or to calculation."[68] The "soul resents the keenest mere intellection, they will not be sought for."[69] And Whitman concluded, "I guess that after all reasoning and analogy, and their most palpable demonstrations of anything, we have the real satisfaction when the soul tells and tests by its own archchemic power—superior to the learnedest proofs as one glance of living sight is more than quarto volumes of description and of maps."[70]

The unconscious will has its own laws, however, and these laws can be apprehended intuitively. Knowledge cannot be transferred from one soul to another, but it can, in Socratic fashion, be called forth out of the soul.[71] The conditions for persuasion are "simple, spiritual, physical, close at hand . . . they are long and arduous and require faith, they exist altogether with the taught and not with the teaching or teacher."[72]

IDENTIFICATION

THE ONLY WAY WE ATTACH IT [ANYTHING] TO OUR FEELINGS IS BY IDENTIFYING IT WITH THE HUMAN SPIRIT—THROUGH LOVE, THROUGH PRIDE, AND THROUGH OUR CRAVING FOR BEAUTY AND HAPPINESS.
—WALT WHITMAN, 1850s[73]

Whitman developed a rhetoric of religious persuasion based on the volitional aspects of the unconscious will. The unconscious will is the "citadel of the primary volitions," the soul.[74] Its natural state is repose and silence.[75] It controls intuitive perception and is the final judge of all things.[76] Any permanent changes in a person's spirituality and character must arise from within and cannot be imposed from without. "The soul," wrote Whitman in the 1855 Preface to *Leaves of Grass*, "has that measureless pride which consists in never acknowledging any lessons but its own."[77] "'Salvation can't be legislated'"; compulsion and force are inefficient means of persuasion. Whitman insisted that "'men are not to be made moral by violent means,'" and he told Horace Traubel in 1889, "'I don't think much of a fellow who is good because somebody tells him he ought to be—who is so and so, does this or that, because he is advised to: the only real good is that which springs out of the man himself spontaneously.'"[78] A person cannot be argued out of a fallacious belief. The principle of amelioration must be applied: the person changed must be encouraged to move on to a "new phase of development" in which the old ideas "fail of themselves."[79] It was upon this principle that Whitman rejected conventional modes of argumentation that promote debate and criticism. His theory of persuasion was a reaction against the direct, legalistic rhetoric of the traditional sermon and the legislative debate. In rejecting appeals to the intellect—the conscious will—Whitman was merely following the contemporary pietistic movement. It was widely believed by the pietists, Romantics, and Transcendentalists that persons could not be argued into changing their religious beliefs.[80] The persuader, Whitman maintained, must put truth into people's minds by using techniques that hint and suggest rather than state or demonstrate.[81] He denounced "partisanship" and "logic" and proclaimed, "'I never knew a controversy of this character—each side ready to swear to its accuracy, full of the arrogance of learning, equipped with book knowledge—to end in anything like a settlement: the problem was always as wide open at the end as at the start.'"[82] The persuader must never argue or debate. Whitman's primary rule for persuasion was "Do not argue at all or compose proofs to demonstrate things."[83] He also denounced bombast,[84] cant,[85] and overly didactic sermonizing[86] as inappropriate for persuasion of the unconscious will.

Whitman believed that persuasion can be accomplished only through the process of identification. "A man only is interested in anything when he identifies himself with it . . . ," he wrote in a notebook prior to the composition of *Leaves of Grass*.[87] This theory of persuasion through identification is the rhetorical counterpart of Whitman's theological assumptions. Since all souls are potentially the same at birth, multiple identifications perfect the "simple experience and association" of the soul and change the individual from within.[88] Experience teaches by dilating the soul; and the greatest person is the one with the most developed and dilated soul. Such a person has made the most progress towards identifying with eidólons and in perceiving the most correspondences between his or her soul and nature. Since the soul dilates and increases its self-divinity by the meditation of eidólons, by identification with nature, or by responding to the influence of other powerful souls, the process of rhetorical identification must operate in a similar fashion.

First, the real tends to identify with the ideal. The process of amelioration creates a hunger in the soul that drives it to identify with eidólons. All of Whitman's efforts were directed to persuade by "victorious fusion" of "Real and Ideal."[89] Moreover, the real (i.e., the body) can be prepared so that identification with eidólons will be stimulated. Consistent with his emphasis on physiology—his belief that the physical state of the body determines the development of the soul—Whitman maintained that the persuader can bring about moral improvement in another's soul simply by encouraging one to acquire "divine health."[90]

On another level, every healthy soul identifies with nonverbal realities. Most of the great verities with which the soul can identify are *"The Untellable,"* that "which cannot be put in fine words[.] Nor in any words or statement or essay or poem."[91] The soul identifies with and is persuaded by the direct influence of nature. Nature, "under favoring circumstances, tallies, perhaps expresses, certainly awakes, those grandest and subtlest element-emotions in the human soul, that all the marble temples and sculptures from Phidias to Thorwaldsen—all paintings, poems, reminiscences, or even music, probably never can."[92] Thus, believing in nature as the direct moral stimulus of the soul, Whitman deified "positive life," "the pleasure of things," and "the eternal realities of things."[93] Natural "things" are "illustrations of growth, continuity, power, amplitude and *exploitation,* almost beyond statement, but proving fact and possibility, outside of argument."[94]

ILLUSTRATION

...HE IS GREATEST FOREVER AND FOREVER WHO CONTRIBUTES THE GREATEST ORIGINAL PRACTICAL EXAMPLE.
—WALT WHITMAN, 1855[95]

fliegd

The soul also tends to identify with other human souls through the power of "Sympathy."[96] Through this attraction, individuals are led to identify with other human beings and thus to relate their own development to that of others.[97] Each person, moreover, through the process of amelioration constantly seeks higher levels of development; nature supplies negative examples of human character that illustrate characteristics to be avoided and superb specimens of human character that serve as models with which less developed individuals can identify. Consequently, the persuader who wishes to aid the process of amelio-

emulate?

ration must offer himself or herself as such a direct model or must attempt to portray such an ideal illustration in his or her discourse. Whitman insisted, of course, that the living model is the most influential. Complete persuasion is assured only when an individual identifies with the living illustration of a perfected personality. There is "a sympathetic germ, probably rapport, lurking in every human eligibility, which no book, no rule, no statement has given or can give inherent knowledge, intuition—not even the best speech, or best put forth, but launch'd out only by powerful personal magnetism. . . ."[98]

Throughout his career Whitman continually emphasized the rhetorical power of illustration. In "The Last of the Sacred Army," a short story that was published in *The Democratic Review* in 1842, Whitman's "philosopher" tells the "young man," "Do not suppose, young man, that it is by sermons and oft-repeated precepts we form a disposition great or good. The model of one pure, upright character, living as a beacon in history, does more benefit than the lumbering tomes of a thousand theorists."[99] In his newspaper editorials, Whitman also advocated the use of models and examples for teaching and persuasion.[100] In what appears to be the last of his short stories, "The Shadow and the Light of a Young Man's Soul," published in the *Union Magazine* in June of 1848, Whitman documented the reformatory power of the model of a great life. Archie Dean, a young man of despondent soul and unsettled character, is reformed into a man of perseverance and insouciance through his awareness of the example of "an ancient, bony, yellow-faced maiden" who had worked diligently to overcome seemingly insuperable odds: "The change was not a sudden one: few great changes are. But his heart was awakened to his weakness; the seed was sown; Archie Dean felt that he *could* expand his nature by means of that very nature itself. Many times he flagged; but at each fretful falling back, he thought of the yellow-faced dame, and roused himself again. . . ."[101] The year before the publication of this story, Whitman had begun the notebooks toward *Leaves of Grass*, and in a note written in the mid-1850s he warned himself:

> *Caution*—Not to blaart constantly for *Native American* models, Literature etc., and bluster out "nothing foreign." The best way to promulge native American models and literature is to supply such forcible and superb specimens of the same that they will, by their own volition, move to the head of all and put foreign models in the second class.

> I to-day think it would be best *not at all* to bother
> with Arguments against the foreign models or to help
> American models—but *just go on supplying American
> models.*[102]

In "The Eighteenth Presidency!"—Whitman's consideration of direct political action—he asserts that ". . . no body of men are fit to
make Presidents, Judges, and Generals, unless they themselves supply
the best specimens of the same, and that supplying one or two such
specimens illuminates the whole body for a thousand years."[103] Such
specimens serve as models for identification. Whitman asserted in 1858,
for example, that oratory could be revolutionized by the model of "a
great leading representative man, with perfect power, perfect confidence
in his power, persevering, with repeated specimens ranging up and
down The States. . . . Let us have the practical sample of a thing, and
look upon it and listen to it, and turn it about for to examine it."[104]

THE DIVINE LITERATUS

AMID THE VAST AND COMPLICATED EDIFICE OF HUMAN BEINGS . . . HE [THE DIVINE
LITERATUS, WHITMAN'S IDEAL RHETOR] BUILDS, AS IT WERE, AN IMPREGNABLE AND
LOFTY TOWER, PART OF ALL WITH THE REST AND OVERLOOKING ALL—THE CITADEL OF
THE PRIMARY VOLITIONS, THE SOUL, THE EVER-RESERVED RIGHT OF A DEATHLESS
INDIVIDUALITY—AND THESE HE OCCUPIES AND DWELLS, AND THENCE MAKES
OBSERVATIONS AND ISSUES VERDICTS.
—WALT WHITMAN, 1856[105]

As documented above, a central principle in Whitman's rhetorical
theory is his insistence on the concrete model. Hence the direct agent
of persuasion in his theory is the model persuader, whom Whitman
came to call the divine literatus. The divine literatus can take others
by their hands, encourage them to develop divine health, show them
nature at firsthand, and influence them through the magnetism of his
or her own fully developed soul. Ethos—the personal influence of the
persuader—is thus the dominant mode of proof. Both Whitman's theory
and practice of persuasion were based on the principle that "I and mine
do not convince by arguments, similes, rhymes. / We convince by our
presence."[106]

Throughout his life Whitman continued to voice his worship of
personal force, human magnetism, and "powerful persons."[107] He
praised persons such as Hicks, Emerson, and Tennyson not so much
for their writings as for their providing illustrations of powerful per-

sonal character.[108] It is through the models provided by the lives of developed and perfected persons that lasting changes can be achieved and the success of reform guaranteed. Whitman's entire program was designed to create such archetypal personalities, and in a poem first published in the "biblical" 1860 edition of *Leaves of Grass* he overtly states his conception of persuasion and reform through personal influence:

To a Pupil.
1. Is reform needed? Is it through you?
   The greater the reform needed, the greater the PER-
   SONALITY you need to accomplish it.
2. You! do you not see how it would serve to have eyes,
   blood, complexion, clean and sweet?
   Do you not see how it would serve to have such a
   body and Soul, that when you enter the crowd,
   an atmosphere of desire and command enters
   with you, and every one is impressed with your
   personality?
3. O the magnet! the flesh over and over!
   Go, mon cher! If need be, give up all else, and com-
   mence to-day to inure yourself to pluck, reality,
   self-esteem, definiteness, elevatedness,
   Rest not, till you rivet and publish yourself of your
   own personality.[109]

Throughout Whitman's writings is the call for the great persons who will unite all reforms in themselves and be the primary agents in the founding of the Religious Democracy. The bulk of his prose writings deal with the outline of these persons, be they called "Redeemer President," "poet," "literatus," "orator," "wander speaker," or "bard."[110] The divine literatus, the messiah of the Religious Democracy, converts and persuades primarily through personal example and personal magnetism. Such a one is a "Vates," priest, prophet, or savior,[111] a medium bearing a divinely inspired message.[112] The particular written or oral medium through which the message is spread is merely a matter of personal choice or individual talent.[113]

Because the divine literatus, Whitman's ideal persuader, is also a model of the physically and spiritually perfected individual who will populate the new order, Whitman went to considerable detail in describing him or her. (Whitman's use of masculine pronouns was usually generic rather than specific; the divine literatus could also be female.

Increasingly Whitman came to use both masculine and feminine pronouns to be sure to include women in his target audience.)[114] Modern
literary critics have tried to interpret this model projected by Whitman
as a literary persona only, but Whitman insisted that the divine literatus
should be a rhetor: an evangelical reformer, a "recruiter," a persuader
who must create new men and women, not just new works of art.[115]
The divine literati must always have a serious purpose and message;
their primary duty is to teach, but by new methods that reject the
"'preacher-priest methods of controversy.'"[116]

Whitman's concept of the divine literatus consisted of more than
just his formulation of the general characteristics of the ideal persuader
as a divinely inspired reformer. He also speculated on the media by
which the literatus was to persuade. From his writings and conversations can be derived his conceptions of the literatus as an orator and
writer and even his concept of the literatus's function as a critic. These
subjects have not infrequently attracted the attention of scholars, particularly Whitman's interest in vocalism as best adapted to the purposes
and methods of the divine literatus.[117] His promotion of vocalism as a
medium of the ideal persuader was the result of two of his key concepts:
his emphasis on ethos, the rhetorical power of personality, and his
identification of sound with spiritual dilation. He associated the perfected voice with personal magnetism,[118] of course, but he went beyond
to stress the nonverbal dimensions of both music and oratory as modes
to dilate the souls of auditors. "Beyond all other power and beauty,"
he wrote, "there is something in the quality and power of the right
voice (*timbre* the schools call it) that touches the soul, the abysms."[119]

But Whitman did not insist that the ideal persuader be an orator
or singer, and he himself was not successful on the public platform.
He spent considerable time thinking about and preparing models for
what he considered new forms of scriptural literature. His rhetorical
theory cannot be divorced from his insistence that literature is primarily
religious. His concept of literature was biblical: religious movements
need "*a book*" to "embody themselves and radiate from."[120] The book
gives permanency to the religion. When the direct models provided by
the prophets of the religion are not present, the book provides a means
of influencing the unconscious wills of other possible converts. "Few
are aware," he wrote in *Democratic Vistas*, "how the great literature
penetrates all, gives hue to all, shapes aggregates and individuals, and,

after subtle ways, with irresistible power, constructs, sustains, demol-
ishes at will."[121] Such works, tallying the identity of "These States,"
were needed as the Bible of the New World.[122]

WHITMAN'S RHETORIC OF INDIRECTION IN DISCOURSE

IT IS TRUE, ANALOGY, COMPARISON, INDIRECTION, SUGGESTIONS ARE PERHAPS ALL
THAT IS POSSIBLE. BUT THE SOUL QUICKLY SEIZES THE DIVINE LIMITS AND ABSORBS
THEM WITH AVIDITY.
—WALT WHITMAN, LATE 1860s OR EARLY 1870s[123]

In addition to his postulation of the role of the literatus as orator,
writer, and critic, Whitman also outlined the methodology by which
discourse could serve as a medium of persuasion of the unconscious
will. Like the Romantics and the Young Americans, Whitman believed
that poetry was less a genre of composition than a human faculty. He
insisted that the "whirling wheel, poetry," was the source of all artistic
expression in music, painting, and acting as well as poetic and prose
verbal composition.[124] In his statements of theory, Whitman gave considerable attention to prose as the most powerful means of establishing
and nourishing the Religious Democracy. Prose was "more flexible,
more eligible . . . freer, vast, diviner" than poetry, narrowly defined as
a literary genre.[125] He believed, nevertheless, that the virtues of oratory
and prose could be absorbed by a new poetic form. He considered
poetry as fundamentally oral. The poet always "utters," "sings," or
"chants" rather than "writes" or "composes."[126] In addition, he insisted
that "the time has arrived to essentially break down the barriers of form
between prose and poetry." By disposing of "arbitrary and rhyming
metre," the "truest and greatest *Poetry*" can unite poetic virtues of
imagery and rhythm with the descriptive and expressive power of prose,
forming a literature of "the truest power and passion."[127] Poetry, in
addition, has the sanction of age. It had originally been the sole medium:
" . . . history, laws, religion, war, were all in the keeping of the poet.—
He was literature.—It was nothing but poems."[128]

Whitman's desire to unite poetry and prose in his scriptural literature resulted from his basic rhetorical dilemma. Direct verbal communication of spiritual meanings to the unconscious will is impossible.
The human soul identifies with the universal spirit as it is perceived
intuitively, in nature, or in other human souls. It responds primarily

to things, not to words. Thus "by curious indirections only can there be any statement of the spiritual world." The most persuasive of verbal communications "after all, can merely hint, or remind, often very indirectly, or at distant removes. Aught of real perfection, or the solution of any deep problem, or any completed statement of the moral, the true, the beautiful, excludes the greatest, deftest poet—flies away like an always uncaught bird."[129]

Whitman, of course, was not reduced to silence by the difficulty of verbal persuasion. An "*indirect mode* of *attack*" is possible and can be used with success.[130] By "removes and indirections" the soul is aided in its efforts to "repel the inconsistent, and gravitate forever toward the absolute, the supernatural, the eternal truth." The soul is constantly seeking "some clue however indirect to itself and to the relations between itself and Time, Space and all the processes and objects that fill them."[131] And while verbal forms are never as persuasive as direct models, they can serve as models for identification. In 1846 Whitman praised Frederika Bremer's novels because "we know nothing more likely to melt and refine the human character—particularly the young character. In the study of the soul—portraits therein delineated—in their motives, actions, and the results of those actions—every youth, of either sex, will make some profitable application to his or her own case."[132] Whitman made similar statements throughout the rest of his career,[133] and his own writings promulgated the model of the archetypal man and woman. The concrete model, though verbal, was a persuasive form for achieving any end. Even bad models teach.[134] Positive verbal models should not be too literal, however. They are not merely copies of existing types, but tallies of the eidólons of the future. They should be developed on the basis of "*law* and *character* more than special cases or partialities." His advice was: "Aim to produce that beautiful resemblance which will excite the motion that the real object might produce—the rest is the mere drippings, the shavings and sawdust."[135]

The primary function of literature is to provide models, but Whitman also envisioned a literature that could achieve religious persuasion through appeals to the soul's "sympathies." The emotional sympathies are "forever eligible to be appeal'd to and relied on."[136] In "A Hint to Preachers and Authors," published in 1874, he advised that persuasion can be achieved through "appeals (each writer, each artist after his kind) to the sympathies of Individualism, its pride, love of grand physique, urge of spiritual development, and the need of comrades. There is something immortal, universal, in these sympathies individualized, all men, all ages: something in the human being that will unerringly respond to them."[137] Among the universal sympathies, Whitman included the primary attributes of the soul—love and pride— plus "the aspirations . . . majesty, delicacy, adhesiveness, amativeness, the dread of being thought mean, [and] the demand for a vogue more and better than practical life affords." Heroism, liberty, justice, and "hatred of meanness" are also "Universalities." Appeals to these sympathies are recognized by the soul, and the individual responds by recalling the corresponding universal spirit latent within his or her soul.[138]

Although Whitman maintained that verbal models for identification and appeals to the sympathies must always remain indirect, he believed that the members of the audience—the group he called the "divine average"—would respond to such indirect persuasion: "Sometimes the bulk of the common people (who are far more 'cute than the critics suppose) relish a well-hidden allusion or hint carelessly dropt, faintly indicated, and left to be disinterr'd or not." In 1885 he wrote, "The propensity to approach a meaning not directly and squarely, but by circuitous styles of expression, seems indeed a born quality of the common people everywhere, evidenced by nick-names, and the inveterate determination of the masses to bestow sub-titles, sometimes ridiculous, sometimes very apt." Thus, he believed that there could be a "poetic style" which is "address'd to the soul" and which is "less definite form, outline, sculpture, and becomes vista, music, half-tints, and even less than half-tints." By such methods the persuader can call forth meanings that are in the souls of the members of the audience.[139]

Because he rejected the inherent defensiveness and partisanship of traditional argumentation, Whitman believed the successful persuader must attempt to stimulate identification between the soul and eidólons, nature, or other souls by methods that counteract the blocking perceptions in the receiving soul. Because an individual may react negatively to direct attempts at persuasion, the persuader should mask his or her method and purpose. In composing his or her discourse, the rhetor must "cover up and involve its real purpose and meanings in folded removes and far recesses."[140] This does not mean, however, that the rhetor abandons rhetorical purposes or forgoes the attempt to achieve specific results. "'The whole point,'" Whitman insisted, "'is, to provide the material—to set it forth so it may be handled—and then turn on the light, which, gathering strength more and more, in its own free way, will drive inevitably to a certain result—is eligible for one result and one only.'"[141] The appeals must always be presented so that the reader or listener feels that the resultant development of character is uniquely his or her own—not something imposed from without. Whitman believed that the persuader could accomplish this task through use of four primary strategies: attention, affirmation, suggestiveness, and tallying.

ATTENTION

"THE PUBLIC . . . IS A THICK-SKINNED BEAST, AND YOU HAVE TO KEEP WHACKING AWAY ON ITS HIDE TO LET IT KNOW YOU'RE THERE."
—WALT WHITMAN, 1880s[142]

According to Whitman, the first step that a persuader must take to achieve proper identification is to ensure attention.[143] This is a difficult task because each soul is different; perception and judgment vary greatly from person to person because each is in a different stage of individual development.[144] The specific audience must, therefore, always be the single soul,[145] and unless the message is on the level of development of the receiving soul there is little chance that the soul will identify with the communication. Individual souls, on the scale from "the minus human" ("animals or very inferior persons") to "the plus human" ("superior persons"), can comprehend only that which is on their level. The rule is that "each is understood only by the like of itself." "The truths I tell to you or to any other may not be plain to you," Whitman wrote, sounding like a General Semanticist, "because I do not translate them fully from my idiom into yours.—If I could do so, and do it well, they would be as apparent to you as they are to me; for they are truths."[146]

In order to ensure attention to the message, the persuader must establish rapport with the person whom he or she is attempting to influence. The primary task is to empathize with the soul of the person addressed, learning its degree of development and thus its "language," and creating the possibility of rapport if and when the reader reciprocates. The reader's empathy with the author can be stimulated by careful adaptation to the specific person being addressed and by embodying in the work an attractive personality with whom the reader can identify.[147] It can also be facilitated through application of the principles of exposure and familiarity of appeal.

The principle of exposure is based on the premise that the more a message is brought to the recipient's attention, for whatever reason, the greater the chance it has to achieve its final result. The persuader must "keep the pot a-boiling" if he or she hopes to achieve anything.[148] If the works are kept before the public, sympathetically disposed souls will seek them out and perhaps will be stimulated to empathize with their author. And persons who might not be prepared for the message at first will have the opportunity to empathize slowly as their physical and moral development increases.

The principle of familiarity of appeal is based on the premise that empathy with the author and identification with the message are most likely if the recipient soul finds something familiar in the message, something with which it has identified in other contexts. A communication should, therefore, contain facts, events, and persons that are familiar to the recipient soul. Whitman's writings were designed to include "subjects disdain'd by solid writers, but interesting to you ["Reader dear"] because they were such as happen to everybody." Whitman also believed that communications increase in effectiveness as they appeal to a greater variety of the sympathies of the soul. The great power of the Bible, for example, lay in its containing "something to touch, or approach every phase of human want, development, tenderness, fanaticism, &c."[149]

Whitman also approved exaggeration for attaining attention, and his practice of persuasion reveals that he had considerable faith in the conventional tactics of promotion as a means of securing public attention.[150]   *which are?*

AFFIRMATION

"BE BOLD! BE BOLD! BE BOLD! BE NOT TOO BOLD!"
—WALT WHITMAN[151]

Rejecting empirical and analytical reasoning, the Romantics and Transcendentalists relied on affirmation. "'I must Create a System or be enslav'd by another Man's. / I will not Reason & Compare: my business is to Create,'" wrote Blake.[152] Emerson asserted, "Truth ceases to be such when polemically stated"; his ideal orator would "electrify us by perpetual affirmations, unexplained."[153] Whitman, too, believed that the spiritual persuader should use only affirmation. The reader or listener must struggle *with* the meaning and not *against* it. Identification must be on the level of the unconscious rather than on the surface level of the conscious will where the reader or listener is disposed to argue with rather than absorb the message. Religious persuasion, therefore, requires "boldness," but a boldness combined with "a modest statement, and proposition of things—as if presented with subdued mind, suggestive, modest, not flaunting and arbitrary." The persuader must "boldly promulge" liberal ideas with a "temper of rounded and good-natured moderation."[154] A moderated boldness allows a persuader to reach the souls of the audience members without provoking them to disagreement. And the persuader must not lose the advantage. He or she must always picture, never explain.[155] The message must be so persuasive that it preempts and disarms all criticism. It must be elevated "far above the views of trivial and commonplace criticism."[156]

Unlimited affirmation promotes redundancy and inconsistency, of course, but Whitman believed that these results were not deleterious. Repetition is a positive value; the more a message is repeated the more likely it will be that identification will take place. And the persuader need not be concerned with possible contradictions.[157] The soul resolves all contradictions by its own laws. The persuader merely follows the method of nature by presenting universal realities. To affirm in the manner of nature requires, in addition, that the persuader present both the good and its paired opposite. Accepting amelioration as per se moral, the religious persuader must present both sides of the continually "conflicting, paradoxical, opposing elements" that contribute to the development of the identities of both individuals and nations.[158] Moreover, by boldly affirming the eidólons of the future, the persuader gives rhetorical force to ideals that synthesize the seeming paradoxes of contemporary life. In short, to avoid didacticism of the "sermonizing sort," the persuader must use a method of pure assertion: "something involving self-esteem, decision, authority—as opposed to the current *third-person style, essayism, didactic,* removed from animation." In a note used to guide the preparation of *Leaves of Grass,* he wrote, "Make *the Works*—Do not go into criticism or arguments at all. Make fullblooded, rich, flush, natural *works.*"[159]

SUGGESTIVENESS

"THE GREATEST POET IS NOT HE WHO HAS DONE THE BEST, IT IS HE WHO SUGGESTS THE MOST; HE, NOT ALL OF WHOSE MEANING IS AT FIRST OBVIOUS, AND WHO LEAVES

YOU MUCH TO DESIRE, TO EXPLAIN, TO STUDY, MUCH TO COMPLETE IN YOUR TURN."
—WALT WHITMAN, QUOTING SAINTE-BEUVE[160]

Whitman used the terms "suggestion" and "suggestiveness" to indicate that persuasive works must not appear polished or complete.
The persuader must always leave a margin of "indefiniteness."[161]
Throughout his life, Whitman preserved an 1848 article in which he
had underscored two passages dealing with suggestion: " . . . the highest
art, which is chiefly dependent for its effect on suggestion, is by no
means universally appreciated, as mere skillful imitation is . . . "; and
the "essential quality of suggestiveness [is that] by which activity on
the part of the reader is absolutely demanded. . . . " In accord with this
principle, the reader or listener must be allowed to feel that he or she
has created the meaning, not that he or she is reading or hearing
something that is complete and finished. The divine literatus, according
to Whitman, " . . . does not give you the usual poems and metaphysics.
He gives you materials for you to form for yourself poems, metaphysics,
politics, behavior, histories, romances, essays and everything else."
Great poems should persuade by "powerful indications—yet loose,
fluid-like, leaving each reader eligible to form the resultant-poem for
herself or himself."[162]

Whitman's theory of suggestion requires that the interaction of
book and reader or of speaker and audience must be an active process.
Spiritual persuasion is effective only when the reading of the poem or
essay or the hearing of the speech or lecture becomes an "Agonistic
arena" or a "gymnast's struggle" in which " . . . the reader is to do
something for himself, must be on the alert, must himself or herself
construct indeed the poem, argument, history, metaphysical essay—
the text furnishing the hints, the clue, the start or frame-work."[163]

According to Whitman, suggestiveness can be achieved through
the use of three primary strategies. First, the nature of poetic language—
symbolic, imagistic, metaphorical—can be used to imply a meaning
rather than to state it directly.[164] Second, conscious ambiguity can be
employed. The persuader can hint that there is an additional meaning
beyond that which may be apparent, something "far away and even
hidden."[165] Metaphorical language and ambiguity can be overused,
however, and Whitman warned himself against the "general mistiness
and gossamer character" of an Ossianic style.[166] The third means of
employing suggestion is through the use of "rough" forms, "collectanea,"
or "melanges." Out of such forms " . . . the modern intelligent reader,

(a new race unknown before our time) can take and adapt & shape for him or herself. . . . "[167]

TALLYING

. . . THE TRUE USE FOR THE IMAGINATIVE FACULTY OF MODERN TIMES IS TO GIVE ULTIMATE VIVIFICATION TO FACTS, TO SCIENCE, AND TO COMMON LIVES, ENDOWING THEM WITH GLOWS AND GLORIES AND FINAL ILLUSTRIOUSNESS WHICH BELONG TO EVERY REAL THING, AND TO REAL THINGS ONLY.
—WALT WHITMAN, 1887[168]

Whitman believed that persuasion should be based on the rhetorical method of nature. Because nature reveals the operation of divine purpose, and because the soul is developed and strengthened by identifying with the universal spirit embodied in nature, the most effective persuasion is that which follows "the secret, sane, non-theatrical quality of the style of nature's workmanship . . . [which] reaches the souls of men by pleasing channels, mysterious, penetrating, as the light, the air, the songs of birds reach the soul, without the soul being conscious of it." And because realities are the signs that awaken the spiritual meanings in the soul, the persuader must discover a method by which words as signs can be used as substitutes for things, creating that "freeing, dilating, joyous" effect which "uncramp'd Nature works on every individual without exception."[169]

As Wilson O. Clough points out in *The Necessary Earth: Nature and Solitude in American Literature,* conventional nineteenth-century poets resorted to "natural scenery enlisted as a handmaiden to hymnology, private quiverings confused wtih cosmic awfulness, tremulous excursions along the banks of some 'humble rill' used to reaffirm household virtues, vague aspirations heaving heavenward while safely anchored in loyalty to parish and kitchen; and all concluding with 'O may this to me a lesson be!'" Such poets did not present nature descriptively, however, but with a "romantic diffuseness."[170] The Romantics, in addition, were not interested in objective nature but in subjective nature.[171] Whitman's method is significantly different. He desired to recreate the spiritual meaning of nature in the soul of the reader or listener. The conversion of "fact" into "feeling," the subjective lesson, must take place in the reader or listener's soul rather than in the mind of the persuader. It is ineffective persuasion for the literatus merely to learn the lesson and put his or her "finished" conclusions into a poem. Rather, the literatus has to present the materials from which each reader or listener makes his or her own poems and learns the lesson for himself or herself.

Whitman knew full well that literature cannot actually present nature. It can only tally it with words.[172] The persuader can use two interrelated types of tallies, one direct and one indirect. The tally of the direct is achieved by the process of actualization or vivification: the reader must be made to feel that he or she is experiencing nature rather than pictures of nature. To achieve such vivification through a verbal medium the persuader must use words to recreate nature accurately and dynamically and not distort "honest shapes" or create "unearthly being or places or contingencies." Nature must be presented in its "ensemble," with no subject "made too pronouncé," and all borrowed, literary themes and ornaments must be avoided. Things are the archetype of poetry: "The United States themselves are essentially the greatest poem," he wrote. Thus, only "those ornaments can be allowed that conform to the perfect facts of the open air and that flow out of the nature of the work and come irrepressibly from it and are necessary to the completion of the work."[173]

While tallies should be transparent and real, they should not be static. To sustain interest and tally time as well as space they must have an "'unhasting and unresting'" sense of movement.[174] And tallies must be presented in a manner that employs the process of suggestion, involving the reader in an active rather than a passive activity. The persuader, therefore, does not attempt to photograph reality but to abstract from it. Nature is presented not literally but in an "elliptical & idiomatic" manner.[175] Ellipticism is not used merely to create an ambiguity with which the reader will have to struggle, however. The persuader desires not to imitate the surface of nature, but to recreate the "spiritual images" behind the face of nature.[176] Primary concern is for the tally of the indirect, the tally of the universal spirit embodied in nature. The persuader must attempt to call forth not only the object but also the object's eidólon, its image. Thus the rhetor is an "image-maker" who abstracts from nature to create a tally that will stimulate the proper spiritual correspondences in the mind of the reader or listener:

> Observing, rapport, and with intuition, the shows and
> forms presented by Nature, the sensuous luxuriance,

the beautiful in living men and women, the actual play
of passions, in history and life—and, above all, from
those developments either in Nature or human personality in which power, (dearest of all to the sense of the
artist,) transacts itself—out of these, and seizing what
is in them, the poet, the esthetic worker in any field,
by the divine magic of his genius, projects them, their
analogies, by curious removes, indirections, in literature
and art. (No useless attempt to repeat the material
creation, by daguerreotyping the exact likeness by mortal mental means.) This is the image-making faculty,
coping with material creation, and rivaling, almost tri-
umphing over it.[177]

The image-making faculty depends upon the function of words to
denote not only an object or event but also the soul, the spiritual
reality, of the object or event. Otherwise, verbal persuasion would be
an impossibility. Whitman maintained, therefore, that words signify
not only their referent but also the universal spirit embodied in the
referent. Words are the "signs" of both physical and spiritual realities.[178]
Or, in the terminology of Whitman's near contemporary Charles Sand-
ers Pierce, they are simultaneously icons and symbols.

For Whitman, the word had first to serve as a clear icon: ". . . I
perceive that words would be a stain, a smutch, except for the stamina
of things."[179] This demands, of course, that the relation of word and
referent be exact. Each word must be the unique icon of the referent
and the unique symbol of the universal spirit embodied in the referent.[180] In consonance with this belief, Whitman insisted that there are
right words and wrong words for things and that only the right word
communicates the spiritual reality. The right word is the one that is
autochthonous, which grows directly from the object or event. He
preferred aboriginal names and slang or argot names over borrowed,
learned, or scientific names. He asserted, for example, that "names of
cities, islands, rivers, new settlements, etc. . . . should (must) assimilate
in sentiment and in sound, to something organic in the place, or
identical with it. It is far better to call a new inhabited island by the
native word, than by its first discoverer, or to call it New anything."
And usage, rather than "abstract construction of the learn'd, or of
dictionary-makers," determines the appropriateness of a word. "Real"
words arise "out of the work, needs, ties, joys, affections, tastes, of
long generations of humanity." The final decisions on matters of lan-

guage "are made by the masses, people nearest to the concrete, having most to do with actual land and sea."[181]

The persuader cannot influence the souls of others by the simple expedient of inventing words. Real words, or right words, follow rather than precede reality. The universal spirit has to be embodied in the referent before its name can have both a physical and spiritual meaning. Words "'cannot be manufactured; [they] must grow as the trees grow.'" There is only "one limitation to the theory of Words—the theory of Things," he concluded.[182] The referent is always more persuasive than its name; both persuader and reader must always test the validity of a tally by comparing it with the model provided by nature.

If the proper words are used, Whitman believed, a tally could approximate the influence of nature. In a passage that itself is an example of his use of a tally, he concluded, "A perfect user of words uses things—they exude in power and beauty from him—miracles from his hands—miracles from his mouth—lilies, clouds, sunshine, woman, poured copiously—things, whirled like chain-shot rocks, defiance, compulsion, horses, iron, locomotive, the oak, the pine, the keen eye, the hairy breast, the Texas ranger, the Boston truckman, the woman that arouses a man, the man that arouses a woman."[183] As the passage illustrates, it is not surprising that Whitman is the favorite poet of twentieth-century filmmakers. His tallies are, in content and in visual placement on the pages of his books, the verbal equivalent of the image-making of the visual montage.[184] Indeed, especially during the period when equipment limitations kept films from being reinforced with natural sound montages, filmmakers often created Whitmanesque narration to accompany their images.[185]

Although Whitman believed that the perfect user of words uses things, he was not so semantically naive as to believe that the word is the thing. He realized that "words are metaphysical beings, and draw on the life of the mind." "Not in these wondrous heiroglyphs of Words, not in these mystic runes, is the power: in the Mind which loads these airy messengers with burdens of meaning is the vis and vivification of speech," he acknowledged. He was aware that names often originated in metaphors, and he praised the metaphorical nature of slang, terming it "indirection, an attempt of common humanity to escape from bald literalism, and express itself illimitably." But words are not "positive and original things in themselves." A word is the "progeny" of the thing it represents, and if the word develops connotations or associations, they too belong to the referent and its soul. If, for example, a word is a metaphor, its meaning is merely that transferred from the spiritual suggestiveness of the implied comparison. Thus, through the power of words to communicate the spiritual as well as the physical meaning of an object or event, verbal persuasion becomes possible.[186] Words can awaken spiritual correspondences in the souls of listeners and readers and dilate them to greater self-divinity. "*Names* are magic"; they "are a test of the esthetic and of spirituality." "A delicate subtle something there is in the right name—," Whitman asserted, "an undemonstrable nourishment that exhilarates the soul. . . . The right name of a city, state, town, man, or woman, is a perpetual feast to the esthetic and moral nature." Such words stimulate the reader or hearer and pour "a flood through the soul." By tallying the method of nature, therefore, the literatus can attain persuasion "worthy the immortal soul of man, and which, while absorbing materials, and, in their own sense, the shows of Nature, will, above all, have, both directly and indirectly, a freeing, fluidizing, expanding, religious character, exulting with science, fructifying the moral elements, and stimulating aspirations, and meditations on the unknown."[187]

In Whitman's theory of tallying, the persuader follows the method of nature by presenting words that stand for natural objects and the spiritual eidólons embodied in those objects. Therefore, the persuader must always use concrete language. Whitman objected to generalizations through ranking, classifying, or giving abstract labels to things or events.[188] And, just as words are unique in origin and signification, they should be used with exactitude. "In most instances a characteristic word once used in a poem, speech, or what not, is then exhausted," he advised; "he who thinks he is going to produce effects by freely using strong words, is ignorant of words. One single name belongs to one single place only—as a key-word of a book may be best used only once in the book."[189]

Although the persuader carefully selects words that signify the spiritual eidólons that he or she is trying to evoke, the manner in which those words are presented is not crucial. Because nature is composed of "irrational forms," irrational structures can be used to tally nature. Indeed, one effective method is merely to present nothing more than a bare list of names. Nature can be tallied by a "bunch and catalogue [of] the affair." Whitman proposed "a new way and the true way of treating in books—History, geography, ethnology, astronomy etc., etc.—by long lists of dates, terms, summary paragraphic statements etc." The great "melange of existence" can be tallied by a "helter-skelter style" with much "skipping and hopping."[190] In biographies Whitman preferred "living glints, samples, autographic letters above all, memoranda of friends &c" rather than "polish'd, formal, consecutive statement." "Nature evidently achieves specimens only . . . ," he reasoned, and thus "specimen-reminiscences" are an appropriate method of presenting a tally.[191]

Literary critics frequently attacked Whitman's inclusions of catalogs and "grocery lists" in his works, and doubtless he would have been pleased with many late-twentieth-century forms of presentation, including perhaps *USA Today*. He believed that individual essays, lectures, stories, or poems should be short, containing only a single *"leading idea or theory."* Gathered together, such short pieces give the proper effect of a tally of specimen reminiscences.[192] If greater structure is necessary, some natural or organic form can be used. Lectures, poems, stories, and prose words can be modeled after conversation, the earth, or the human body. Moreover, the journey motif can be used, in which the reader or listener is led to recreate a chronological or spatial movement through nature. Moving through time and space the persuader can merely tally a "list of all that is seen."[193] The most effective of such descriptions are those that are properly suggestive and elliptical and which are written "at the time and on the spot." Such descriptions or lists, "with all the associations of those scenes and places brought back, will not only go directest to the right spot, but give a clearer and more actual sight . . . than anything else."[194] And such tallies not only capture the persuasiveness of nature, but also give identity to the subject that is tallied. Thus it is, according to Whitman, that the ideal persuader, the divine literatus, uses the tally of past and present to create the future.

WHITMAN'S RHETORIC TODAY

"THE LEAVES DO NOT NEED ANY EXCUSE; THEY DO NEED TO BE UNDERSTOOD. IF I DID NOT UNDERSTAND THEM I WOULD DISLIKE THEM MYSELF, GOD KNOWS!"
—WALT WHITMAN, 1888[195]

Long before the multitudinous new rhetorics of the twentieth century, Whitman abandoned traditional rhetorical theories and practices, all of which he knew well by both study and practice as a speaker, debater, and—most extensively—political journalist. Long before the explosion of antirationalistic rhetoric in electronic media, he used terms and explored topics such as sympathy, identification, image-making, indirection, and suggestion. His theory and use of the tally is a written equivalent of the film montage, and his conception of the function of language—central to his rhetorical practice—is semiotically highly sophisticated. The existence in the mid-nineteenth century of a rhetoric based consciously on such concepts as identification, indirection, and suggestion helps place in context the sudden expansion of rhetorical theories in the twentieth century.

It is significant that Whitman published very few of the manuscripts dealing with the divine literatus or his proposed dictionary for a new American language, an outgrowth of his interest in the tallying power of words. His theory of persuasion was more the private outline of his own efforts than a theory proposed for study and use by others. In formulating the models of the ideal persuader and the ideal rhetorical literature, he was sketching a pattern for use in perfecting his own life and writings. He could not reveal too much of his purpose or method and still remain indirect and suggestive. His practice of persuasion followed his models, however, and throughout his life he struggled to live up to his ideal of the divine literatus. But to live the life of the literatus, he not only had to exert personal magnetism and use direct persuasion; he also had to create the ideal work of scriptural literature. Once written, that work, *Leaves of Grass,* became an inseparable part of his other rhetorical efforts.

A hundred years after his death, Walt Whitman's writings, and even the man himself, have been absorbed into "literary literature," something he detested. The man and his message are almost impossible to decipher in modern editions of his works, with their heavy baggage of erudite introductions, unsympathetic arrangement and presentation of poems, and academic footnotes.[196] That he has been appropriated by advocates of a particular sexual preference, which he denied and feared as irrelevant but potentially distracting to his rhetorical purposes, cuts him off from much of his potential audience.[197] Few have a chance to approach him on his own terms, but are given only fragments of his works in school classes along with labels such as "lyric epic poet," "language experimenter," or "homosexual poet."

Writing as early as 1963, Sculley Bradley concluded, "So much has been written of Whitman's aesthetic ideas and his theory of poetry that unless one were to discover a new rationale there is little to add."[198]

Is there a new rationale for studying Whitman? In this essay the proposition has been put forward that Whitman's own rhetorical standpoint be explicated as the most appropriate way to understand him. Understanding him, perhaps then we can better judge him. But understanding him, we know that he did not want readers to judge him but to respond to him. He wanted to move people, to dilate their souls, to prepare them for life in the Religious Democracy. He did so reach many who kept alive his nonliterary influence for several generations. Could he still persuade if he could be approached from a nonliterary perspective? If a reader could escape a hundred years of focus on Whitman through distorting literary lenses, could he or she today react as did Richard Maurice Bucke, Eugene V. Debs, Clarence Darrow, Horace Traubel, Louis H. Sullivan, Hamlin Garland, and hundreds of others who responded as Whitman intended? If you, Dear Reader, would like to try with your own soul, you have only to find a copy of *Leaves of Grass* that Walt Whitman personally edited and published in or before 1892. Then you may dally with the divine literatus, though

> You will hardly know who I am or what I mean,
> But I shall be good health to you nevertheless,
> And filter and fibre your blood.

> Failing to fetch me at first keep encouraged,
> Missing me one place search another,
> I stop somewhere waiting for you.[199]

LINCOLN AND DOUGLAS RESPOND TO THE ANTISLAVERY MOVEMENT

David Zarefsky and Ann E. Burnette

One obvious feature of movements is that they move. Over time they experience stages of development, each stage having its rhetorical needs and opportunities. Griffin identified three distinct phases of a movement: inception, during which movement leaders reject the existing order, identify an alternative, and propagate the alternative through discourse in search of converts; rhetorical crisis, in which audience members, unable to maintain mental balance between the new movement and the old order, must choose between them; and consummation, during which the success or failure of the movement is validated and its goals are either incorporated into mainstream society or abandoned.[1] Discourse during each of these stages will reflect the needs of the time and circumstance.

But discourse generated in response to a situation also has a life of its own, and may even become functionally autonomous of the context from which it grew. In this sense discursive forms—arguments and appeals, images and metaphors, structures and patterns—also can be said to move. A text is not only a response to a situation but also contains the motive for its own further development and extension.[2] So, for example, the term "slavery," which was used in political rhetoric prior to the American Revolution to suggest a relationship between sovereign nations and their colonies, also nurtured the argument that chattel slavery was inconsistent with republican ideals. Initially the presence of slavery in the American republic did not seem so odd, and the signers of the Declaration of Independence could continue to hold slaves in good conscience even while they declared that "all men are created equal." But discourse

112

moves, and the dialectical terms "freedom" and "slavery" could lead naturally to support different arguments in a different situation from that in which they obtained currency.

Griffin used the term "rhetorical trajectory" to refer to this course of development of a term or theme.[3] Borrowing an analogy from the physical sciences, he proposed that discourse has its own curve of development. A text not only says or does something; it leads somewhere. And where it might lead is not just explained after the fact— it can be sensed by the astute rhetor or listener even in the midst of ongoing public discussion. Those with prescience recognized in the late eighteenth century that slavery was an unstable element in a nation founded on the basis of political liberty, just as their counterparts during the 1940s recognized that the invention of nuclear weapons did not just mean bigger bombs but a dramatic change in how we talk about peace and war, national sovereignty, and the permanent and the transient in life. Griffin argued that "we are moved by our rhetoric as our rhetoric is designed to move others,"[4] and the verb "moved" can be read both as "changed" and as "influenced." Rhetoric affects how we organize, describe, and reason about people and events, although these effects are less commonly recognized than is the working of discourse in a specific situation or context.

To talk of rhetorical trajectories, however, is not to imply determinism. Trajectories are not foreordained, and they do not lead only to a single result. The implicit motives in an argument pattern can be acted upon or left latent; they may be accepted by audiences or dismissed and ignored. Part of the rhetorical art, then, lies in identifying and utilizing the rhetorical trajectories of a person, time, or culture. That is true for movement leaders, like those in the civil rights movement in the 1950s and early 1960s who were able to see how the call for inclusion in American society "led naturally" into a call for transforming society. It is also true of the targets of movements, such as Southern politicians in the aftermath of the Voting Rights Act who recognized that their traditional arguments about the Constitution and civil rights somehow must accommodate the reality of black political participation.

Social movements, in some sense, always target the established political system, seeking acceptance of their goals or transformation of the system. Holders of or aspirants to public office therefore must be particularly sensitive to movements and to the movement of discourse.

Their own statements should be relevant to the situation at hand but should also be capable of incorporating likely change based on the movement's rhetorical trajectory. The successful political response is likely to be that which, while maintaining a consistent principle, moves along with or even precedes the rhetorical trajectory.

In this essay we will explore these ideas by examining the responses of Stephen A. Douglas and Abraham Lincoln to the antislavery movement during the 1850s. That decade witnessed Douglas's dramatic rise and fall and Lincoln's emergence from obscure Illinois state politics. Douglas was the preeminent politician of the early 1850s, seeking formulas to remove the slavery question from the sphere of national politics and subsuming it under procedural questions about who had the right to choose. But he failed to anticipate the revival of moral concerns about slavery and hence was unable to respond to the growing radicalism of Northern opinion. By contrast, Lincoln, while never advocating abolition, was able to ground his position in the immorality of slavery. His argument was more constitutive of later trends in American culture, largely because it was more sensitive to the movement's rhetorical trajectory. We shall pursue these claims by sketching the antislavery movement and then examining speeches and documents by each man in 1854, as well as their famous joint debates of 1858.

THE ANTISLAVERY ARGUMENT

The "antislavery movement" is something of a misnomer. There was no single, consistent movement toward a constant goal. Rather, there were a series of fits and starts which seemed often to end in failure. The antislavery effort was made up at various times of revivalist abolitionists, antislavery politicians willing to compromise for the sake of efficacy, and mainstream politicians who concentrated on stopping the expansion of slavery rather than on its abolition. More than a social movement, then, what is involved is the movement of antislavery discourse along a trajectory between the 1830s and the Civil War.

At its inception the American antislavery movement stemmed from the evangelical effort of the Great Revival of the early nineteenth century. The birth of an organized campaign against slavery can be dated to the appearance of the first issue of *The Liberator* on

January 1, 1831. In this issue publisher William Lloyd Garrison proclaimed his doctrine of "immediatism"—the immediate abolition of
slavery. The newspaper provided a rallying point for like-minded
Americans who subsequently organized into regional and, later, national antislavery organizations. In January 1832 the New England
Anti-Slavery Society was founded in Boston. In December 1833, delegates from nine states came together to form the American Anti-
Slavery Society (AASS), for which Garrison wrote a Declaration of
Sentiments.

The early organized abolition campaign was clearly part of a Christian reform effort. Members at first sought to advance the cause of
immediatism by persuading nonslaveholding citizens in the North to
denounce slavery as a sin. This effort to convert individuals and thereby
change society was consistent with the philosophies of other Christian
reform efforts that grew out of the Great Revival, such as the temperance
movement. In addition to channeling energy toward changing the
individual instead of toward political solutions, this focus also cast the
issue of slavery into simple moral terms. One needed only to denounce
slavery in order to obtain salvation. And, by the same moral equation,
one who did not condemn slavery as a sin was assumed to support it
and hence implicated in sin.

Such an explicitly moralistic approach alienated far more people
than it converted. Few listeners enjoyed being called to account for
moral lapses in any case. Many Northern citizens did not perceive
the doctrine of immediatism as being either feasible or desirable. Abolitionists' commitment to immediatism regardless of the consequences for the Constitution (already a highly revered document)
offended many of their audience members.[5] Because immediatism
was a threat to the Constitution, abolitionism was likewise perceived
as radical.

The AASS's primary strategy of emphasizing moral argument in
preference to other kinds of persuasion caused a profound rift
among its members. Garrison and his followers maintained that
"nonresistance" was the only moral position open to true abolitionists. According to the nonresistance principle, reformers should willingly renounce their loyalties to any human government that
violated God's laws. Garrison consistently resisted the impulse to
adapt antislavery messages to political audiences or to use political
means to achieve his ends. By 1838 the AASS was in serious finan-

cial trouble and losing the organizational power that it needed to
recruit, train, and send forth abolitionists to convert citizens.

Although the argument of the abolitionists did not carry the day,
their element of moral suasion drew upon familiar god terms such
as "liberty." The alternative to Garrisonism was the expression of
moral impulses through political channels, and in 1840 the Liberty
Party was formed for this purpose. This new voice for antislavery
sentiment needed new arguments for abolition because it could not
afford to alienate large numbers of citizens. The Liberty Party, dependent on constituents for support and political power, toned
down the radical and fiercely moral antislavery arguments as party
speakers urged more moderate ways of addressing the problem.

The Liberty Party, however, never was able to secure widespread
support. Some of its most prominent advocates realized that a party
that sought to advance antislavery goals might have to broaden its
platform even further to retain a politically viable constituency.
Salmon P. Chase, for one, worked to build a coalition between Liberty Party members and antislavery activists in the major parties in
an effort to create an antislavery faction that could garner mass
support.

In 1848 a group made up largely of the "Barnburner" Democrats
formed the Free Soil Party. Like the Liberty Party, the Free Soil
Party was committed to the antislavery cause, but that was only one
of its major tenets. The Free Soilers were also committed to im-
proving the conditions of working-class white citizens and increasing
their access to the benefits of a "free soil" society. Their identification with antislavery was not the primary bond that drew them together. In fact, many of the party leaders, including Chase, made
special efforts to separate their own antislavery goals from the abolitionist doctrines that still were associated with radical moralistic
groups.

The channeling of the antislavery message into more politically
acceptable arguments was the result of the convergence of two
rhetorical trajectories. Although the elements of the antislavery trajectory clearly arose from abolitionist sentiment, the political framework into which this message was cast represented the rhetorical
trajectory of a larger public sentiment: the belief of people who
might have acknowledged that slavery was wrong but preferred that
it not be debated politically as a moral issue. Because of the intense,

Not a "discursive form" – cf 112

personal ethical considerations and the sectional divisiveness of the slavery issue, many politicians and constituents saw slavery as an inappropriate issue for public argument. The Democratic Party especially held tenaciously to the view that all political questions should be settled in a way that would preserve the sanctity of the Union and the Constitution. In this context, notes Joel Silbey, antislavery agitation was perceived as "superfluous, dangerous, and outside the pale of reasonable concern."[6] Stephen A. Douglas was the principal spokesperson for this point of view.

But what became of the moral fervor that had been the motivating principle behind the early antislavery movement? Although antislavery activists and politicians after 1840 did not maintain the moral framework that the radical abolitionists had created, the moral elements of their rhetorical trajectory nevertheless resurfaced in debates over the expansion of slavery rather than over slavery itself. As the two established sections of the country developed increasingly exclusionary ideologies and competed for influence in the rapidly expanding U.S. territories, the debates over slavery in the territories took on the moral significance that the earliest abolitionists had assigned to slavery itself. And as the moral stakes of slavery's expansion heightened, the tenor of the arguments became more absolute. Thus, a new moral dimension of the slavery argument emerged as a result of the convergence of the antislavery rhetorical trajectory with the escalating debates over the issue of extension. *[how new?]*

Frustrated by the annexation of Texas and recognizing that the war with Mexico might result in additional slave territory, Pennsylvania Congressional Representative David Wilmot introduced in 1846 a proviso calling for the exclusion of slavery from all territory to be gained from Mexico. The Wilmot Proviso, which was attached routinely to bills in the House, would have an impact beyond its determination of the status of slavery in other territories acquired from Mexico. It signaled a willingness on the part of Congress to dictate the future of slavery extension, particularly in Southern territories.

The debate sparked by the introduction of the Wilmot Proviso demonstrated how much the slavery issue had escalated in importance. The political stakes were high; the moral terms in the debate were correspondingly elevated. "The aura of morality thrown over the whole northern sectional position in connection with the slavery issue," observes John Wright, "engendered an attitude of greater rigidity, of greater reluctance to compromise over the territorial question than at any time since the Missouri controversy."[7]

The events of 1846–50, however, heralded a change in the ethos of antislavery politicians that reflected the constraints of the rhetorical trajectory emphasizing union. Avery Craven notes: "The politician could now be a practical abolitionist and yet deny the charge he was one. He could draw to his support all the moral forces behind the opposition to slavery and phrase his political programs in terms of right and wrong."[8] As Craven explains, the issue of slavery was now fully legitimate in the context of political argument, as long as it was the dimension of the extension of slavery that was being discussed. The rhetorical trajectory of antislavery arguments was still influential in public discourse, provided it was channeled into acceptable political terms.

That the Compromise of 1850 worked out the practical issues of the debate over slavery and territorial expansion suggests that the collective arguments privileging terms such as "union," "the Constitution," and "compromise" still formed the dominant rhetorical trajectory in public discourse and therefore determined public arguments. The union-saving peace that was won, however, was tenuous. Eric Foner observes that the Compromise of 1850 was "the last attempt of the political system to expel the disease of sectional ideology by finally settling all the points at which slavery and national politics intersected."[9] This is the primary set of terms that the antislavery trajectory would challenge.

Early in 1854 Douglas introduced a bill to organize the territories of Kansas and Nebraska, eschewing any declaration of their slave or free status but leaving this question for the inhabitants of each territory to decide through their popular vote. The Nebraska bill brought two competing trajectories into collision. By the early 1850s the sentiment that the morality of slavery was not an appropriate subject for general political debate had calcified in many sectors of the audience. This feeling dictated the reaction of many to Douglas's Nebraska bill, since the morality of slavery was raised as an issue in the debate over the measure. Wright argues that among many citizens of Illinois the popular feeling "was regret shading into anger that the slavery question had been reopened at all."[10] At the same time, antislavery feeling seemed to be intensifying. The moral aspect of the antislavery appeal, previously championed only by radicals such as Garrison and subsequently sublimated in debates over expansion, was gaining enough force to pose

a challenge to the prevailing view that slavery was not a moral issue
that could be discussed in the political realm.

THE RESPONSES: 1854   (1) *immorality*

Two rhetorical curves, previously thought separate, came to a
point of intersection, perhaps even collision. The task for a speaker
was to respond to this new circumstance in a way that might also
anticipate and be deemed appropriate to the future course of either
trajectory. Both Stephen A. Douglas and Abraham Lincoln spoke to
this need during 1854. Their texts provide an opportunity to examine how each politician framed his argument in response to the
meeting of the two trajectories. In his April 6 letter to twenty-five   *Douglas*
Chicago clergy, Douglas's arguments reflected the general aversion to
debating substantive moral questions in the political forum, and
privileged procedural over substantive morality. Lincoln, however,
speaking on October 16 in Peoria, tried to create an ethical stance
that borrowed the substantive moral argument from antislavery rhet-   *Lincoln*
oric as well as the procedural and constitutional priorities of the
more general rhetorical context.[11]

Douglas, as the Nebraska bill's author, was naturally in a position
of explaining and defending the principle of popular sovereignty.
Among the constituents who responded to their senator's legislative
solution to the question of expansion were a group of Illinois clergy
who met in Chicago on March 27 to draft a resolution objecting to
the Nebraska bill. The ministers issued their objections "in the name
of Almighty God"[12] and sent the letter to the Chicago *Tribune* and
Democratic Press, both of which published the letter on March 29.
Douglas's reaction to the resolution was angry and imperious: he objected to the ministers' attempt to invoke God's authority in their
judgment of a public question, and he felt that they misrepresented
the aims of popular sovereignty. Douglas countered their criticisms in
a public letter that appeared in the *Chicago Northwestern Christian
Advocate,* the Boston *Christian Watchman and Reflector,* and the *Congressional Globe.*

In his letter to the Chicago clergy, Douglas unequivocally marked
out the domain of the principle of popular sovereignty. The will of the
people, as expressed through their representative government, was the
ultimate moral authority in governmental matters—it took precedence

over the divine insight of any religious leaders. Furthermore, the clergy's attempt to influence legislation in their capacity as religious leaders not only confused the issue of popular self-government but undermined and threatened it. Douglas rejected their assertion that they had a privileged perspective from which to argue for the public good: "Your claims for the supremacy of this divinely-appointed institution are subversive of the fundamental principles upon which our whole republican system rests" (*DL*, 312).

Because Douglas viewed popular sovereignty as his moral absolute, he subordinated to it the dilemma of slavery as a moral issue. Douglas responded to his correspondents' criticism of the Kansas bill by saying, "Your opposition is confined exclusively to the principle of popular sovereignty. It does not vary the question, in any degree, that human slavery is, in your opinion, a great moral wrong" (*DL*, 318). Douglas defended popular sovereignty as an acceptable way to arbitrate the question of slavery by focusing on two arguments: first, that the principle of popular sovereignty was a moral absolute, and second, that slavery was no more pressing a moral issue than other matters of legislation determined regularly by local government.

According to Douglas, the framers of the Constitution "held that the people were the only true source of all political power." The "great principle" of popular sovereignty was not only historically sanctioned but was perpetually "recognized and affirmed in the constitution of the United States and of every state in the Union" (*DL*, 313). Douglas feared that tyranny would result, not so much from the violation of protected liberties as from the abrogation of the people's right to determine their own laws.

The Nebraska bill, in Douglas's view, was not legislation concerning slavery but "purely a question of self-government, involving the right and capacity of the people to make their own laws and manage their own local and domestic concerns" (*DL*, 320). Because Douglas defined the question of self-government as preeminent in any debate of public or legislative morality, he contended that the issue of slavery was merely an adjunct to the more important issue of popular sovereignty.

Douglas buttressed his claim that popular sovereignty rather than slavery was the important issue by demonstrating that slavery was only one of many issues citizens must decide for themselves. To this end, he made analogies between slavery and other social issues that had moral significance. People of the states and territories determined their laws governing the distribution of alcohol, the transaction of business on the Sabbath, gambling, and even their criminal codes—it was accepted that popular sovereignty was an appropriate way to decide these issues. "Inasmuch as you are willing to leave these questions, and all others which are supposed to be interests of society, in the hands of the people of the respective States and Territories," Douglas inquired, "would it not be better and wiser to entrust the slavery question to the arbitrament of the same authority, rather than to violate the great principle of self-government which lies at the foundation of all our free institutions?" (*DL*, 319). Douglas repeatedly defended the moral right of the people of a state, territory, or community to decide their policy toward slavery, irrespective of the decisions of other localities or the sentiments of national leaders.

While Douglas was frequently called upon to defend his vision of popular sovereignty, Lincoln used the debate over the Nebraska bill as an opportunity to issue his own views on the expansion of slavery. Lincoln was campaigning in 1854 for a seat in the Illinois legislature and indirectly promoting his candidacy for a Senate seat that would be open in 1855. He used the turbulent political situation of 1854 as a backdrop for his first public criticism of slavery on moral grounds. Lincoln made a series of campaign speeches in the late summer and fall. His speech in Peoria on October 16 was characteristic in that he concentrated on the question of slavery expansion almost to the exclusion of other campaign issues.[13]

Lincoln based his objection to slavery's expansion in part on the tenet that slavery was morally wrong. He responded to the Nebraska bill by proclaiming in his Peoria speech, "I object to it because it assumes there CAN BE MORAL RIGHT in the enslaving of one man by another" (*LS*, 274). The simplicity of this statement, however, belied a more complicated position. While Lincoln incorporated the moral revulsion to slavery that was part of the antislavery argument, his stance on slavery included many subtle distinctions. Although he believed that the institution of slavery ultimately would be extinguished, he was concerned publicly with preventing the *spread* of slavery rather than with eradicating it. At the outset of his speech, Lincoln noted that he was "arguing against the EXTENSION of a bad thing, which where it already exists, we must of necessity manage as best as we can" (*LS*, 266). In this respect, Lincoln did not contradict the general belief that it would be unconstitutional to interfere with slavery where it already existed. But his view also encompassed the somewhat radical view that blacks deserved basic human rights, as well as the more prevalent opinion that blacks were inferior to whites and that society should legislate accordingly.

Because his views about blacks and their role in society served as one premise for his stance on slavery, Lincoln referred to them several times in the course of his Peoria speech. Lincoln believed that blacks were human beings and thus entitled to the rights, privileges, and obligations enumerated in the Declaration of Independence. He attempted to demonstrate to his audience that the basic humanity of blacks was evident to all, even to Southern slave owners, citing as evidence legislation ending the African slave trade, Southerners' pronounced distaste in dealing with slave dealers, and the existence of presumably valuable free blacks. "In all these cases," judged Lincoln, "it is your sense of justice, and human sympathy, continually telling you, that the poor negro has some natural right to himself—that those who deny it, and make mere merchandise of him, deserve kickings, contempt and death" (*LS*, 265).

Lincoln's belief in the humanity of blacks, while convincingly expressed in relation to basic legal rights, did not extend to issues of social and political equality. Indeed, he acknowledged his ambivalence about the status blacks should assume in society: "What next? Free them, and make them politically and socially our equals? My own feelings will not admit of this" (*LS*, 256). He suggested colonization as one solution that appealed to him, but granted that the logistics of such a plan probably would preclude its implementation (*LS*, 255).

It was only at this level that Lincoln addressed procedural issues. Sometimes his unwillingness to accept political equality for blacks was expressed as an act of deference toward his audience. He noted that "the great mass of white people" could not accept blacks as their political and social equals. He further observed, "Whether this feeling accords with justice and sound judgment, is not the sole question, if indeed, it is any part of it. A universal feeling, whether well or ill-founded, can not be safely disregarded. We can not, then, make them equals" (*LS*, 256). Moreover, Lincoln at times framed the question of nonextension exclusively in terms of the benefits it would afford whites. He argued that the new western territories were intended for the white population only. "We want them for the homes of free white people," he noted, adding, "Slave States are places for poor white people to remove FROM . . . New free States are the places for poor people to remove TO" (*LS*, 268). Lincoln's assessment of his audience, however, also included the observation that "the great mass of mankind" believed slavery immoral. "They consider slavery a great moral wrong; and their feelings against it, [are] not evanescent, but eternal" (*LS*, 281–82). In his analysis of his audience, Lincoln projected a rhetorical climate that was receptive to his own ambivalence to the nature and rights of blacks.

Lincoln's arguments about the immorality of slavery and the inferiority of blacks enabled him to respond to the moral momentum of the antislavery movement while also accommodating his audience's beliefs about white superiority. He pronounced slavery categorically wrong because the enslavement of persons entitled to fundamental human rights was immoral. Using the god terms "liberty" and "humanity," which had great resonance in American political discourse, he was able to assimilate the antislavery rhetorical trajectory. Yet simultaneously Lincoln successfully dissociated himself from radical abolitionists, who advocated political empowerment of blacks—a position that the vast majority of Americans in 1854 found extreme and dangerous.

To be sure, Lincoln's negotiation of these competing trajectories required him to take ambiguous positions. He condemned slavery, but worked against it only where it did not exist. He defended the humanity of blacks, but sharply limited the range of human rights to which they were entitled. Far from being a reckless visionary on either issue, Lincoln couched both of these positions in terms of what "the great mass" of white constituents would tolerate. Still, his fundamental underlying premise was that slavery was a moral evil.

Douglas's decision to make popular sovereignty the higher morality in the debate over slavery, however, rendered him incapable of issuing a moral evaluation of slavery. This incapacity, while consistent with Douglas's hierarchy of moral values, meant that he could not directly address—either to reject or to endorse—the antislavery arguments that were used to attack popular sovereignty. Nor could he point out or exploit the tensions in Lincoln's positions on the substantive issues. Douglas's strategy of constructing a moral framework that left substantive questions to be decided by procedural mechanisms that had the weight of moral sanction was potentially viable in the rhetorical

climate of 1854. But the strategy prevented Douglas from either stopping or utilizing the moral force of the antislavery rhetorical trajectory,
a force that Lincoln was in a position to appropriate.

THE RESPONSES: 1858

The years between 1854 and 1858 witnessed the intensification of
the slavery issue to the point that it overwhelmed most other topics
on the political agenda. The push for the settlement of Kansas and the
controversy over the Lecompton constitution severely tested the meaning of popular sovereignty. The break between Douglas and the Buch-
anan administration had altered the senator's standing on the issue,
making him suddenly more popular among opponents of slavery, and
increased the concern of Illinois Republicans that they be sure to
distinguish their program from his. The Dred Scott decision, holding
that Congress lacked the power to prohibit slavery in the territories,
seemingly undercut the platforms of both Lincoln and Douglas and
sent each scurrying for a way to reconcile his principles with the
decision of the Supreme Court. Moreover, in an age in which conspiracy
rhetoric and suspicion of "designing" politicians were widespread, this
decision was seen by many as preparing the way for a second decision
which would legalize slavery in all the states as well. Fears had been
reawakened of the "slave power," a Southern conspiracy to remake
America into a slave society and in the process trample on the rights
of free white northerners.[14] Transformed from innocent bystanders into
potential victims, northerners took a great interest in the controversy.
Moderate Northern opinion, if not abolitionist, moved gradually toward
accepting the premise that slavery was wrong as a presupposition in
discussions about what should be done. This shift, though it hastened
in the years after 1858, had begun by the time of the Lincoln-Douglas
debates.

Lincoln's rhetorical stance was more able to accommodate this
movement of the antislavery argument along the rhetorical trajectory.
Indeed, Douglas's emphasis on the procedure of popular sovereignty
as his fundamental value precluded his adaptation to shifts in public
sentiment. After all, the essence of his position was indifference to the
substantive outcome. He had to remain as neutral as he had been in
1854, even though neutrality could now be portrayed much more easily
as moral obtuseness.

Douglas approached the slavery question as a pragmatist. If slavery was economically beneficial, it was fine; if not, he was opposed. When Lincoln cited the prohibition in the Northwest Ordinance as evidence of the founders' moral sanction against slavery, Douglas replied that moral sanction must mean little since the institution was introduced to Illinois anyway. As he said in the Alton debate, "We in Illinois . . . tried slavery, kept it up for 12 years, and finding that it was not profitable we abolished it *for that reason*, and became a free state" (emphasis added).[15] He was disdainful of all who claimed to know the nature of morality and to impose it on others. Consequently, as one biographer put it, he opposed all "who on their own assumption of superior moral rectitude and judgment were bent on removing motes from the eyes of their brothers."[16] To assert a moral claim as the basis for public policy was to display intolerance, since knowledge of morality was not given to mortals. Against all such displays, Douglas championed the right of a community to regulate its own affairs.

For Douglas, procedure itself was moral. He found authority for his own view in the second chapter of Genesis, in which God set good and evil before man and empowered him to choose between them.[17] Like any procedural issue, Douglas's was preemptive. It subsumed the morality of slavery by focusing on who had the right to determine whether the institution was moral or not. That right, to Douglas, lay with the inhabitants of a state or territory, who after all would have to live with the consequences of their decision. By taking this position, of course, he was rendered incapable of revealing his own moral judgment, much less trying to impress it upon others. He could not adapt to or even acknowledge the gradual shifts in his audience's view of the moral issue.

This orientation shaped Douglas's moral argument in the debates. He mixed the prevalent anti-black sentiment of the time with concern for their well-being. At Ottawa, for instance, he proclaimed, "I am opposed to negro citizenship in any and every form. I believe this government was made on the white basis. I believe it was made by white men, for the benefit of white men and their posterity for ever." But he immediately added, "I do not hold that because the negro is our inferior that therefore he ought to be a slave. . . . On the contrary, I hold that humanity and Christianity both require that the negro shall have and enjoy every right, every privilege, and every immunity consistent with the safety of the society in which he lives" (*Debates*, 111–

12).[18] The key question was *which* rights, privileges, and immunities were compatible with the public good, and that question could best be answered by the inhabitants of each territory or state. Some might make them slaves; some might make them citizens; and some, like the state of Illinois, might follow a middle course.

Little difference can be detected, then, between the Douglas of 1854 and the incumbent in the Lincoln-Douglas debates. If anything, he had become more strident in his insistence that he "don't care" whether slavery is voted down or up in Kansas. Many voters, too, still held to this position, although it is uncertain how many did so because they could imagine no alternative to abolition. Douglas's object remained to banish the slavery dispute from the halls of Congress so that the country could get on with the business of growth and expansion, tasks that would subsume the controversy anyway.

In contrast, significant movement can be found in Lincoln's argument. As in 1854, he began with the premise that slavery was a moral wrong. He gave this premise greater salience by linking it to Douglas's position. Lincoln's argument was energized by the conviction that Douglas's professed neutrality actually served to legitimize a wrong and thereby paved the way for the nationalization of slavery. As the challenger viewed matters, Douglas could say that he "don't care" only if he did not deem slavery wrong, since to profess a right to do wrong would be a contradiction in terms. In the debates Lincoln repeatedly denied that slavery was a trivial issue whose resolution could be left to the normal course of politics. Not condemning slavery as wrong necessarily meant condoning it as right. And if it were right, why should it not be permitted to go on indefinitely? Lincoln sought to portray Douglas as sanctioning slavery forever—knowing that even the conservative Whigs, however much they might hate abolition, were moving to the belief that slavery was wrong and would disappear in God's good time. By narcotizing public opinion as to the morality of slavery, Douglas was effectively removing the only obstacle to its spread across the land.

Interestingly, however, Lincoln did not develop his moral claim until late in the debates. Except for a brief mention in the Ottawa debate, he did not introduce the issue until Galesburg, the fifth debate. Even there he only pointed out the incumbent's lack of a moral position. In the next debate, at Quincy, he chided Douglas for enabling slavery to go on forever, and he fully articulated his own moral position only in the final debate, at Alton. He was constrained both by his awareness of the complexities of audience sentiment and by his own commitment to the value of compromise. He still disavowed any commitment to black citizenship or to racial equality, even though the arguments he used for emancipation would generally apply to those actions as well.

These constraints created for Lincoln a paradox of rhetorical strategy. He faced the same dilemma as in 1854, but it was now more salient. His moral beliefs, derived from a theory of natural rights, seemed to be absolute, but the actions he supported were limited and gradual. He resolved the discrepancy by appealing to a theory of public opinion that evolved during the debates. At Ottawa he said, "In this and like communities, public sentiment is everything. With public sentiment, nothing can fail; without it nothing can succeed. Consequently, he who moulds public sentiment, goes deeper than he who enacts statutes or pronounces decisions" (*Debates*, 128). From this standpoint, the necessary and sufficient condition for Lincoln's program was public confidence that slavery, however gradually, would disappear—or, as he carefully phrased it, slavery must be placed "where the public mind shall rest in the belief that it is in course of ultimate extinction" (*Debates*, 2).[19]   vs popular sovereignty

Yet how could the public conclude that slavery was on the way out? The answer, for Lincoln, lay in public condemnation of the institution on moral grounds. Refusal to extend it would symbolize that the country intends for it to end, and since it is immoral it should not be extended. In this way morality and practical action were joined. The concept of the "public mind" created a conceptual space between acquiescence and abolition. Just as Lincoln in 1854 had appealed to public opinion as his reason for stopping short of abolition or black equality, he now castigated Douglas for interfering with a settled matter of public conviction and judgment through the introduciton of the Nebraska bill. That consensus, in the Republican's view, was what had sustained the confidence that slavery eventually would die out, even while its continued existence was tolerated.

A second adaptation Lincoln made was to make the villain in the moral drama not the slaveowner, who really was an innocent victim, but political opponents like Douglas who kept the slavery issue unsettled by trying to rid it of its basic moral dimension. Frequently Lincoln asserted that the whole country had regarded the slavery question as settled until Douglas introduced the Kansas-Nebraska Act,

↳ But — Clay had only deferred

which repealed the Missouri Compromise. Plaintively Lincoln asked in the Jonesboro debate "why he could not have left that Compromise alone" (*Debates*, 207).

Focusing on Douglas enabled Lincoln to redefine the candidates' position on the moral issue. Lincoln was not at one extreme, favoring abolition. Rather, Douglas was at the *other* extreme, opposing any end to slavery, ever. If Douglas could be portrayed as a dangerous radical, then Lincoln would appear moderate by comparison—an important result because the Illinois audience was still hostile to abolition.

As in 1854, then, Lincoln took a somewhat ambiguous position. He tied universal moral appeals to a limited political program and justified his doing so by reference to the power of public opinion. But he gave greater prominence to the moral issue, asserting that the central difference between him and Douglas was that he viewed slavery as wrong whereas Douglas accepted it as right. Moreover, he clearly implicated Douglas in a pattern of events which, by anesthetizing the public, would prepare the country for the nationalization of slavery, in opposition both to the wishes of the nation's founders and to the prevailing belief of the public all the way back to 1854. Whereas Douglas's position remained exactly the same as it had been four years earlier and precluded consideration of slavery as a moral issue, Lincoln had moved toward a more prominent and more fully developed moral argument, taking care to ensure that his rhetorical trajectory did not outpace the evolution of moderate public opinion.

CONCLUSION

Both Lincoln and Douglas represented views that were popular with voters during the 1850s, and even in 1858 it was Douglas who came out ahead. Lincoln may have spoken more to the ages, but Douglas was more effective at acknowledging voters' immediate anxieties. He raised the specter of abolitionism and convinced enough of the swing voters that he rather than Lincoln was the true ideological descendant of Henry Clay in his moderation on the issue. He made popular sovereignty seem an acceptable way to settle the slavery question, particularly once it was clear that Kansas would be free under either his or Lincoln's program.

Yet when, following Griffin's lead, one views the trajectory of the arguments, it becomes clear that the kernel of Lincoln's philosophical position was more in keeping with the spirit of the time and harder to refute than was Douglas's. He gave voice to the still latent moral concerns of the North and yet was able to reconcile them with prevailing views of history, legality, and race. He anticipated emergent views and gave them voice, espousing the unspoken claims toward which the moderates gradually were tending. Moreover, although his appeals were not always persuasive at the time and became moot soon afterward, he did carefully distinguish his commitment from both abolition and social equality. He did so first by placing the Constitution in a privileged position and acquiescing in its sanction for the peculiar institution. Lincoln justified his refusal to advocate abolition immediately by asserting that it would come only when the public mind was ready. Second, he regarded freedom, or "the right to rise," as fundamentally an economic rather than a social or political right. This distinction made it possible for him to stop short of the full implications of equality while clearly defending his own position. As he put the matter in the Ottawa debate:

> I agree with Judge Douglas [that the negro] is not my equal in many respects—certainly not in color, perhaps not in moral or intellectual endowment. But in the right to eat the bread, without leave of anybody else, which his own hand earns, *he is my equal and the equal of Judge Douglas, and the equal of every living man.* (*Debates,* 117)

When times changed, moreover, and Lincoln's distinctions were no longer relevant, they could be excised without detracting from the main point of his argument. When, near the end of the Civil War, the Constitution was amended to outlaw slavery, reverence for the Constitution and opposition to slavery were no longer at odds. What would be recalled through the ages was not Lincoln's legalistic deference to a historical document but his forthright defense of individual human rights. Similarly, as the distinction between economic advancement and social and political equality was seen as less compelling, Lincoln's disclaimers have been conveniently forgotten. What is collectively remembered is his masterful statement at Alton: "The real issue in this controversy—the one pressing upon every mind—is the sentiment on the part of one class that looks upon the institution of slavery *as a wrong,* and of another class that *does not* look upon it *as a wrong*" (*Debates,* 390). Douglas, without knowing it, spoke the language and values of a time already passing him by. Lincoln's argument was able both to speak to his own time and to anticipate the future. By bringing his rhetorical trajectory in line with the evolution of the antislavery argument, Lincoln was able, in the light of history, to win the clash with Douglas which occupied both men for much of the 1850s.

◆ ◆ ◆

Burkean Rites and the Gettysburg Address

Thomas F. Mader

In his afterword to Leland M. Griffin's "A Dramatistic Theory of the Rhetoric of Movements," William H. Rueckert says that Griffin is attempting to "develop a model or abstraction from Burke for the study of a specific subject."[1] In this essay I try to do much the same thing, although my specific subject is the rhetorical analysis of a single speech rather than of a movement. Lest I appear unmoved by Griffin's keen interest in movement studies, I note that Griffin has broadened his own definition of movement, so that in his analysis of Lee Harvey Oswald's assassination of John F. Kennedy Griffin observes that Oswald "saw himself as the leader of a movement, imaginary though it was."[2]

However, my interest is not in claiming that concepts can evolve and change. My goal is to establish a model for rhetorical criticism and to apply that model to Lincoln's Gettysburg Address. Although there have been numerous essays written about Burkean concepts, few of them have focused on applying those concepts to the analysis of speechmaking.[3] It may be, as Thomas B. Farrell contends, that "the practitioners and advocates of rhetorical criticism are often more pleased to discuss their methods and assumptions than to examine their particular objects of study."[4] To make matters worse, one searches desperately for the critic who has said anything about style, which Burke sees as an element of substance.

Although there has been little application of Burkean concepts to speechmaking, the Gettysburg Address has been dissected by a number of competent critics.[5] My primary reason for choosing the Gettysburg Address is that its brevity allows me to demonstrate how Burke's ideas can be used to explain the "movement" of a speech.

In developing my Burkean model, I consider the function of identification and persuasion in communication. First, I will consider identification and its relationship to religion and symbolic action. Second, I
will explain Burke's perspective on style and its relationship to ritual.
Third, I will move from *rhetorica docens* to *rhetorica utens* and apply
Burke's concepts to the Gettysburg Address.

IDENTIFICATION AND DRAMATISM

Aristotle posits that "Rhetoric is the counterpart [antistrophos] of
dialectic."[6] He means that rhetoric and dialectic are similar but distinct
functions of communication. Burke contends that persuasion is the
counterpart of identification: "A speaker persuades an audience by the
use of stylistic identifications."[7] In Burkean terms, Aristotle's approach
focuses on agency, whereas Burke focuses on act: rhetoric (agency) is
the art of persuasion (act); dialectic (agency) is the art of identification
(act).

Of course, both Aristotle and Burke talk about agency and act, but
the difference in emphasis is significant. For Aristotle, rhetoric and
dialectic are primarily matters of technique; for Burke, rhetoric and
dialectic are primarily matters of *being*, of ontological concern. In
addition, Burke sees persuasion and identification as distinct but related
acts, which makes his perspective on antistrophos more Greek than
Aristotle's. The classical concept of antistrophe refers to distinct op-
erations blended together to achieve single purpose, as in the Greek
choric dance. Because there could not be an antistrophe without a
strophe, this means that the strophe provides support for the antistrophe, and that both together give meaning to the dance. Analogously,
we can say that identification supports persuasion in the attempt to
goad audiences to action.

Burke calls his theory of language "dramatism" primarily because
drama focuses on the human being's capacity to act, to say yes or no
to a specific behavior. Action is essential to drama; characters on a
stage come alive insofar as they make decisions and carry them out.
Making decisions necessitates language, and language therefore is a
form of action—symbolic action.[8]

Each act that we perform flows from our conception of self, our
self-identity. However, we are not born with a self-concept, nor can
we create one in isolation. Therefore, we reach out to others to confirm

that what we have done is characteristic of us and therefore makes sense. This reaching out requires us to speak the language of the group significant to us. If we speak a common language and can understand one another, it seems to follow that we are pretty much the same. It is this sameness that allows us to identify with one another, to say not only "I understand" but also "I understand *you*." In short, we develop our self-concept by identifying with others who confirm our self-concept. At the same time, we help others develop their self-concepts.

When we identify with another person, we feel as one with that person. Yet this unity, or social cohesion, confirms our self-identity, that which makes us unique and separate from the other. Thus we are individuals insofar as we confront one another, stand in one another's presence, talk to one another. Although communication implies (and necessitates) social cohesion, communication also verifies our separation from others. In other words, in unity there is separation. Only if we are together in the oneness of identification can we sense the distinctiveness of self. In short, identification is a dialectical operation because it "proves opposites" (*Motives*, 44–46).

IDENTIFICATION AND UNIVERSAL MOTIVES

Why are we able to identify with one another? Burke contends that identification is possible because all of us have the same motives, or inherent needs, and that the terms for these motives name "relationships and developments that, *mutatis mutandis*, are likely to figure in all human association."[9] Moreover, we justify our behavior by referring to these motives, and we attempt to induce others to behave in a certain fashion by framing our message in terms of these motives. Although we usually have no difficulty separately identifying these motives, they are like arcs of a circle that interlock and radiate from a central point, the ultimate motive—or motive of motives—order. Our need for order determines what choices we make and how we explain and justify these choices to others (*Motives*, 194–97).

Burke says that we must focus on religion, "a center from which all other forms of human motivation gradually diverged," to discover the terms for the universal motives of humanity.[10] Yet our focus will not be on religion per se but rather on the terminology of religion, which means that our interest is not people's relationship to God but their relationship to the word "God." Burke's rationale for such an approach is that "theological doctrine . . . is words about God. In being words about so 'ultimate' or 'radical' a subject, it [is] an example of words used with thoroughness. Since words-about-God would be as far-reaching as words can be, the 'rhetoric of religion' will provide us with good insight into the nature of language itself as a motive" (*Religion*, vi).

What it comes down to is this: We are who we are because we share basic internal needs; this allows us to identify with one another and to confirm our self-identity. We know who we are because we know where we stand. But where do we stand? What is our "substance"? What is permanent about us that allows us to identify with one another and thereby determine our self-identity? What is permanent about us is that we change. On the one hand, we grow (in experience, strength, knowledge, authority, virtue); on the other hand, we deteriorate (lose hair, teeth, tolerance, enthusiasm, resistance to disease). Deterioration is perverse growth and therefore negative (in our perception). Positive growth actively engages all people who are normal and healthy. People with such an outlook want to live for a long time and be happy; the longer the better, provided one is happy.

Now religion offers us an eternal life of perfect happiness—an enticement that is the ultimate persuasion. It is for this reason that Burke views the biblical story of creation as "an ultimate source of motives,"[11] and he identifies these internal needs of humanity as hierarchy, guilt, victimage, and redemption. From a theological perspective, these motives symbolize the covenant God made with Adam and Eve that provides them and their progeny (i.e., all of us) with an orientation, a sense of order. In the following sections I will discuss these universal motives of humankind.

Hierarchy and Guilt

The Bible spells out the rights and obligations of the human being: "Increase and multiply and fill the earth, and make it yours; take command of the fishes in the sea and all that flies through the air, and all the living things that move on the earth" (Gen. 1:28). In addition, the covenant spells out human beings' obligations to God: "And this was the command which the Lord God gave [them], Thou mayest eat thy fill of all the trees in the garden except the tree which brings knowledge of good and evil; if ever thou eatest of this, thy doom is death" (Gen. 2:16–17). God's covenant provides guidelines by which Adam and Eve could conduct their lives. In regard to inferiors, these guides are positive. But in regard to the Creator, the sole guide is negative; the first time God speaks to them concerning their relationship, God commands what is *not* to be done.

Burke sees this use of the negative as "a peculiarly linguistic invention, not a 'fact' of nature, but a function of a symbol-system, as intrinsically symbolic as the square root of minus one" (*Religion*, 20). However, God's use of the hortatory negative establishes two "facts" about humankind: (1) each human being possesses free will, and (2) each human being can reject God's commands and thereby sin. If Adam and Eve do not have free will, God's command to them is meaningless; the command has meaning because they can disobey. As Burke explains, "The possibility of a 'Fall' is implied in the idea of a Covenant insofar as the idea of a Covenant implies the possibility of its being violated. One does not make a covenant with stones or trees or fire—for such things cannot break agreements or defy commands, since they cannot even understand agreements or commands" (*Religion*, 174).

While the hortatory negative defines human beings' capabilities, it places limits on their actions as a symbol of their obedience to God. Yet such restraints also encompass their biological behavior, since God tells them not to eat of the forbidden fruit as a *symbol* of willingness to obey God's commands. Therefore, whatever property needs they have as animals, and whatever property rights they have as symbol users, they may not satisfy these needs and rights by eating from the tree of knowledge of good and evil. When they violate God's command and eat the forbidden fruit, this "original sin" indicts them both in their generic state as animals and in their specific state as symbol users. Their original sin is an action that proclaims their irrelevance because they reject the principle of hierarchy, the principle that sustains their existence as purposive human beings. When they realize their error, Adam and Eve become anxious—they experience guilt, which is primarily a sense of loss. They have alienated themselves from God and are therefore alone and undefined. In addition, they have condemned themselves to extinction.

The biblical myth of original sin is significant because it implies that Adam and Eve's sin is the sin of all humankind. Their guilt, then, has a universal application that transcends person and time: All people in all ages share it. This means that each person feels not partly, but wholly, responsible for Adam and Eve's sin. This is also because they are not merely *a* representative of humankind but *the* representative of humankind. They are the symbol of all symbol-using animals who choose to reject the symbol of God's authority, who choose to deny the principle of hierarchy. To speculate that some other symbol of humankind might have acted differently ignores the fact that they were the ultimate symbol of humankind, the symbol that sums up completely what it means to be human. As such, they represent the principle of identification. They are at one and the same time the symbol of each human being and of all human beings. They therefore symbolize both the principle of division (i.e., self-identity, what makes each of us distinct and separate) and the principle of cohesion (i.e., what we have in common that makes us the same and allows us to identify with one another).

We are different because each of us is capable of making his or her own decisions. We are the same because each of us has this capability. And if we are to be human, we are faced with this agonizing reality: we *must* choose. Even the refusal to choose is a choice. Prior to their original sin, Adam and Eve exist in a state of innocence, a lobotomized, rather than a rapturous, state, one in which they move, rather than act. Until the serpent endows them with the light (*lux,* Lucifer) of consciousness, they are not actually human. The serpent introduces Adam and Eve to conflict: consciousness, thought, choice, and guilt. Burke notes that consciousness "occurs in situations marked by conflict," and he further posits the gradations of consciousness: simple consciousness of deliberate choice, deep conscientiousness that one has made a wrong choice, and aggravated crises of conscience (*Permanence,* 30).[12] Human beings choose in the belief that they have made the right choice, but with the awareness that their choice may be wrong.[13] It is this awareness that constitutes their sense of guilt.

Victimage and Redemption

Ultimately, Adam and Eve's sense of guilt results from the conflict between freedom and necessity. When they say "no" to the hortatory negative, they choose to reject what is necessary to their existence as purposive, symbol-using animals. They can make this choice, but they should not choose to reject the authority necessary to their existence. It is the conflict between "can" and "should not" that evokes their conscience, their awareness of their relationship to God and the responsibilities that relationship imposes.

No person can endure guilt permanently, because guilt is like a sickness that courts death. Therefore, the part of oneself that is threatening one's existence must be "killed." This can be done in two ways. First, through mortification: penances, fasts, and other restraints upon the body to offer oneself in sacrifice to appease God, who has been wronged. Such appeasement also "kills" the weakness that tempts one to offend God. Mortification symbolizes one's sense of justice. Something has been taken that belongs to God, so now something must be given up that is intrinsically one's own: the power to do evil, to make the wrong choice.

Second, one can attempt to kill this sense of guilt through victimage, the sacrifice of a scapegoat. The scapegoat has its origins in the Old Testament: "On the Day of Atonement, which was the tenth day of the seventh month, the Jewish high-priest laid both his hands on the head of a live goat, confessed over it all the iniquities of the Children of Israel, and, having thereby transferred the sins of the people to the beast, sent it away into the wilderness."[14] Both social cohesion and division (the dual function of identification, which simultaneously separates and brings together) are exemplified in the scapegoat mechanism. First, those individuals burdened with a sense of guilt view the sacrificial victim as sharing this burden with them. Second, having made this identification, they cleanse themselves of their guilt by loading the entire burden of their sins upon the sacrificial victim, thus alienating themselves from it. Their subsequent destruction of the scapegoat confirms their purgation. Third, such purgation, or catharsis, introduces "a new principle of merger, this time in the unification of those whose purified identity is defined in dialectical opposition to the sacrificial offering" (*Grammar*, 406). The three steps in victimage, then, are (1) a consciousness of guilt, both individual and communal; (2) an alienation from guilt by communal sacrifice of a scapegoat; and (3) a new identification resulting from redemption, "for the alienating of iniquities from the self to the scapegoat amounts to a rebirth of the self" (*Grammar*, 406).

DIALECTIC AND SUBSTANCE

As symbol-using animals, we accept the principle of hierarchy because we understand the purpose of a hierarchy: to establish relationships and bring into being a code of rights and obligations that tells us where we stand and what choices we should make. Social

relationships are characterized by division into classes or ranks, and
this division is enhanced by mystery, whereby each of us is aware that
we are different from one another. While division is needed for individual action, social cohesion is needed for cooperation. We achieve
social cohesion through identification, or consubstantiality, wherein
we are able to transcend our differences by realizing that all positions
on the hierarchical pyramid serve the purpose of maintaining social
order.

For Burke, the concept of substance introduces the principle of
the negative: One determines what a thing is by reference to what it
is not. Although the word "substance" is used to signify the essence of
a thing—its intrinsic nature—"substance" nevertheless means that
which "stands under" or "supports." Therefore, "substance" actually
refers to what is extrinsic to a thing, to the thing's context. And a thing
is not its context (*Grammar*, 23).

The principle of the negative is peculiar to language. Negatives
simply do not exist in nature. Nature is whatever it is, whether we
describe our attitudes toward specific natural processes such as death
and deterioration negatively or positively. The relationship of words
to nature, therefore, requires that language be "discounted" it if is to
be used properly. As Burke writes,

> Whatever correspondence there is between a word and
> the thing it names, the word is not the thing. The word
> "tree" is not a tree. And just as effects that can be got
> with the thing can't be got with the word, so effects
> that can be got with the word can't be got with the
> thing. But because these two realms coincide sponta-
> neously at certain points, we tend to overlook the areas
> where they radically diverge. We gravitate spontane-
> ously to naive verbal realism. (*Religion*, 18)

Discounting the negative is a form of transcendence because one
must stand above the word and the thing to understand that "word"
and "thing" are in reality a relationship and not an identity. In the
same way, each of us must transcend division to achieve social cohesion,
and we must transcend social cohesion to maintain division. If in
transcending division an individual becomes lost in the unity of social
cohesion, this phenomenon would be dissolution, not identification.

In physical reality, two substances cannot become one substance
and simultaneously remain two distinct substances. But symbolically,

such a phenomenon is possible. It is in the realm of symbolization, therefore, that opposites meet and are resolved by transcendence. The confrontation of opposites is the province of dialectic, and Burke therefore chooses the term "dialectic substance" to describe the form of the dramatistic approach:

> [Dialectic substance] derives its character from the systematic contemplation of the antinomies attendant upon the fact that we necessarily define a thing in terms of something else. "Dialectic substance" would thus be the over-all category of dramatism, which treats of human motives in the terms of verbal action. By this statement we most decidedly do not mean that human motives are confined to the realm of verbal action. We mean rather that the dramatistic analysis of motives has its point of departure in the subject of verbal action (in thought, speech, and document). (*Grammar,* 33)

In other words, the dramatistic form is dialectical, and the dialectical structure brings together thesis and antithesis in order to define "what is." On the whole, dialectic enables us to determine possibilities by analyzing the relationship between opposing concepts.

Whence come the concepts, given that Burke describes dialectic as "systematic contemplation"? The opposing concepts flow from the speaker's interpretation of the universal motives. The speaker uses such concepts to define these motives as they pertain to a given situation or a specific problem with which speaker and audience are concerned. For example, I will show that Lincoln develops his perspective on hierarchy by examining the opposition between dedication *of* a cemetery and dedication *to* principles, and his perspective on guilt by examining the opposition between saying and doing. In articulating his perspectives, Lincoln attempts to establish that his definition of each universal motive and the implications flowing from such definitions are true. If Lincoln and his listeners are able to agree on "what is" the situation, they identify with one another because they "speak the same language," or interpret reality similarly. Such identification does not make Lincoln and his listeners the same; rather, people who identify with one another understand their relationship and the implications of that relationship for the preservation of the hierarchy.

At the same time, identification does make Lincoln and his listeners equal insofar as the reality they share has been structured through reasoning. As H. D. Duncan points out, reasoning is possible only among equals, among people who are willing to forego the superior and inferior roles they usually play to engage in another kind of play whose rules primarily fall under the heading of the epistemological, and therefore are characteristically methodical.[15] Method, however, of necessity (or by definition) must be neutral, or nonpartisan.[16] Such neutrality allows mathematics to achieve certainty within the closed system of its axioms.

Dialectic, however, lacks the rigidity of mathematics because dialectic focuses not on axioms but on presuppositions. In short, mathematics deals in "givens" and dialectic deals in "what ifs." Ideally, the goal of dialectic is to convert tentativeness ("what if") into certainty ("what is"), although the conversion usually goes no further than probability ("what is more likely to be true than not true"). But if this goal is purely consummatory—if, for example, Lincoln and his audience are satisfied merely with Lincoln's supporting his claims—then the truth arrived at by dialectical means is trivial, simply argument for the sake of argument or talk for the sake of talk. An audience that acknowledges that Lincoln has proved his point need not identify with him or pursue any course of action. Their acknowledgment says that they believe him to be methodically exact, as if he had solved a complicated crossword puzzle and should be complimented for his exertions.

RHETORIC AND ACTION

Speakers must complement dialectical method with rhetorical technique to have any hope of persuading their audiences to participate in a specific course of action. Rhetoric requires speakers to select language that will appeal to audiences, language that will transcend the implicit competitiveness of dialectic and encourage cooperation. As Burke explains, rhetoric "is rooted in an essential function of language itself, a function that is wholly realistic, and is continually born anew; the use of language as a symbolic means of inducing in beings that by nature respond to symbols" (*Motives*, 43). In a later passage Burke says that rhetoric is a linguistic function that "is essentially a realism of the act" (*Motives*, 44). By this he means that rhetoric's focus is on what should be done rather than on what is true or false. Rhetoric is grounded in the moral, the persuasive. Its concern is not to make the true false or the false true, but rather to use language in a way that will lead to identification and the social cohesion necessary for action. The need for action implies a present exigence that places stress not on what is, but on what should be.

One of Burke's most significant contributions to rhetorical theory is his stress on identification as a state of being rather than a strategy of linguistic embellishment. Since identification acknowledges a state of being, and since being transcends time, identification has the character of what is eternally present. For example, when Lincoln attempts to identify with his audience, he does not persuade them to *change* their state of being but to become *aware* of their state of being. According to Burkean theory, this awareness results from the speaker's bringing to the audience's attention a common concern for the preservation of social order, a concern that requires both speaker and audience to respond as the kind of people they are. And what kind of people are Lincoln and his audience? They are individuals capable of identifying with one another because they share a universe of discourse expressive of their values, principles, and attitudes. As a result, whatever directives Lincoln enumerates regarding what they should and should not do will appear reasonable and forceful because what they should do is grounded in who they are. Human action, in short, does not result from directives but flows from our state of being and is therefore constitutive.

Burke points to the difference between the directive and the constitutive in his analysis of the statement "Let us have peace." Burke says that "Let us have peace" can be either "a directive for existence" or "mandatory for being." As a directive, "peace is but an ideal, a general direction towards which one should incline when plotting a course . . . not an integral-part-of [but] an annex-to." By contrast, peace as "mandatory for being" is "substance—and only insofar as one was consubstantial with it [is] he truly alive" (*Grammar*, 332–33). For people to be consubstantial with peace, peace must provide them with a sense of personal identity as well as an identification with all those people for whom peace is part of being. Consubstantiality, therefore, expresses the universal act of being rather than specific acts of doing. Or, as Burke puts it, "Find out what now *is* within you, and you have found what will be." In this perspective, the future becomes the present, and Burke sees this transformation as characteristic of religious orientations (*Grammar*, 334). As a result, "the present forever is," and out of the eternal present flows the activity expressive of a way of life.

THE ART OF RHETORIC

However, peace is not the sole value that people have, and in certain situations peace may conflict with other values that are equally important. In such cases, people may be uncertain about how they should act or, having decided what course of action to follow, may be anxious to have their decision reinforced by someone else. If an individual, such as Lincoln, attempts to persuade them to pursue a specific course of action, he must do more than merely posit a set of directives. Directives are useful in teaching a person how to drive a car, tie a shoelace, or get a college degree—objectives that are not essential manifestations of character. But, as previously noted, Burke believes that action is substantival or constitutive, and therefore "involves character" (*Grammar,* 310). Character implies not only values, attitudes, and beliefs but also an enthusiasm to demonstrate personal qualities, all of which makes sense if one feels that something is being achieved, if there is some meaning to this kind of activity.

In the classical view of substance, character imposes a form upon substance, gives substance a shape that makes substance identifiable and meaningful and better, without at the same time changing substance into something different. Imposing form upon substance without changing the substance is an artistic activity. Moreover, the artist's imposition of form upon substance not only gives structure to substance but also *completes* substance, for the artist takes "what is" and transforms it into "what should be," the transformation being the actualizing of a potentiality. The potential is real, which means that the seeds of "what should be" are contained within "what is."

Transforming a piece of marble into a statue, however, is a minor accomplishment compared to persuading an audience to choose a specific course of action. We can manipulate marble, but, if persuasion has any meaning, we must appeal to audiences. The appeal must be to the human being's "striving towards . . . perfection," a continuing pursuit of redemption, rebirth, growth, or completion (*Motives,* 333). The road to redemption is a matter of personal choice and therefore solely the responsibility of each individual. The basis upon which individuals choose to strive toward perfection is their capacity for symbol using, that singular trait that separates them from all other animals. The persuader must appeal to this symbol-using capacity because symbolic action will necessarily precede any other type of action.

THE NATURE OF SYMBOLIC ACTION

Burke says that the symbol "might be called a word invented by the artist to specify a particular grouping or pattern or emphasizing of experiences."[17] While the symbol expresses an attitude, symbolic action is "the dancing of an attitude,"[18] meaningful movement aimed at causing delight that will be a goad to action (recall antistrophos). As the guiding principle to action, the symbol is appealing in that it provides a rationale for dealing with a situation. The symbol stresses the relevant elements of a particular need and discounts those elements that are not relevant. It focuses on what must be done to maintain order, because a symbol not only names a pattern of experience but also proposes a program of action. Yet while it deals with aspects of a particular need, with a specific problem facing individuals at an identifiable moment in time, the symbol is grounded in universal needs that transcend time, "the notion that at bottom the aims and genius of man have remained fundamentally the same, that temporal events may cause him to stray far from his sources but that he repeatedly struggles to restore, under new particularities, the same basic patterns of the 'good life'" (*Permanence*, 163).

The symbol, then, serves as a means of identification because it finds its source in universal needs. Moreover, in the same way that an individual's prayer to God expresses the relationship of inferior to superior, the symbol, as "secular prayer," acknowledges the transcendent equality of all symbol-using animals in their continuing pursuit to maintain the hierarchical division that is the basis of social cohesion. Insofar as the symbol transcends division to maintain social cohesion (and contrariwise) it is dialectical, since it resolves the clash between thesis (division) and antithesis (cohesion) by a synthesis that demonstrates a potentiality, an ideal, beyond the reality of the opposing forces. Insofar as the symbol expresses an attitude, it is partisan and therefore rhetorical, and is intended to induce cooperation among symbol users in order to have them transform symbolic action into concrete behavior. Logically, the dialectical precedes the rhetorical, or identification precedes persuasion. Temporally, persuasion and identification are simultaneous, since the social cohesion that is the mark of identification is an awareness that results from the effectiveness of the speaker's appeal. Although we need to separate identification and persuasion for purposes of analysis, in reality one does not identify

with an audience and then persuade them. One persuades by identifying, and identifies by persuading. Symbolic action is a process in the
same way that dialectic and rhetoric form a process describing the
nature of human communication.

Symbol and Style

A speaker begins with a plan, and the plan will be a symbol. Or
as Burke says, "the symbol is a formula" (*Counter-Statement*, 153). A
formula provides the speaker with a way of dealing with a situation
and also expresses the speaker's attitude toward the situation. In this
sense, the symbol has power because it not only points a direction but
also represents a state of mind. Such power can contribute to the
effectiveness of a solution, provided the power is not suggestive of
rigidity and monotony. "Black Power," "ERA," or "Gay Rights" may
capture the imagination and point a direction, but if these formulas
for action become the substitute for both thought and action there is
little chance that the symbols will maintain their impact. At best they
will become slogans; at worst, clichés. To depend totally on the power
of a symbol is to see the symbol as an accomplished fact, as though
Black Power were an achievement rather than an objective. A symbol,
however, is a representation of attitudes and therefore a guide to action.

Once the speaker has chosen a symbol, he or she must help the
audience appreciate the complexity, as well as the power, of the symbol.
Primarily, the complexity of a symbol is equivalent to its implications.
For example, Black Power implies that blacks take pride in their race,
that they work together to achieve common goals, and that they emphasize their strengths rather than their weaknesses. But Black Power
implies even more: imagination, persistence, courage, progress, community, and so on. If people are to appreciate the complexity of Black
Power, they must understand its implications, especially as those implications pertain to how they behave.

Burke says that "the peril of complexity is diffusion" (*Counter-
Statement*, 160). The speaker's analysis of Black Power becomes diffuse
when he or she puts forth implications that are confusing, tangential,
directionless, and overblown. The speaker attempts to avoid the pitfalls
of diffusion through style. Burke defines style as "ingratiation."[19] Style
is not something added to the person, but flows from the person; it is
a state of being, a way of doing things. Although ingratiation requires

the speaker to say the right thing, it "is no obsequious matter, but is best managed by the boldest minds."[20] If Lincoln is an obsequious speaker he will attempt to pacify his audience. By doing so he takes no risks because he refuses to confront the audience. A speaker who will not confront the audience is avoiding argument, and in effect avoiding him- or herself as an individual capable of right choices. Henry W. Johnstone, Jr., writes that "a person who chooses argument does in fact choose himself" because one's argument expresses one's self.[21] In addition, Johnstone contends that "to argue is inherently to risk failure." The argument that is well developed, clear, honest, and confrontational will probably receive high marks for boldness, but it nevertheless may be rejected by an audience. Presumably, the audience at least will understand what it is rejecting. By contrast, the speaker may couch an argument in language intended to manipulate, and the audience may accept the argument. Obviously, the audience accepts what it does not really understand.

As a "bold" speaker, Lincoln will risk confrontation with his audience, fully aware that the audience may reject or ignore his challenge. He will ask his audience to shift perspective, to see what is old with new eyes, to embark upon an adventure that, despite its dangers, will probably prove rewarding. Admittedly, not all messages approach such stirring heights, but I think the Gettysburg Address does.

Style and Ritual

How do speakers attempt to ingratiate themselves with audiences? As symbol-using animals, human beings express their needs through ritual, or what Langer calls "a symbolic transformation of experiences."[22] Similarly, Burke says that artists convert their revelations into a symbolic process he describes as the "ritualizing of a revelation" (*Counter-Statement*, 168). As a result, the revelation becomes an aesthetic truth in contrast to a scientific truth. Scientific truths are beliefs or facts, what the artist "knows." Scientific truths are transformed into aesthetic truths by treating "with ceremony [facts] considered of importance," finding "a correspondingly important setting for them" (*Counter-Statement*, 168). A ritual is a code of verbal and nonverbal stylistic gestures developed by a community of believers over a period of time that makes human experience significant.[23] Ritual is a means by which a community of believers talk to God (remember that Burke focuses on the word "God" and its implications). Burke views rhetoric as the secular equivalent of ritual, a way in which people can talk to each other. Religious communities use ritual to please God; speakers use rhetoric to please audiences. God can be appropriately addressed by various nonverbal gestures—standing, kneeling, bowing, singing—together with verbal gestures (prayers) that constitute the ritual.

Rituals dramatize the individual's membership in a community, a community with a tradition and a commitment to the future. The dramatization expresses the universal motives, or internal needs, of human beings. For example, in a religious service members of the community come together to acknowledge the principle of hierarchy. They all believe in God, and they recognize the priest, minister, or rabbi (the orator, the "one who prays") as God's special representative, one whose function sets him or her apart as the master or mistress of ceremonies. They acknowledge their wrongdoings or shortcomings as an indication of their guilt. They indicate their willingness to sacrifice as a symbol of their promise to do better and thereby become better than they are (redemption). Both the officiating minister and the faithful must be adept in the "religious dance"—the various verbal and non-verbal gestures that constitute the ritual.

Style and Form

Both ritual and rhetoric require the use of stylistic gestures that will appeal to audiences. The speaker communicates these gestures to an audience through various forms. *Form* is a way of experiencing, an approach to language that spells out the meaning and consequences of the symbol. In addition, form enables the speaker to deal with the symbol in a way that expresses his or her individuality in attempting to please the audience.

The speaker needs to integrate the various forms to achieve the intended effect. Although we can describe the characteristics of a specific form, the form is meaningless unless it is part of the process that transforms pedestrian sounds into a work of art. Burke defines form as "an arousing and fulfillment of desires. A work has form insofar as one part of it leads a reader to anticipate another part, to be gratified by the sequence" (*Counter-Statement,* 124). In other words, a specific form is not satisfying in itself; it is part of the whole and depends upon other parts (or forms) to make sense.

Forms are not merely stylistic embellishments but persuasive structures that have "great functional urgency" (*Motives,* 66). Burke says that "the expressing of a proposition in one or another of these rhetorical forms would involve 'identification,' first by inducing the auditor to participate in the form, as a 'universal' locus of appeal, and next by trying to include a partisan statement within this same pale of assent" (*Motives,* 59).

In the Gettysburg Address, Lincoln attempts to share his "property"—his style—with the audience, in the hope that they will therefore take vicarious delight in participating in his endeavors. As a result, the audience may realize that, in reality, it shares with Lincoln not only the superficial manifestations of his thoughts but also the thoughts themselves. His property is their property; his action is their action. They identify, cooperate, and act together with him in the pursuit of a common goal that satisfies their universal needs.

FORM AND THE GETTYSBURG ADDRESS

In the following sections I will discuss conventional form, syllogistic progression, repetitive form, qualitative progression, and incidental form, applying each to various sections of the Gettysburg Address.

Conventional Form

ignore epideictic issues

When a speaker uses conventional form, he or she offers to the audience the appeal of form as form (*Counter-Statement,* 126). For example, an audience usually anticipates that a speech will have an introduction, a development, and a conclusion. If a speech satisfies this expectation the audience will probably be gratified by the well-made form. Conventional form satisfies expectancies that exist before the specific act of communication. Expectancies relevant to the other Burkean forms arise during the act of communication (*Counter-Statement,* 126).

Any of these forms can become conventional if the audience expects the speaker to use the form and the speaker employs the form properly. The effectiveness of conventional form depends upon the audience's being aware of the form and appreciating its employment. But other forms "may be effective even though the reader has no awareness of their formality" (*Counter-Statement,* 126).

If the effectiveness of the speech is due to the speaker's satisfying audience expectations that exist before the speech is presented, then the audience is responding primarily to conventional form, whether the audience anticipates that the speaker will be simple and clear or orotund and complicated. Strictly speaking, we can identify a specific section of a speech as conventional form only if we can be sure that the audience was struck by its familiarity. For example, in the Gettysburg Address Lincoln's overall structure stresses temporal divisions. He moves from the past, to the present, to the future ("Fourscore and seven years ago . . . Now we are engaged in a great civil war . . . the unfinished work . . ."). If the audience is aware of this structure and takes delight in it, we can call the temporal divisions conventional form. In addition, we might guess that Lincoln structured the speech to satisfy the audience's expectations regarding formal appeal. In short, we can conjecture about what Lincoln attempted to do to satisfy his audience and indicate that certain constructions have potential as conventional form. But unless we know the audience's delight in form *as* form, those constructions will be classified differently. For example, the temporal divisions of Lincoln's speech might appeal to the audience's sense of the familiar (i.e., the audience expects the speaker to go from the past to the present to the future), but they also are a tremendous aid to the logical development of the speech, which Burke calls syllogistic progression. It is probably easier to see the temporal divisions of the speech as syllogistic progression than as conventional form, unless a case can be made for the tremendous delight the audience took in Lincoln's satisfying their demands for such temporal divisions.

If we are able to cite many examples of conventional form in the Gettysburg Address, then the speech probably serves a consummatory, rather than an instrumental, purpose. In such case, the beauty of the speech—how well it was put together—would overshadow its practical effect on the audience. The categorical expectancies of an audience at times demand that a speech have a consummatory purpose; that is, that the speech be satisfying as a speech because it satisfies its audience. As a result, politicians harshly criticize their opponents, oversimplify or ignore issues, lavishly praise their constituencies, and make promises they cannot keep. None of this fools their listeners; they have in fact demanded it. In short, the conventional form of a speech may result from the speaker's acceding to audience demands because the speaker has no other option.

Syllogistic Progression

Syllogistic progression appeals to an audience by its "connect-the-dots" development of ideas. The classical syllogism invites the audience to grasp the relationship between a major premise and a minor premise and infer a conclusion. As a result, the audience joins with the speaker in creating the message. If all the dots are connected in the right sequence, a clear picture emerges. Of course, all the dots are necessary to one another if any one dot is to have any meaning. For example, there is no such thing as a cause unless there is an effect; nor is there an effect unless there is a cause. In the same way, a pattern of conduct cannot be called a solution unless a problem exists. And, strictly speaking, a set of circumstances cannot be labeled a problem unless a solution can be offered (an "insolvable problem" is a "predicament"). Although a speaker may discuss an effect before identifying the cause or a solution before identifying a problem, the audience anticipates that a discussion of effect will lead to the identification of cause, and similarly with solution and problem.

In the first part of the Gettysburg Address, Lincoln invites the audience to share in the following conclusion: "It is altogether fitting and proper that we should do this [dedicate the field]." He guides them to the conclusion by stating that the nation was founded upon equality, that this foundation has been threatened, and that men have died trying to remove that threat. Therefore, these men deserve to rest in consecrated ground.

In the second part of the speech, Lincoln reverses the situation: "But, in a larger sense, we cannot dedicate, we cannot consecrate, we cannot hallow this ground." Burke contends that "the peripety, or reversal of the situation . . . is obviously one of the keenest manifestations of syllogistic progression" (*Counter-Statement*, 124).[24] The peripety in this case yokes two opposing ideas together. On the one hand, it is appropriate that we dedicate the field. On the other hand, we cannot dedicate the field because it has already been dedicated. Lincoln and the audience must arrive at a synthesis of these opposing ideas. The peripety also points to the difference between the logical consistency of a speech and the categorical expectations (conventional form) of the audience. With the peripety the speaker attempts to change the audience's expectations.

Because Lincoln has changed the audience's expectations of the speech's development, the audience now anticipates Lincoln's justifying this reversal. Lincoln previously led his audience to the reasonableness of dedicating the field; he now claims that it cannot be done because it has already been consecrated by those who struggled at Gettysburg. Therefore, "what we say here" is insignificant ("the world will little note nor long remember"). Lincoln then says that what we really should be doing is dedicating ourselves to "the unfinished work," so that "these dead shall not have died in vain" and this nation "shall not perish from the earth." If the audience is astute enough, it will understand that the dedication of "a final resting place for those who here gave their lives" is meaningless unless the audience is dedicated "here to the unfinished work."

Repetitive Form

Repetitive form is variation on a theme, a demonstration of the speaker's virtuosity in exploring imaginative ways of saying the same thing over and over in ways that maintain the audience's curiosity and attention. Repetitive form is the means by which the speaker pursues the audience. Such pursuit demands that the speaker have both a sense of wonder and a penchant for discovery, lest repetitive form devolve into repetitiousness. Anything we look at long enough we inevitably take for granted—unless we continue to see with new eyes—because novelty is within us, not outside us. Musicians appreciate repetitive form, which is why Brahms would take a pleasant $\frac{2}{4}$ theme by Paganini and run it through fourteen variations, positing changes in meter ($\frac{2}{8}$, $\frac{3}{8}$, $\frac{6}{8}$) and tempo (anywhere from poco animato through poco piu vivace to feroce-energico, and a few other pocos, prestos, and vivaces) that say a lot for Paganini but even more for Brahms.

How did Lincoln use repetitive form? There are ten sentences in the speech. "Dedicate" or "dedicated" appears six times; equivalent words ("consecrate," "hallow," "devotion") appear a total of five times. "Dedication," then, seems to be Lincoln's "plan," or symbol, that enables him to structure the speech in *his* way. For example, in the first sentence the birth of the nation and its dedication to equality are simultaneous; without such dedication, the nation would be undefined and therefore meaningless. As a result, the failure of the nation to honor its dedication leads to expressions of guilt, alienation, and war. The sacrifice necessary to erase this guilt requires numerous deaths, each death a witness to the nation's striving to confirm its dedication to equality, its reason for being—the source (birth) of its distinctiveness and individuality.

In the fourth sentence, however, "dedication" takes on a different meaning: "We have come to dedicate a portion of that field," to set it aside—to make it holy—by saying words that symbolically transform dirt into a temple of martyrs. Lincoln subsequently says, "It is fitting and proper that we should do this." Dedication to equality is a commitment to act in a certain way. Dedication of the burial ground at Gettysburg is an acknowledgment that a number of Americans have already fulfilled that commitment.

Then follows a disturbing thought; in fact, a questioning of how fitting and proper it is to proceed further. Lincoln says, "But in a larger sense, we cannot dedicate, we cannot consecrate, we cannot hallow this ground." Dedication is more than a matter of words, and Lincoln uses the next two sentences to stress this point. The men who struggled at Gettysburg, who were willing to sacrifice their lives, have already consecrated the ground, and nothing that can be said will come close to the significance of their deeds.

Dedication, then, "in a larger sense," is a willingness to act. Thus Lincoln moves from a dedication *of* a piece of earth to a dedication *to* "the unfinished work . . . the great task remaining." And it is dedication seen primarily as a form of action that will bring redemption, "a new birth of freedom."

(weak)

Qualitative Progression

Qualitative progression is basically a tonal form that sets a mood, as in a play. At the same time, qualitative progression may evoke a number of moods sequentially that, however different, make sense— at least after the fact. Shakespeare, for example, touches us deeply with his depiction of Ophelia's suicide in *Hamlet,* yet follows this scene with the graveyard comedy. The contrast offers balance, if nothing else.

Qualitative progression may require that either syllogistic progression or conventional form be violated, as is the case in the Gettysburg Address. Lincoln violated conventional form by delivering a speech so brief that many of his listeners could not believe he had finished. He was establishing a tone, and took risks to do so.

The mood or tone of Lincoln's speech is more than solemn or

profound—it is prayerful. The beginning words of the speech prepare us for what is to follow: "Fourscore and seven years ago . . . our fathers . . . dedicated to the proposition." The language is a mixture of the archaic and the simple, and the biblical tones are evident. Since dedication is the thread that pulls together the entire speech, the prayerful tone gives to dedication a mystical aura. The mysticism also serves to intensify the larger meaning of dedication, because dedication to equality is dedication to a community of people who brought the nation into being, to people who presently struggle for its survival, and to people yet to come who will experience freedom in a country that will never perish. The mysticism and prayerfulness bind together all those who constitute the nation. Whether they are living or dead or of the future, they are present as members of the community.[25] For example, Lincoln says that the dead continue to provide us with a model of what dedication means ("that from these honored dead we take increased devotion"), and he equates dedication with action to ensure that "these dead shall not have died in vain," as though the dead anticipated that we would respond appropriately to their deeds.

Incidental Form

Repetitive form is emphatic, qualitative progression is tonal, and incidental form is memorable, at times spectacular. Whereas conventional form appeals to an audience *as* form, minor form appeals to an audience as form *within* form. Burke explains:

> Thus a paradox, by carrying an argument one step forward, may have its use as progressive form; and by its continuation of a certain theme may have its use as repetitive form—yet it may be so formally complete in itself that the reader will memorize it as an event valid apart from its setting. A monologue by Shakespeare can be detached from its context and recited with enjoyment because, however integrally it contributes to the whole of which it is a part, it is also an independent curve of plot enclosed by its own beginning and end.
> (*Counter-Statement*, 127)

Minor or incidental form does not so much emphasize as enhance what the speaker says. And it is probably felicitous that Burke calls the form minor or incidental, despite its frequent dramatic intensity.

The spectacular has its place in speechmaking, but only as a means to an end. If the spectacular becomes more than incidental to the whole, what is said may become secondary to how it is said.

Lincoln's attempts at spectacle make use of contrast and rhythm. First, there is the contrast of words and action that provides the perspective on dedication. Second, there is the contrast between the living and the dead, which gives the dead an advantage: "The world will little note, nor long remember, what we say here, but it can never forget what they did here." And if you stay with those words a while, you realize that the dead live because they have acted and because their action continues in its demand that we respond to what they did. If the living do not respond by dedicating themselves to the "unfinished work," then the living have no significance—which is worse than being dead, because the living merely exist, as do animals without obligations.[26]

Third, Lincoln makes use of incidental form by using rhetorical devices that emphasize rhythm. The Gettysburg Address is like a litany or chant (this especially comes through in its repetitive form), which is most appropriate (and therefore satisfies elements of conventional form) for a prayer. Gilbert Highet's analysis of the Gettysburg Address points to Lincoln's use of the tricolon, a rhetorical device in which an idea is divided into three harmonious parts, generally of increasing power.[27] Lincoln uses the tricolon structure three times, and in each case the emphasis is on the meaning of "dedication." The first tricolon allows Lincoln to shift the perspective on the meaning of "dedication":

> we cannot dedicate
> we cannot consecrate
> we cannot hallow [this ground]

The second tricolon is a stirring restatement of the nation's original dedication:

> [we here highly resolve]
> that these dead shall not have died in vain
> that this nation, under God, shall have a new birth of
>   freedom
> and that government [what follows is the third tricolon]
> of the people
> by the people [and]
> for the people
> [shall not perish from the earth]

This threefold use of the tricolon rather neatly parallels the birth-redemption cycle. Each tricolon is a way of looking at "dedication," the nation's reason for being (birth). The first tricolon focuses on guilt, the second on sacrifice, and the third on rebirth and redemption. Burke says that birth, guilt, sacrifice, and redemption are internal symbolic needs, or motives, that goad us to act as human beings.[28] Even though Lincoln never read Burke, Lincoln probably had a sure sense of what might make an audience act.

CONCLUSION

The Gettysburg Address develops a theme (repetitive form), establishes a tone (qualitative progression), and attempts to be timeless (incidental form). It is orderly and consistent (syllogistic progression), but it violates audience expectancy by being too brief (conventional form). However, Lincoln's violation of conventional form probably gives us the clue to the artistry of his speech. He demonstrates his virtuosity by variations on a theme disciplined by the need for brevity. Brevity also enhanced the prayerful tone of his speech. And in regard to incidental form, Lincoln's violation of conventional form—what would satisfy his immediate audience—probably points to his real audience.

The Gettysburg Address is timeless in being addressed to a universal audience, one that will eventually understand and appreciate what the speaker said and will respect him for being the kind of person who took the stand he did. Lincoln's ability to persuade the universal audience is possible if the audience not only agrees with Lincoln's perspective but also identifies with Lincoln as a person, which it does when it appreciates the symbolic action of the speech, specifically the complexity and implications of "dedication." The audience will probably have this appreciation if it understands dedication as relevant to the satisfying of their needs. Although the message that Lincoln presented was specific to a time and place, his ritualizing of his revelation, his transforming scientific truth into aesthetic truth, enables him and his ideas to transcend time and therefore to be present to others in different ages.

Manifesting Perspectives: Rhetoric in the Movements of Modern Art

Thomas B. Farrell

> The movement's Negative is in essence the
> announcement of a stand, a "standing together,"
> an *understanding*. It may be called a constitution,
> manifesto, covenant, program, proclamation,
> declaration, tract for the times, statement, or
> counterstatement.
> —Leland Griffin, 1969[1]

Leland Griffin's finest work has shown scholars how to better appreciate the constitutive function of rhetoric within the fabric of our social history, even while attending to traditional features of choice, tactics, and judgment within rhetorical forms. It is in this spirit that I ask what the inventional capacities of rhetoric are within the context of a rather unlikely example of a historical movement: the modernist art movements of the early twentieth century. The question is prompted both by my own interest in how rhetoric "works" in this relatively ungrounded context and by a provocative analogy I detect between Griffin's sense of history and recent visions of modernism.

I. Art and Rhetoric

The question of how rhetoric works in the modernist art movement is interesting because it reintroduces the age-old paradoxes among rhetoric, cognitivity, and art. At the height of its power, rhetoric never really answered the Platonic objections so much as danced around them. Rhetoric didn't have to imitate the form of a truth (as Plato's Socrates had demanded) because it was already lodged inextricably

155

within the world of the recognizable. In fact, rhetoric was already "in fact." Its materials were those *phainomena* in which we all participated. Its artistry was dependent upon how the public thought, how the *doxa* of its audience[2] might be engaged and brought to bear upon recurring social issues in real-life settings. In other words, rhetoric cannot be attacked for being at odds with the form of truth so long as we accept a more realistic Aristotelian ontology locating rhetoric as one efficient cause of reason within these very same forms. Ironically enough, the very worldliness of rhetoric, its referentiality, becomes for the art a saving grace.

But what changes drastically with the rise of modernity is the whole question of what might be imitated, what might usefully be presupposed, even what might be recognizable enough to be shared. Regimes of order move through the centuries and, with all their arrogance, move in an increasingly interiorized direction. From nature to culture, from culture to history and "reason," from histories of reason to will and subjectivity itself. And so, it is—to me—fascinating to inquire just what shape a rhetoric might take when its very context of meaning is comprised of sharp, even irreconcilable differences.

This uncertain shape of rhetoric might lend some force to the loose analogy I detect between Griffin's view of rhetoric in history and modernism's own developing vision of itself in art. Goaded as he is by the Burkean worldview throughout his study of social movements, Griffin also senses a tragic turning away from an order once frozen and pure but now "strained by impiety, and irrelevance of its rhetoric; an order tending toward Death, the ultimate failure of communication—toward disunity, disintegration, Disorder." Thus the "rhetorical striving," the "becoming" of a social movement.[3] Like all fine scholarly writing, these passages work on multiple levels. Surely they have religious undertones, a haunting sense of the futility of secular order. But I think they might be read just as sharply as a commentary on the Aristotelian polis after the intervention of history. Orders are not stable; virtues are not grounded in unquestioning subservience to *archai*. The ancient striving toward archetypal ends can no longer be presupposed to unfold without intervention and of its own teleological accord. History literally displaces the moods of design and judgment from the hermetically sealed environs of texts and the boundary conditions of the public regime. Disaffiliation becomes a temporal possibility. The rhetorical movement is born.

More than simply a theory of social movements, Griffin's dramatism gives us a philosophy of the world in which social movements are possible. Nowhere is this clearer than in the way he employs classical concepts and terminology to study the movement itself. The stages of inception, crisis, and consummation are not derived from the vocabulary of classical rhetoric as much as they are finely tuned dramatistic adaptations from classical poetic. And it is in keeping with this poetic turn that Griffin has located the penultimate dialogue of moods within the social movement as that of tragedy and comedy. Griffin writes:

> So the wheel forever turns. Man's movements, in time, come to an end. And they come to an end in tragedy— for tragedy involves defeat, "the failure of our ends," the ultimate death of the "good." Yet if his movements are tragic, the fate of man himself is comic—for tragedy also involves triumph, "the beyond of resurrection," an ultimate "prosperous end." And if the wheel forever turns, it is man who does the turning—forever striving, in an "imperfect world," for a world of perfection.[4]

This meditation on poetic form is doubly appropriate to Griffin's subject. It brings the archetypal categories of drama to a historical world that finally replicates our own flawed vision in every attempted transformation. In a world where timeless truths can no longer be imitated, truth itself is an urgent project, forever inviting, forever eluding our grasp.

And, unlikely or not, there seems to be a rather striking parallel between Griffin's sense of the movement displaced from the timeless order, and modernism in art, displaced from the tranquility of styles and schools. Much like the schools of oratory that flourished in ancient Greece, pre-nineteenth-century art also worked within a recognizable framework of training and teaching, for which the term "school" was an appropriate ascription. The idea of a school in art presupposed a master and a style or method, a shared background understanding of relevant tradition, and above all, a clear pattern of pedagogical authority. From art master to art apprentice.[5] Teaching and training resembled less the acquisition of a skill and more the discovery and refinement of a gift. Like the polis itself, the art school is inherently conservative in its resonance. It holds to a rather static notion of time and meaning. It searches for forms and truths that do not change quickly.

But with the turning of the centuries, the industrialization of culture, and the general decline of the ancien régime, the art movement
is born. The art movement is very strange as movements go. Although
blessed with a static, outmoded tradition to serve as foil (the art
"schools"), it has no overt political program. In fact, as has been noted
many times, the frenzy of exuberance unleashed by the likes of futurism,
dadaism, constructivism, surrealism, and (the granddaddy of them all)
cubism seems applicable in form to either radical end of the political
spectrum. Also, and with very few exceptions, there are no bureaucrats
or social engineers involved in the typical art movement. There are
ongoing tensions between the respectability of institutional acceptance
(the museum) and the public relations needs of the movement (the
artist as renegade), but these tensions provide the occasions for self-
promotion rather than the institutional rearrangements typically sought
by overtly political movements. And this is the major curiosity afflicting
a movement that is guided by an aesthetic. If we might borrow from
Kierkegaard for a moment, the aesthetic impulse is informed above all
by the free play of possibility, the unconstrained imaginings of the free
consciousness.[6] For the most part, artists do not function well following
predetermined platforms and scripts. In other words, the very sense of
compulsion, the onesidedness of the art movement would seem to run
counter to the aesthetic impulse itself. Perhaps that is why art movements seem almost to parody the rhetoric of revolution; they take shape
and agitate seemingly for no other end than their own existence, the
sheer joy of dynamism. Informed only by a dissatisfaction with the
past, a taste for adventure, and an appetite for risk, art movements
give us the original "revolution for the hell of it."

For all these contradictions, art movements are undeniably of rhetorical significance, both in their impetus and in their modus operandi.
Nikos Stangos observes:

> Modern art movements and concepts were intentional,
> purposeful, directed and programmed from the very
> start. They were accompanied by a plethora of mani-
> festoes, documents and programmatic declarations.
> Each movement was deliberately created to make a
> point; artists, and often critics, formed platforms to
> launch movements, they formulated concepts. Modern
> art movements were essentially "conceptual": works of
> art were considered in terms of concepts which they
> exemplify.[7]

This continual strain between a strict piety to the orthodoxy of the avant-garde on the one hand and the exuberant commitment to aesthetic possibility on the other might help to explain the tremendous sense of acceleration and then exhaustion accompanying each new wave in the art movements of modernism. Each new concept is seized and set upon in a collective effort to extract from the concept all aesthetic possibilities. But when the possibilities have all been extracted the concept is longer valued. The movement has come to an end.

This creates, of course, a problem for anyone who would seek to chronicle and explain the art movement. For proponents of the movement there was very little intention of making lasting transformations in the institutional practices of one's time and place. In a highly transitory sense, each art movement did wish to change the way its audience looked at things, but only for the time being. The problem was straightforward. Once the movement had been named and chronicled by an outsider, it was dead; it had already been assimilated into the decadent bourgeois culture the artist-radicals purported to loathe. And so it would be necessary to keep things dense, at a distance, and ever-changing. But even after the dust had settled, it is difficult for those outside the movement to know how properly to chart its course.

II. A "RHETORIC" OF ART?

My preferred procedure will be to apply Griffin's own movement phases to the individuated art movements themselves; for instance, futurism, constructivism, dadaism, and surrealism. However, before undertaking such an effort, even by way of illustration, I must pause to examine two important alternative approaches to the phases and rhetorical content of modern art movements. The two classic texts requiring our attention are Renato Poggioli's *Theory of the Avant-garde*[8] and Marjorie Perloff's *The Futurist Moment*.[9] My aim is not so much to take issue with either text as it is to show how a specifically rhetorical perspective on historical movements might differ from them.

In *The Theory of the Avant-garde*, Poggioli traces the development of modern art movements to a concerted reaction of artists to the repressive bourgeois landscape of the nineteenth century. Employing a loose Marxian frame of analysis, he argues that the various individual art movements of the early twentieth century (i.e., cubism, futurism, constructivism, dadaism, and surrealism) are actually phases in the larger developmental "movement" of modernism itself. The stages he selects provide an interesting contrast with Griffin's stages of a historical movement. Poggioli's stages develop as follows:

Activistic moment>>>Antagonistic
moment>>>Nihilistic moment>>>
Agonistic moment (the gesture or social symbol)[10]

Poggioli seems to have captured something about the way movements try to ward off institutional legitimacy, often deliberately alienating possible sympathizers. But he has difficulty explaining the match among categories to art developments; moreover, his terminology tends to flatten out the disturbances and disruptions among movements themselves. The categories would be more useful for my purposes if they were reframed through Griffin's rhetorical terminology. Instead of viewing cubism or constructivism as itself a phase in modernism, we might consider each episode in art history as a microcosmic movement with inception, crisis, and consummation phases. We might employ Griffin's use of the Burkean negative to show how differing art movements reacted to one another during this turbulent time. Finally, and I think most important, reading the movement stages offered by Poggioli (i.e., activism, antagonism, nihilism, agonism) in terms of the more generalizable phases introduced by Griffin (i.e., inception, crisis, consummation)[11] might allow us to identify three loci of turmoil or disturbance within each art movement. These loci would be regions or "places" of creative choice within the art movements themselves. Consider, as one crude hypothesis, the following array:

1. Inception—————Activistic>>>><<<<Antagonistic
2. Crisis—————Antagonistic>>>> <<<<Nihilistic
3. Consummation——Nihilistic>>>>><<<<<Agonistic

Art movements with very short lifespans (for instance, the Berlin dada movement) might pass very quickly into nihilism and then gesture. But contrast this with surrealism, which managed to prolong tensions among antagonism and nihilism for decades. These are sweeping generalizations, of course, and any careful study of contemporary art movements would have to allow for the individual differences of character, style, execution, local conditions, and so forth. But that is precisely my point. A synthesis of the rhetorical categories of the historical movement with the more dialectical phases of Poggioli at least allows

for regions of creativity and choice, perhaps opening up the possibility
of studying the rhetoric of invention in modern art.

A second important object of inquiry has to do with the curious
status of rhetorical content in the art movement. As the citation from
Stangos indicated, most art movements were themselves instrumental
and purposive by their very nature. They sought to overturn the conventions of tradition, in part through the forceful exemplar of their
own art "product." But the role of rhetoric is much more complex than
this. For, as Griffin's quotation at the beginning of this essay suggested,
the rhetorical movement also requires a kind of caption as its own
expressed negative, whether these be constitutions, slogans, manifestos,
covenants, proclamations, or tracts. Put another way, within any
rhetorical movement there is at least a tripartite level of rhetorical
operation. First, there is the symbolic action of a movement's representatives, their overt conduct. Second, there is the quite conventional
exhortation, ceremony, sloganeering, and advocacy accompanying any
partisan cause. But third, there is also an interpretive, attending discourse to explain what this conduct, and even these messages, actually
mean. We have until very recently paid no attention to anything in
modern art other than the actual gallery of works. But Perloff's recent
study, *The Futurist Moment*, also requires our attention. As I was first
developing my own interest in the art movements of twentieth-century
Europe, Perloff's essay "Violence and Precision" appeared in 1984 in
the *Chicago Review*.[12] At the time it was the only work I had seen that
was concerned with the artistry of the movement manifesto. Although
in a preliminary condition, that discussion is still the best research on
this underexplored topic. The later work, *The Futurist Moment*, includes
Perloff's earlier essay, together with an analysis of one specific art
movement, futurism.[13] The work is so comprehensive and fascinating
as to complicate considerably the more exploratory study I am attempting here. I can best summarize Perloff's overall agenda and argument to show how it parallels and where it deviates from my own.

Part of the agenda of *The Futurist Moment* is undoubtedly to revise
and improve upon the conventional reception given to the futurists
themselves. This is apparent from the preface, where Perloff invites
the reader to share empathically the millenialist euphoria accompanying
the aesthetic experience of early twentieth-century Europe:

Seventy years and two world wars later, it is almost

impossible to understand this peculiar mixture of radicalism and patriotism, of a worldly international outlook and a violently nationalist faith. Yet we find this
paradox everywhere in the arts of the *avant guerre.*
Before we dismiss as a contemptible proto-fascist the
Marinetti who declared, in the first Futurist manifesto
(1909), "We will glorify war—the world's only hy-
giene," we must look at the context in which such
statements were made.[14]

Perloff's revisionist aims also show themselves in a 1988 essay, "Why
Futurism Now,"[15] where she attempts to appropriate the futurist antiliterary style of shock and parody for everything from countercultural
art journals to performance artists such as Laurie Anderson and David
Byrne. The agenda itself does not invite indictment, of course; such
monumental depth of research and detail as Perloff's can only be a
result of some camaraderie and kinship for the subject matter.

Perloff's argumentative claims for futurism are something else
again. She alleges that the futurists virtually invented the genre of art
manifesto, that they exercised a lasting and decisive influence upon
art styles, and thus in large part authored the initial euphoric moment
of literary modernism. These are bold claims that reach considerably
beyond the admittedly encyclopedic case Perloff makes for the importance of futurist literature itself.

My own essay employs Griffin's dramatistic perspective on social
movements in order to make a constructive qualification of Perloff's
argument. From Griffin's perspective, the initial moment of a social
movement, its inception stage, would understandably take on a euphoric mood of zeal, and anticipatory energy. To the extent that the
futurists were able to identify and define this initial euphoria, theirs
may indeed be a lasting contribution to the literary genre of the art
manifesto, in part because of their historical positioning. Yet the story
of modernist art movements is more complex than that of a single narrative trajectory. Each individual movement found itself absorbed with
the expression of an individual identity, as well as a differentiation from
what went on before. It is my contention that each individual movement
comprised a kind of microcosm of movements generally: to be in a kind
of ongoing tension with the conventions and critique of polite society,
all the while exploring the tripartite sequence of inception—crisis—
consummation.[16] To the extent that the individuality of each movement
must consist in a partisan program of rebellion as well as an unfinished

program of aesthetic (or even anti-aesthetic) objectives, every art movement will bear some resemblance to the futurist attitude.

Hence, there appears to be something of a self-confirming character to Perloff's thesis. Since Perloff looks at the manifesto of each art movement from its own common perspective of frenzied zeal, and exuberance toward an unfinished productive life, each movement discloses to her an undeniably futurist attitude. But this is precisely because such movements all possess a euphoric attitude toward the future. And so, from her own unfinished historical vantage, all early twentieth century art movements (constructivism, suprematism, even dadaism and surrealism) become brands of futurism. It is not my intention in this exploratory essay to reject Perloff's arguments for a revised appreciation of the futurist contribution to the development of modern art; in my opinion, those arguments are unassailable. Instead, I wish to offer an alternative appreciation of the development of the art manifesto, and its own relationship to the individual phenomenon and status of each art movement.

A somewhat more temperate version of the futurists' role in the development of manifesto as genre would seem to require that we also offer an alternative hypothesis of causal agency: developmental influences upon the genre of manifesto itself. If it can be shown, for instance, that the central qualities of the manifesto were at work before the earliest embodiment of futurist art, and if it can be shown convincingly that alternative parallel developments could explain the individuated qualities of manifesto in each modernist art movement, then our own version of the manifesto as rhetoric may acquire some force. This two-part analysis previews my more extensive consideration of the manifesto as movement genre.

Central to the sense of manifesto proposed here is the changing relationships among art practice and aesthetic theory and criticism during the nineteenth century. Wendy Steiner has shown that practitioners of discourse have struggled over the centuries with the problem of capturing the meaning of painterly craft within prose and poetic form. As early as the seventeenth century, Lessing divided up the arts into spatial and temporal forms.[17] Much earlier, Simonides is said to have claimed that painting was "mute poetry," while poetry was a "speaking picture."[18] This is all metaphor, of course, but it is worth remembering that the inter-art comparison of media (prose to poetry; discursive to presentational) is not a recent invention. When William

Carlos Williams attempted (in a famous series of poems) to translate
and express the core meanings of Brueghel, he was only the latest to
wrestle with this historical dilemma.[19]

With a growing awakening to history's own urgings, manifestos of
nationalism, revolution, and religious reform were prominent forms of
expression from the seventeenth century forward. As a kind of codification of principles, an expression of shared convictions, there is little
formal difference between the notorious Marx-Lenin polemic and the
most exuberant pronouncements of the Berlin dada movement. The
more speculative question has to do with the placement of aesthetics
as critical discourse. Here it is important to keep in mind that aesthetic
theory had always had something of a polemical character. Even the
most rigorous such treatise ever written—Aristotle's *Poetics*—was interpreted for centuries as a set of ironclad prescriptions for what artists
should do. Aristotle's famous predecessor had already politicized the
discussion by exiling all artists from his own utopian polity in the
Republic.[20]

The two most important developments that sealed the advocacy
orientation of aesthetic discourse are the public, presentational quality
and the recognizable cultural identity of art.[21] With the appearance of
art in a prearranged, public space, such as the exhibit, it became possible
to crystalize and codify principles applicable both to the techniques of
craft and to the conventions of appreciation. The discourse of critical
appraisal thus moves over into an advocacy mode; it clearly speaks on
behalf of appreciative "others" who depict and embody a culturally
identifiable audience. It also clearly speaks *to* other artists. In the year
1822, Adolphe Thiers writes of a Paris exhibition, "Corinne at Mis-
enum," by Gerard:

> Human nature has always been clothed in ancient form,
> and no matter how handsome David's Greeks and Ro-
> mans are, I see in them foreigners, abstract drawings
> depicting moral abstractions, and even though over-
> come by admiration, I am not convinced. What!
> Through the misfortune of our clothing and our habits,
> can we possess neither grandeur nor exterior nobility?
> The generous feelings that sometimes animate our
> hearts, the deep thoughts that occupy us, cannot be
> depicted with our faces and our clothing! Are there no
> more noble features today, no more beautiful shapes,
> and no way of throwing about us graceful veils which
> will decorate our bodies without disfiguring them?[22]

Thiers goes on to suggest that until recently the painter Gerard was unable to challenge this mystification of the tradition. But now he has moved beyond it. The critic moves on to the technical properties, and the cultural legacy, concluding: "I do not deplore an aberration of taste, on the contrary, I see with a nationalistic joy a mark of progress in art that honors, at the same time, the artist, the country, and the century."[23]

With the single exception (significant, to be sure) of an aesthetic steeped in the traditions of beauty and grandeur, this document anticipates virtually all of the formal qualities of the art manifesto. It is exuberant and declamatory in tone. It collectivizes aesthetic experience as an expressed quality. It employs liberal doses of irony to distance art from its heritage. It clearly mediates between audience and artist with the aim of captioning art (within the present historical era—an era, by the way, that represents progress). Yet, because this is authored not by an artistic community or movement but rather by a critic steeped in traditions, this is not yet a manifesto.

What remained for the growth and full emergence of the manifesto was a complete break with the schools, traditions, and styles of the past, as well as a codification of principles and conventions by artists themselves. The break came before the end of the nineteenth century. The early and late impressionist periods, the fauvists, and the breathtaking geometry of Cézanne all worked to distance the arts from natural attitudes and conventions of the time. Increasingly, artists were asked what in the world they were doing. And when, as in the cases of Matisse and Picasso, they refused to answer, the need for interpreters was palpable. As for theory, it had moved into the front lines. Tolstoy wrote his remarkable polemic "What is Art" as a virtual onslaught directed at the conflicting cultural tendencies of the age.[24] Criticism had virtually abandoned any pretense of aesthetic distance, and presented odes or diatribes about all aspects of culture. All of these developments had occurred several decades before the futurists authored their notorious manifestos.

As I interpret the rhetoric of the art manifesto, then, it is an outcome of at least four interrelated developments: (1) the developing inter-art tension between discursive and presentational forms; (2) the breakdown of any mimetic relationship between art works and commonsense apprehensions of the outside world, the so-called "natural attitude"; (3) the increasingly public nature of the art exhibit, and its presentational quality; and (4) the increasingly dogmatic and polemical quality

✝ of art theory and critical discourse. With these influences in place, we might begin to face and interpret the curious rhetorical genre of the art manifesto.

III. THE MANIFESTOS

Futurists

It is a matter of general consensus that what we call modernism in art, insofar as painting is concerned, was the result of the late-nineteenth-century fauvists (such as Gauguin and Matisse), as well as two individual artists who defied all movement characterizations: Picasso and Cezanne. In the case of earlier artists, frequent letters and other communiques (such as lectures, notes accompanying exhibitions) served many of the same functions as that of the manifesto. Other groups of artists, such as die Brucke, der Sturm, or die Blau Rieter, associated themselves with a journal or general program of aesthetic ambition. In the case of Picasso (who was decidedly less forthcoming about his principles and aims), a kind of theorist of cubism arose in the person of Juan Gris.[25] But what makes the futurists a particularly ironic aggregate for the honor of inventing the manifesto is not only the fact that they were preceded by all these others. It is the fact that their belligerent statements were originally declaimed before any actual "futurist" art had ever been created. In at least a technical sense, their provocations were those of frustrated critics and theorists rather than programs of a thriving art community. Art historian Norbert Lynton describes the futurists' conditions and problem:

> It was to take some time for the futurist painters, early on augmented by Giacomo Balla (1871–1958) and Gina Severini (1883–1965), to find the pictorial vehicle for their ideas. When Boccioni showed forty-two works in Venice in July they were quite well received by the critics, not striking anyone as particularly revolutionary; indeed, one commentator noted the wide gap between Boccioni's bold words and his temperate pictures. At this point the futurists' knowledge of avant-garde art north of the Alps was negligible. For lack of more adventurous forerunners they admired the pictures of Segantini and Previati, and they stirred their imaginations through reading Nietzsche.[26]

Insofar as we find the art manifesto to be a genre that somehow mediates
between art theory and art practice, between artist and potential audience, then this unlikely stream of vitriol is manifesto in name alone.
Still, what it lacks in concrete referentiality it more than makes up for
in pretension. Here is an excerpt from the most notorious publicist
and provocateur of the futurist movement, Filippo Tommaso Marinetti:

> We declare that the splendour of the world has been
> increased by a new beauty: the beauty of speed. A racing
> car, its body ornamented by great pipes that resemble
> snakes with explosive breath . . . a screaming automo-
> bile that seems to run on grapeshot, is more beautiful
> than the *Winged Victory of Semothrace*.[27]

He continues very much in the same vein:

> Beauty now exists only in struggle. A work that is not
> aggressive in character cannot be a masterpiece. . . .
> We want to glorify war—the world's only hygiene—
> militarism, patriotism, the destructive act of the anar-
> chists, the beautiful ideas for which one dies, and con-
> tempt for women. We want to destroy museums,
> libraries, and academies of all kinds, and to make war
> on moralism, feminism, and on every opportunistic and
> utilitarian vileness. We shall sing the great crowds ex-
> cited by work, pleasure or rioting, the multi-coloured,
> many-voiced tides of revolution in modern capitals.[28]

And so it continues, a kind of dark Whitmanesque ode to the id. It
does not take an art theorist to recognize that there is no program or
principle for art practice here. It is the same adolescent romanticism
for power that one finds today in heavy metal bands. One cannot help
also to notice a curiously old-fashioned sense of heritage in all this
bluster. So art is still about beauty; it is only that the category of beauty
has broadened its meanings. This is, by the way, nonsense. Aristotle
wrote two thousand years earlier that tragedy finds beauty in things
that are, objectively, not only ugly but gruesome. Note also the codicil:
"A work that is not aggressive in character cannot be a masterpiece."
Forgetting the double-negatives, this is an amusing retrogression to
the nineteenth-century preoccupation with the same genius categories
of museum, pantheons of canonical works, and pretenses toward permanence that twentieth-century art movements sought to demolish.
Contradictory or not, the codicil could just as surely have sprung from
the pen of Horace.

This ode, for all its hostility toward tradition, is a product of all the influences we have noted thus far. Still, Perloff is convincing about one thing. Politically naive, imprudent, and even dense to a fault, the document is nonetheless powerful. Why? In keeping with the overall genre of manifesto, it invokes a kind of consensual authority to cement and fulfill its own declarations. But by whom, one wonders? Who would endorse anarchism as well as patriotism, war, and revolution, ideologies in all their nefarious quarrelsome differences? Only an un-bridled aesthetic attitude that refused to be intimidated by any possi-bility, that saw the world itself as on the verge of arbitrarily bursting, that actively enjoyed the sound of all the splinters falling. What Mar-inetti is celebrating, and moral conventions be damned, is freedom in all its Dionysian manifestations. This is, I suspect, the source of its power.

But it is also the reason for its very contemporary aura of "flaming out" as a definition of significance. Marinetti seems intent upon being the twentieth century's first fifteen-minute celebrity. And he succeeded. Since there was really no substantive doctrine to the futurist message, what apparently survives this movement's relatively perishable contri-bution to art history is a highly controversial individuation of form, as well as an undeniable sense of attitude. This is the single respect in which Perloff can be said to have isolated something enduring in this art group. Here was a group with a millenialist attitude, and the right name, even as the centuries changed. By definition, this does not happen very often.

Dadaists

Any sense of meta-narrative to the progress of modernism in art would be dispelled by the short-lived dadaist movement. Emerging among a group of expatriate artists who had fled their respective countries to avoid the war, the dadaist movement might be described as a single, clamorous gesture of futility at all the cultural collaboration with the militarization of Europe. It is interesting, as a sidelight, to note that Perloff finds remarkably similar traits in the discourse strat-egies of both futurists and dadaists, concluding that the former deci-sively influenced the latter. Such may well be the case. In his early chronicle/diary of the dadaists, for instance, Richard Huelsenbeck writes:

Through Tzara we were also in relation with the futurist movement and carried on a correspondence with Marinetti. By that time Boccioni had been killed, but all of us knew his thick book, *Pittura e scultura futuriste* [1914]. We regarded Marinetti's position as realistic, and were opposed to it, although we were glad to take over the concept of simultaneity of which he had made ←———— so much use. Tzara for the first time had poems recited simultaneously on the stage, and these performances were a great success, although the *poeme simultane* had already been introduced in France by Derreme and others.[29]

At least one lesson to be drawn from these reflections is that there were doubtless multiple influences on the dadaists, futurism surely among others.

The claim that the dadaist manifesto is entirely derivative from futurism requires a more guarded response. Certainly, there are superficial similarities, but it is unclear how many of these are specific individuations derived from futurism and how many are simply genre characteristics common to all manifestos. Furthermore, there is a paradoxical temporal relationship between dadaist practice and its manifestos. In an odd inversion of the futurist course, dadaist acts were ongoing for several years prior to the appearance of any manifesto proclaiming the principles of their significance. This may be because dadaists were suspicious of anything so pretentious as to *have* purported significance. Long before the European war had run its course, and long before its own manifestos were ever written, the Cabaret Voltaire was a public platform for the ongoing parody of every dominant tendency in art and politics. The dadaist performer-artist co-opted the "art of noise" to poke lethal fun at the brute propaganda still gushing forth from the aging colonial powers. There is every reason to believe, if one early dadaist manifesto may be taken as evidence, that in its own propaganda, too, the dadaist movement was parodying the prewar euphoria of futurism and even communism. Note the following "articles" of faith:

> 2. *The Central Council* demands:
>   a. Daily meals at public expense for all creative and intellectual men and women on the Potsdamer Platz (Berlin);

     b. Compulsary adherence of all clergymen and
teachers to the Dadaist articles of faith; . . .
     e. Introduction of the simultaneist poem as a Com-
munist state prayer;
     f. Requisition of churches for the performance of
bruitism, simultaneist and Dadaist poems;
     g. Establishment of a Dadaist advisory council for
the remodeling of life in every city of over 50,000
inhabitants;
     h. Immediate organization of a large scale Dadaist
propaganda campaign with 150 circuses for the enlightenment of the proletariat.[30]

To this we might add the fact that dadaism saw itself as a spirit or
attitude common to many different tendencies in art. One dadaist
manifesto praises the constructivist Tatlin. Another praises the expressionists and avers that anything abstract is dadaist. With the futurists, dadaism espoused a kind of brute vitalism, believing that
energy expressed is the most fundamental force of life. Yet it can
scarcely be denied that the positioning of its attitude, however eu-
phorically expressed, was diametrically opposed to the program of
futurism. The interesting question for the rhetoric of modern art is
whether the cognitive differences in position imply any corollary differences in the individuated style for their (i.e., futurist and dadaist)
manifestos.
    We know, for instance, that the "art" of the dadaists possessed a
very different, subversive attitude toward the machinery of everyday
life than did that of the futurists. The futurists were technological
romantics. With guns, tanks, speeding cars, and factories they would
transform the dull legacy of cultural tradition. In a very primitive sense,
alien to the logic of the machine, they had not yet experienced violence
as a waste. How much different are the ready-mades of former futurist
Duchamps: machines that could never work, that systematically frustrated their conventional task. Other dadaist devices included an iron
with tacks protruding from the base, and a mannequin's head equipped
with tape-measure, rulers, and spools, entitled "The Spirit of Our Time."
Kurt Schwitters culled bits of urban junk, by-products of the machine,
for his own modest compositions. What style of manifesto could pos-
sibly capture and celebrate this radical displacement?
    In overviewing some very different variations of the dadaist man-
ifesto, we might begin to sense some of its own permutations as genre.

We have already noted the programmatic codicils of the dadaist Central Council. Here we find a calculated sense of the absurd, articles drafted and proclaimed so as to ensure their own unreality. It may help to remember that such gibberish as this emerged within the same historical milieu as Wilson's Fourteen Points and the Treaty of Versailles. Yet along with dadaism's obvious stunts, we find the apparently more urgent tones of the following Berlin manifesto of 1918. It reads, in part:

> The highest art will be the one which in its conscious content presents the thousandfold problems of the day, the art which has been visibly shattered by the explosions of last week, which is forever trying to collect its limbs after yesterday's crash. Has expressionism fulfilled our expectations of such an art, which should be an expression of our most vital concerns?
> NO! NO! NO![31]

The rhetorical questions continued:

> Have the expressionists fulfilled our expectation of an art that burns the essence of life into our flesh?
> NO! NO! NO![32]

Having pronounced these explicit and emphatic charges, the indictment of their immediate cultural heritage must be detailed. The crime?

> Under the guise of turning inward, the expressionists have banded together into a generation which is already looking forward to honourable mention in the histories of literature and art. . . . Hatred of the press, hatred of advertizing, hatred of *sensations* are typical of people who prefer their armchair to the noise of the street.[33]

And then, of course, the collective enactment of an alternative:

> The signatories of this manifesto have, under the battle cry
> DADA!!!
> gathered together to put forward a new art. What, then, is Dadaism? The word "Dada" signifies the most primitive relation to the reality of the environment. . . . Life appears as a simultaneous muddle of noises, colours, and spiritual rhythms, which is taken unmodified with all the sensational screams and fevers of its reckless everyday psyche and with all its brutal reality. . . . Dada is the international expression of our times, the great

> rebellion of artistic movements, the artistic reflex of all
> these offenses, peace congresses, riots in the vegetable
> market.[34]

Here we find, in raw urgency, the tensions of a developing art movement crystallized. Much more clearly voiced than in the futurist movement is a specific disenchantment with the past. Whereas the futurists were rejecting the heritage of the past as a matter of general principle (and, for that matter, etymology), the dadaists of Berlin had, by 1918, rejected their very specific cultural heritage of expressionism. Since dadaism initially seemed to endorse the expressionist spirit, along with everything else it considered abstract, it is worth asking what had framed this disenchantment.

The opening of the manifesto is forceful exhortative rhetoric, phrased almost as a forensic brief, or at least as the sort of brief one might present to a "hanging judge." The inferential movement of the "exordium" is as unmistakable as it is rhetorical. The highest of art is to have a "conscious content" as worldly, transitory, and perishable as life itself: it is to be responsive to its own ongoing history. Then, following a lurid reference to the anarchistic spirit of the times, there are two rhetorical questions addressed—so it would seem—to the collectivity of sentiment standing outside the dadaist signatories. It is especially interesting to note that, in each case, the expressionists are convicted, as it were, for having failed to "fulfill our expectations." I hardly need to add that this suggests a rhetorical appropriation of aesthetic form entirely in keeping with the fifty years of criticism since Kenneth Burke. Now consider the indictments themselves. They are a shrewd combination of the moral and the ad hominem. "Under the guise of turning inward" (i.e., even their most distinctive trait may be only a pose), this group "has banded together into a generation which is already looking forward to honourable mention in the histories of literature and art." This is, I think, a lethal stab at the one thing all art movements fear; irrelevance, a failure to respond to the historical demands of the age. Further, there is just enough referentiality to make the attack plausible; expressionism does "turn inward." Whether this necessitates a preference for the "armchair" over the "noise of the street" may be highly debatable, but this does not matter in the present moment of urgency. At such times, one function of rhetoric is to identify qualities of character with other qualities "bordering on them," as Aristotle said.[35]

One final point about the strategy of this message. The signatories are very shrewd in their locus of temporal placement. The expressionists are referred to as a "generation," looking forward to recognition (honorable mention in the histories of art and literature). This is another way of suggesting that their moment has passed; they are already part of a narrative retrospection that will recede in favor of the present moment. All together, then, the strategies of tone, mood, and temporal locale serve to distance the expressionists from the present moment, while defining present history as the proper occasion for the dadaist spirit.

As for the actual principles unifying the dadaists, they are every bit as prescriptive and no less ambiguous than the landmarks of aesthetic theory they would supplant. In an attempt to define "Dada," the signatories simply take over from the futurists and expressionists the dynamism of an unfinished historical episode. To use Poggioli's terms, dadaism is unvarnished activism, but as a sort of "gesture."[36] It is, as all movements, antagonistic toward its immediate predecessors. Because the futurists presented their proclamations first, they were able to reject everything that had come before. Yet even the futurists needed to turn back to cubist insights in order to generate actual artifacts. The dadaists were able to reject expressionism and the protofascist doctrines of futurism. Yet here, too, we have the claim that dadaism is "the international expression of our time,"[37] an interesting co-optation of their immediate predecessors.

It would doubtless be dangerous to generalize from these few early samples to the larger contours of the art manifesto as genre. But it should be possible to learn something about the genre from this peculiar individuation. As a kind of gesture, dadaism ensured its own perishability. Moreover, its highly reflective sense of the absurd seemed out of sorts. Where the ringing proclamations of manifesto seemed to call for solidarity, the dadaist could not resist a whimsical disclaimer. Hugo Ball wrote the following shortly before he left the movement:

> I write a manifesto and I want nothing, yet I say certain things, and in principle I am against manifestoes, as I am also against principles. I write this manifesto to show that people can perform contrary while taking one fresh gulp of air; I am against action. . . . If I cry out:
> *Ideal, ideal, ideal*
> *Knowledge, knowledge, knowledge*
> *Boomboom, boomboom, boomboom*

> I have given a pretty faithful version of progress, law,
> morality, and all other fine qualities that various highly
> intelligent men have discussed in so many books,
> only to conclude that everyone dances to his own
> boomboom.[38]

Within the very tensions characterizing the relationship between dadaist content as art and the art movement manifesto as form, we begin
to grasp some recurring features of the manifesto's style and function.
I now hazard several hypotheses about these features.

1. Manifestos are, first and foremost, collectivist documents. Even
though they may have a single author, they are intended as a declaration
shared in common with other members of the movement. In fact, the
manifesto attains whatever weight of credibility it might possess as a
result of its status as "covenant," the demonstrative authority of beliefs
held in common with others. This is another way of saying that the
membership of an art movement functions both as surrogate authors
of the art manifesto and as audience-witnesses for the force of its
expression. One reason for the curious quality of Ball's "antimanifesto"
is that it is presented in an individual voice, reflecting upon its own
ongoing status as discourse. This individual quality has the effect of
relativizing the force of a manifesto's oracular pronouncements. After
a while, one "boomboom" sounds quite a bit like another.

2. As to the force of the manifesto, it is undeniably perlocutionary
in intent and active by design. Unlike the traditional aesthetic theory,
the manifesto is less a form of explanation than a form of enactment.
Indeed, in exhorting its reader-witness to erase the distinction between
art and life, to look at both in an entirely new way, the manifesto
would—as in Plato's allegory of the cave—seize our attention in a
moment of urgency and literally force us to see things differently. This
sense of exhortation becomes easier to understand when we recall that
the link between art and worldly appearance has been ruptured with
the rise of modernity. The traditional pleasures of recognizing beauty
in coherent form have given way to something more ominous and
disturbing. The content of modern art demands our attention, even as
it defies easy assimilation. The manifesto expresses this new paradox
in the most contentious manner imaginable.

3. Since the manifesto is asserting vision as a kind of imperative,
its style typically reflects this partisanship. What were once principles

or rules of thumb are now presented as commands. The admittedly prescriptive language of critical aesthetics yields to something deliberately designed to provoke and scandalize. Hyperbole and slogan are mixed with gratuitous attacks on differing traditions and movements. The manifesto is less an attempt to argue persuasively than a refusal to be ignored. Whether or not it forces a favorable judgment, some decisive reaction must be forthcoming. It is a discourse designed to polarize. This does not mean that manifestos only proceed noninferentially. The first dadaist manifesto of 1918[39] quite explicitly presses reasoned grounds for its attack on the expressionists: They have not fulfilled our expectations for an art that is responsive to our age. They have already retreated from the historical challenge. We shall take up the fight. My point is that these reasons are all shaped quite explicitly to meet the thematic needs of the art movement itself.

4. Perhaps the least programmatic aspect of the manifesto is the function it performs for the modern art movement. No longer a theory of art, the manifesto remains inextricably tied to the art practices of the movement. In a volatile period of history, with a competing babel of nationalisms, cultures, and avant-gardes, the manifesto presents itself as a combination of harbinger and interpretive voice. In the role of harbinger, it is ready and willing to stir things up, to propagandize and outrage, all the better to reap publicity for its "products." But its polemical tone is qualified by another, more conventional need. To the extent that art practices themselves are abandoning any mimetic or referential domain of meaning, it falls to the manifesto to proclaim (usually with great urgency) just what these highly diffuse works are doing. To anyone steeped in the natural attitude, this must seem an ironic sort of pastime; works of art begin to be created for no other reason than to illustrate a point. For all this, there seems to be a problematic tension at the heart of the relationship between manifestos and art practice. The manifesto occupies a highly tenuous middle ground between provocation and coherent interpretation. If the movement in question contains a point or message that might be assimilated fully by discourse, the movement will have become a "legacy" and effectively passed into art history. Put somewhat more colorfully by the ubiquitous poet and modern art groupie, Appolinaire, "It is useless to paint what can already be described."[40] But from the other side of the tension, a manifesto that is utterly incoherent, which bespeaks no

referentiality at all, will have failed in its function of pointing toward an identifiable tendency, a novelty worth attending to, in art practice. My fifth hypothesis expresses one consequence of this tension.

5. There seems to be a temporal gap between the flourishing of an art practice and the pronouncement of an art manifesto. Perhaps for political reasons, the freedom of an aesthetic imagination is always uncomfortable with the regimen of solidarity. Ball's departure from the dadaist movement seems almost a logical consequence of his antimanifesto celebration of the absurd. And as we have seen, the futurist manifesto predated the actual appearance of any futurist art. By an ironic juxtaposition, the dadaist spirit swept Europe years before any actual manifesto appeared signifying its meaning. And once a serious attempt was made to capture and decipher that meaning, the movement was effectively over. In light of modernism's subsequent history, it is interesting to inquire whether the art manifesto may work in genuine temporal conjunction with the flourishing of an art movement.

Constructivists

Until recently, it was common to think of the constructivists as representing little more than a short-lived episode in the history of modern art.[41] The reasons for this misunderstanding are obvious enough. Unlike the vociferous and self-aggrandizing futurists, the constructivists were preoccupied with the material work of art rather than its outward manifestation as style. Moreover, the constructivists were preoccupied with the transformational mission of a previously closed and virtually medieval culture—Russia, soon to be the Soviet Union. Although influenced by the futurists and the cubists, there was another, more revolutionary political manifesto to which they owed their allegiance, the famous *Communist Manifesto* of Marx and Engels. More than any other art movement of the twentieth century, then, the constructivists were presented with an occasion and a vanguard of activists with genuine revolutionary significance. They found themselves able to celebrate the technologies of modernity not as an instrument of speed and death, but rather as an epochal moment of both political and historical liberation.

The constructivists thus have significance as a conspicuous counterexample to our intuition of displacement. Because they were in a position to act collectively and effectively, their words could charge their actual work with immediate felt significance. At the same time, they worked from an implied theory of art that had a direct causal relationship to the impending revolutionary transformation. While their pronouncements may appear somewhat naive in retrospect, theirs was a world where the movement of history and the task of art all seemed to be pointing in the same exhilarating direction.

In 1920, Nahum Gabo and Antoine Pevsner published a constructivist manifesto, in conjunction with the Moscow constructivist exhibition of the same year. Here are excerpts from their pronouncements:

> The "fundamental bases of art" must rest on solid
> ground: real life.
> In fact (actuality) space and time are two elements
> which exclusively fill real life (reality).
> Therefore, if art wishes to grasp real life, it must, like-
> wise, be based on these two fundamental elements.
> To realize our creative life in terms of space and time:
> such is the unique aim of our creative art.[42]

Here we find several of the characteristic generic features of the manifesto, given a unique cultural and political individuation inspired by setting and purpose. Note first the postulational quality of these "fundamental bases." They are the same sort of bedrock principles we might have found in any traditional aesthetic theory. But here they are presented as part of a program and issued as commands. Note too the sense of an inferential pattern culminating in an exhortation of mission. Not unlike the dadaist indictment of expressionism, this more affirmative statement presents us with general truths about art and reality; it therefore becomes the "unique aim" of constructivists generally to realize these creative truths.

Yet all this apparent rigor raises the same question as to the rhetorical point of the constructivist document. As a statement of principles, it is evocative. But is it intended to recruit more constructivists, to undermine more traditional approaches to art (as venerable symbol, perhaps), to divide supporters from opponents in the manner of the dadaists and futurists? The answer appears to be none of the above. As near as we are able to tell, the constructivists took a very traditional view of art as object and converted it to an understanding of art as revolutionary utility. Unique among early modern art movements is the presence of a direct and mediating theory of art within their own art manifestos. The 1920 manifesto continues:

> We hold our sextant in our hand, our eyes look straight
> before them, our minds are stretched like a bow, and
> we shape our work as the world its creation, the en-
> gineer his bridge, the mathematician his formulas of a
> planetary orbit.
>
> We know that every object has its own individu-
> ality. Table, chair, lamp, book, telephone, house—each
> of them constitutes a world in itself, a world having its
> own rhythm and its own planetary orbit. . . .
>
> We deny volume as an expression of space. Space
> can be as little measured by a volume as a liquid by
> linear measure. What can space be if not impenetrable
> depth? Depth is the unique form by which space can
> be expressed.[43]

What can be the point of these theoretical pronouncements? The
members conceptualized art as the making of objects, a process equally
compatible with the work of nature and culture (and Aristotle's *Physics,*
for that matter). This much may be gleaned by the euphoric equation
of sextant and mind to arrow and bow, the eager drive to shape and
mold the objects of present and future life. More is implied than the
simple "form follows function" formula of late architectural modernism. The constructivists brought together two powerful and related
concepts in a bold dialectical synthesis to guide their work: the tec-
tonic, overall concept—a synthesis of form and content based upon
the overall idea materialized in use, and *factura,* the propensity and
tendency of materials themselves, given their own natural condition
and availability.[44] With the two terms synthesized, art would move
beyond mere abstraction and the dilettantish games of dadaists. It
would be an art for and of the people.

This is what is presented to us in the collective pronouncements
of the constructivist manifesto. "We hold . . . We know . . . We an-
nounce . . . We deny . . ." In affirming what they call the "individuality"
of every object, they are forcefully denying the art conventions that treat
objects as recognizable background for a plane surface. In affirming the
indissolubility of space, they are demanding that art take its place outside the studios and stages and attach its creations to the unfolding
horizon of history. Subsequent years would witness a dizzying array of
art experiments: in sculptures as functional architecture, in the remarkable prouns (i.e., three-dimensional paintings) of Lissitzky and others.[45]
The collective emergence of theory and speech-act conviction in the

constructivist manifesto seems particularly well suited to the willful direction of art as social program.

In the present interpretive synopsis, then, the constructivist use of art theory as a movement program places this phase of modernism firmly in the activism-antagonism/range of social experience. And yet there is an unnerving paradox directly related to the immanence of constructivism's performative mission. Earlier art movements had, one might suggest, the freedom of their own indeterminacy. The futurists and dadaists, particularly, were able to celebrate or reject the historical and cultural forces of their time with the unbounded confidence that comes from having absolutely no power over their outcome. This is, it might be added, part of the larger paradox deriving from the synthesis of aesthetic spirit with the movement prerogative for programmatic action. In the utopian inception stage of a movement, all are charged with the aesthetic spirit of unlimited possibility: "Sisterhood is powerful!" "Let a hundred flowers bloom!" "The whole world is watching!" It is only when concrete conditions dictate policy choices, irrevocable commitments and programs, that freedom must give way to more painful imperatives, as in "The people's army does not shoot the people."[46] In this more tragic sense, it might be said that the dadaists and futurists, for all their playful exhilaration, finally were able to manifest the good sense of their own futility. By failing historically, they were purged of the delicate problem of serving the twentieth century's two great idols: the autonomy of individual "conscience" and the proper consciousness of the "people." The constructivists, poised on the threshold of historical transformation, did not have this option of avoidance.

A personal notation may help to add some resonance to the human dimension of this art movement and its denouement. Several years ago I attended a showing of the George Costakis Collection of Russian constructivist art.[47] In many ways, the exhibit was a prototype of the retrospective status attributed to once vibrant and incendiary art movements once their moment of euphoria had passed. And, in true modernist fashion, the name of the collector and curator (Costakis) had greater prominence and celebrity value than any specific artist featured by the exhibit itself. But for all this, what seemed most poignant was the contrast between powerful vision—the proud concreteness and certitude of these visual architectonics—and the manifest uncertainty of personal fate. As name after name passed—Loganson, Medunetsky,

Grinberg—there would be a birth date with only a question mark following as to fate or date of death. In some cases there were deaths of scarlet fever, in exile, in labor camps; in others, the statement, "almost none of his work has survived."[48] Of course, the immersion of self in collective solidarity is characteristic of the art movement's appeal. But here this same immersion has been sealed by the very literalism of state power. Such seems to be the tragic dilemma beckoning any seriously political art movement.

Surrealism

There is one art movement that seems to have almost flaunted the norms of politics and fate that bedevil aesthetic modernism. In some cases it has made a dilettantish pastime of feigning radical affiliations, while in others it has laughed all the way to the bank. The broad chronological outlines of surrealism are well enough known. Founded on the ashes of dadaism[49] and rooted in an artful misreading of Freud, surrealism offered the immodest proposition that life itself might be made more artful than its conscious manifestations had hitherto suggested. By probing and evoking the resources, themes, and methods of the unconscious, a new hyper- or surreality might be generated that would bring together both the conscious and unconscious manifestations of the real. Rather than being an attempt to subvert the workings of rational consciousness, then, surrealism presented itself as a bold new synthesis of reality with a deeper, participatory dimension.

There is a sense in which the surrealists presented a logical extension of previous moments in modern art movements. If we grant that the cubists and dadaists had given new participatory meaning to space and time as aesthetic constructs, and if the dadaists and constructivists had founded an aesthetic divorced from conventions of meaning and "fine art" value appreciation, then the surrealists had discovered the ultimate underground for Western modernity: the uncharted territory of the self and its unconscious life. But this is more than a simple extension. For all their pronouncements of transformation, each previous art movement purported to be giving its adherents and audiences an appreciation of reality in dimensions that were truer and more complete than what had come before; this is one reason often presented for the eventual exhaustion of aesthetic modernity.[50] The artistic imagination finally cannot transcend the recurring finitude of its own material world.

To all this the surrealists offered a revolutionary counterproposal. It is only reason, that great residue of modernity, that continually binds and constrains art to the manifestations of conscious existence. Heretofore, even the most radical art movements had been unable to resist their own implication in the forward development of modern consciousness. This fact explains both their urgency and their notoriously brief duration. Once their point is understood and encapsulated, their vitality is done. To be understood and thus explained is to be reintegrated into the regime of ratiocination. To this developmental sense of art's manifestations the surrealists opposed one further step that might erase all the ones made before: consciousness itself must yield to the deeper reality of dreams, the forbidden territory of the nonrational.[51]

More than in any other art movement, the manifestos of surrealism attempt a direct relationship between theory (which defines the movement) and aesthetic practice (which enacts the theory). Perhaps for this reason, it is difficult to encapsulate the prototypical surrealist manifesto. In *Manifestoes of Surrealism,* for instance, Andre Breton includes everything from long stream-of-consciousness antinarrative to conventional declarations of postulates to boldface aphorisms that would do Jenny Holzer proud.[52] Here is Breton writing more or less plainly on the theory behind the movement:

> What reason, I ask, a reason so much vaster than the other, makes dreams seem so natural and allows me to welcome unreservedly a welter of episodes so strange that they confound me now as I write? And yet I can believe my eyes, my ears; this great day has arrived, this beast has spoken . . . we may hope that the mysteries which really are not will give way to the great mystery. I believe in the future resolution of these two great states, dream and reality, which are seemingly so contradictory, into a kind of absolute reality, a *surreality*, if one may so speak. It is in quest of this reality that I am going, certain not to find it but too unmindful of my death not to calculate to some slight degree the joys of its possession.[53]

At the same time, and occasionally within the same document, the surrealist manifesto will accompany its theory with extravagant parodistic claims for its doctrinal tenets, and even protocol: "Let us not mince words: the marvelous is always beautiful, anything marvelous is beautiful, in fact only the marvelous is beautiful."[54] There is no point in logic chopping here. The point is that a euphoria of new discovery had come on the modernist scene, one particularly suited to what remained of the aesthetic impetus behind contemporary art.

Surrealism replaced the initial dadaist quest for the nature of meaning with an equally disturbing quest for the nature of freedom. The work of the surrealists thus counts as an innovation and extension on what had come before in art practice, even as it manages to unearth additional truths about the aesthetic spirit. Characteristically, the surrealists even sought to institutionalize their program with something called The Bureau of Surrealistic Research. Flaunting its own contrariety, the Bureau really does seem to have been a serious attempt to sponsor ever more elaborate forms of aesthetic subversion. The first director of the Bureau was the notorious surrealist director, founder of the "Theater of Cruelty," Antonin Artaud. In a letter Artaud wrote to the chancellors of the European universities, we find the ominous, almost prophetic stirrings of the surrealists' irrationalist spirit:

> Further away than science will ever reach, there where arrows of reason break against the clouds, this labyrinth exists, a central point where the forces of being and the ultimate nerves of the spirit converge. In this maze of moving and always changing walls, outside all known forms of thought, our spirit stirs, watching for its most secret and spontaneous movements—those with the character of revelation, an air of having come from elsewhere, of having fallen from the sky. . . . Europe crystalizes, slowly mummifies herself beneath the trappings of her frontiers, her factories, her courts of justice, her universities. The fault lies with your mouldy systems, your logic of two plus two equals four; the fault lies with you chancellors. The least act of spontaneous creation is more complex and revelatory than any metaphysics.[55]

One can only imagine what a typical university chancellor might make of such an epistle. But in their search for the "act of spontaneous creation," the surrealists had fastened upon one of the enduring features of the aesthetic consciousness, even as they set traditional issues of quality and competency aside.

It was Theodor Adorno who most effectively captured the essence of the surrealist consciousness, especially in relation to its own apparently subjective rendering of freedom. The modern world of the enlightenment, noted Adorno, had a completely secular and materialistic understanding of freedom.[56] Freedom was the ability to make egalitarian, comfortable and, above all, convenient institutional arrangements. For a long time, the so-called modernist aesthetic consciousness simply became absorbed in the infinite promise of secular or outer freedom. It followed its whimsical, self-indulgent appetites; it wrote poems to technology. As we have seen, it even praised and glorified war, and when war would not cooperate by meeting its inflated expectations it even rebelled childishly and celebrated nonsense. But while this aesthetic consciousness was following freely its own inclinations and congratulating itself for destroying one taboo after another, it finally began to discover that the real material world had become capable of stifling and totally depersonalizing human possibility. According to Adorno, this discovery—and perhaps the related sense of shock, dismay, and even shame—is what the surrealist consciousness is all about. The only solution is to show in dramatic terms the degree to which reality, as it ambles about in its programmatic, routinized way, is radically incomplete on its own terms. Nor might it be countered effectively by the subjective, autonomous ego; the scales are too unbalanced. Only the free, involuntary expression of the unconscious might allow an effective counter, completion, and synthesis of these appearances. And so, even as one might question the enduring aesthetic quality of surrealist works themselves, there is an enduring conceptual insight to their message. If all great art is finally about art, the greatest insight from the manifesto as art is finally about its own constitutive medium: language. Here is Breton again: "Language was given to man to use in a surrealist way. The surrealist image is born of the chance juxtaposition of two different realities, and it is on the spark struck by their meeting that the beauty of the image depends; the more different the two terms of the image are, the brighter the spark will be."[57] This is metaphor, but without any precondition for resemblance; an exquisitely modern terrain for the activity of invention. One may also think of this rendering as an explicit counterstatement to Kenneth Burke's and Griffin's understanding of form: the arousal of appetite and its fulfillment.[58] Instead of this notion, we have something very close to a continual and recurrent search for the perspective by incongruity.

Having said this much, I am not entirely certain that the surrealists found exactly what they were looking for. Surely they are, if not entirely correct about language, at least highly prophetic as to its preeminent contemporary understanding. But why is it that language was given to us to be used this way? And for that matter, why is it that surrealism— alone among all movements in modern art—seems translatable into almost every conceivable art medium: the film of Dali and Bunuel, surely the poetry of Breton and Aragon, the theater of Artaud, the music of Satie. To answer this question is, to an extent, to qualify the mystique of the surrealist vision. Surrealists have found, within the languages of art, the historicity and relativity of convention. And so, in its characteristic way, each of the art media seems almost to mock Plato's original indictments of art by converting its false mimetic prop- erties into a kind of subversion of expectation. Theirs was a uniquely modern rhetoric of aesthetic invention.[59] But the last irony may have belonged to art history itself. This powerfully euphoric aesthetic of liberation would not have been possible without some residual vitality of the conventions of art practice.

IV. CONCLUSION

This exploratory essay has sought to apply Leland Griffin's dra- matistic theory of social movements to the relatively uncharted rhe- torical territory of the twentieth-century art movement. To do this, I have had to extend upon and yet qualify the three-stage approach that Griffin suggests for interpreting the diachronic qualities of a movement. At the same time, I have had to be mindful of the curious metanarrative quality of the purported modernist movement itself, supposedly crys- tallized in the individuated episodic outbursts of futurism, construc- tivism, dadaism, and surrealism (as well as many others). This curious synthesis of the instrumental with the expressive, the break with the developmental, placed unusual rhetorical demands upon the movement practitioners. They had to articulate a vision of practice that was new, a previously unexplored expression of modernity's consciousness. At the same time, they had to hover around an identifiable core of doctrinal tenets, something that characterized the movement. Thus the paradox. To follow the muse of creativity alone was to be a renegade, an outsider, but strict adherence to the developing doctrinal momentum of an art movement had the restrictive effect of reducing the artist to a sort of aesthetic functionary.

This doctrinal paradox may also help to explain why the most fully realized political art movement, constructivism, also turned out to be the most completely anonymous art movement so far as the identity of real live artists was concerned. At the same time, the two artists who arguably exerted the most lasting qualitative influence upon modern aesthetic practice, Picasso and Matisse, never completely subordinated their creations to a single set of doctrinal tenets.

Was aesthetic modernism, then, simply a project that was doomed to exhaust itself, willfully contrary and wrongheaded from the very beginning?[60] I cannot subscribe to this tempting and popular thesis. Without doubt, the more radical experiments of the art movements, those interested in shock value alone, dated themselves with each expression, not unlike the scandal-sheet journalism they sought to parody. And yet, there is a disturbing resonance to the idea of modern art as a movement, fallen headlong into history, fated to leave no taboo unbroken in its ongoing romance with creative adventurism. In an odd way, the broken dialectic among perception (the cubists), time (the futurists), power (the constructivists), meaning (the dadaists), and consciousness (the surrealists) parallels and expresses the aura of this epoch as no other "time capsule" could do. Against the perennial vision of all art, it is simply too easy to remind one and all of their failed social responsibilities.

Griffin's theory of the social movement, like his powerful theory of the rhetorical trajectory, derives from the tragic realization that art and life can never be one and the same thing. But ironically, this same insight applies to the conceptual lessons drawn in the late twentieth century about the ostensive failure of aesthetic modernism. As Van Gogh's "Irises" threatens to tip the $100 million mark, as Andy Warhol's cookie jar collection evokes passions formerly reserved for Cezanne's mountain, and as Miro and Picasso facsimiles dot and shape the aura of every "postmodern" landscape, the last ghostly laugh of a fetishistic age may be on all of us.

◆   ◆   ◆

for/structure

THE STRATEGY OF NARRATIVE AND METAPHOR IN INTERVENTIONIST RHETORIC: INTERNATIONAL CASE STUDIES

D. Ray Heisey

In their analysis of "consummatory" versus "justificatory" crisis rhetoric, Cherwitz and Zagacki find that, in American presidential responses, "rhetoric plays a paramount role in defining, shaping and responding to international crises." They argue that how presidents talk about international crises may be more important than the crises themselves. This is true, they say, whether it is consummatory rhetoric, where no military response is necessary because "discourse *is* the response," or justificatory rhetoric, where "presidential remarks focus on explanation and rationalization of military retaliation."[1] Their study is a good example of the many that have been done on crisis rhetoric in the 1980s.[2]

Although critics have examined American foreign policy rhetoric to a considerable degree, the same cannot be said for the rhetoric of international leaders. My study in the Special Issue of the *Western Journal of Speech Communication* compared the rhetoric of President Mitterrand with that of President Reagan in their defenses of military intervention on foreign soil in Chad and Grenada as well as peacekeeping forces in Beirut.[3] The present essay is an expansion of that effort to increase our understanding of how various national leaders rhetorically defend their use of military involvement in the resolution of international conflict. I will do this by determining whether Cherwitz and Zagacki's conclusion about U.S. presidents also applies to foreign leaders when we look only at justificatory rhetoric.

Specifically, how do the official leaders of large, industrialized nations structure their rhetoric, and what function does their linguistic

186

style serve in the speeches they present to their national/international audiences when they are called upon to defend their military action on behalf of, or within, a smaller, developing nation? What are the similarities and the differences in their rhetoric in light of the differing national circumstances in each conflict, the differing cultural/political backgrounds of the audiences addressed as well as the spokespersons themselves, and what conclusions can be drawn in light of these similarities and differences?

The nations chosen are four of the five permanent members of the UN Security Council, plus one other. All are current world powers, symbolically if not in fact; all are highly industrialized; all are highly structured or developed politically; all intervened militarily in a smaller or weaker territory perceived to be within their sphere of political influence; and all interventions took place approximately within the decade of the 1980s. They are the Soviet Union in Afghanistan, England in the Falklands, Israel in Lebanon, France in Chad, and the United States in Grenada. Although military strikes were made against Libya, assistance was provided to the Contras in Nicaragua, and armed ships intervened in the Persian Gulf, these cases were not included because armed personnel were not landed on foreign soil to take over the territory.

These cases were chosen, then, because both their similarities and their differences are significant. If, in spite of cultural and political differences, a common rhetorical pattern of response can be discovered in such cases, what might that response be? On the other hand, if there are significant differences, are they culture specific or simply due to the particular circumstances? Will we find that rhetoric plays a crucial role in "defining, shaping, and responding to international crises" among foreign leaders as well? The hope is to advance our understanding of the dimensions of foreign policy rhetoric used across international boundaries, not just within the United States.

The approach I used was to examine the text of a major foreign policy address or rhetorical effort used in defense of the intervention by the elected leaders of these five nations, analyze the structure or form of the address, determine the use of linguistic style with particular attention being given to the metaphor in several cases, and compare these dimensions internationally.[4] I am not concerned with the variables of the speakers as individuals or with the effects of the speeches on selected audiences. My concern in this study is with the message found in the text. I have assumed that the rhetorical structure of interventionist speeches and the metaphors used by the rhetors disclose the essential argument of that nation-state. Is it primarily a rational or narrative structure, and what stylistic devices stand out in the speaker's language to enforce that argument?

The central finding in these cases was that the narrative structure was prominently used. I also found that linguistic terms chosen, which serve as metaphors and as examples of compressed language, disclose as much about the nature of the speaker's rhetoric and the national ideology as they do about the situation being described. The latter is consistent with the claim by Hawkes that "metaphors 'create' reality for us, but . . . [it] is not a new reality, so much as the reinforcement and restatement of an older one which our total way of life presupposes."[5] Metaphors, sometimes more implied than explicit, are used in these speeches along with strategic compressed terms to focus on the perceived reality of the rhetor.

In the case of narrative structure, I use Fisher's "narrative probability," which "refers to formal features of a story conceived as a discrete sequence of thought and/or action in life" that holds coherence, and "narrative fidelity," which concerns "the degree to which it accords with the logic of good reasons." A "good reason" is one that is accepted as a warrant for the values advocated. "To weigh the values," argues Fisher, "one considers questions of fact, relevance, consequence, consistency, and transcendent issue."[6] In all cases the speakers attempted to build a coherent and value-oriented story that fit the audience's frame of reference. The narrative structure is especially appropriate for justificatory rhetoric because it allows the rhetor to develop a coherent and sound sequence of events after the fact. It is a way of constructing perceptions and interpretations of action taken that are consistent with the higher values held by the members of the national audience.

The essay will proceed in chronological fashion, beginning with the interventionist rhetoric of the Soviet invasion of Afghanistan in 1979–80 and ending with the U.S. intervention in Grenada in 1983. A second section will offer implications and a final section a conclusion.

INTERVENTIONIST RHETORIC

Brezhnev and Afghanistan

The world would hardly have guessed in July 1979, when President Carter and Chairman Brezhnev met at the Vienna summit, that within months they would be calling each other names, accusing each other of abominable international behavior, and taking unilateral actions against the other's interests. Without warning, Soviet troops and tanks crossed the southern border into neighboring Afghanistan on December 29, 1979. In the following weeks massive armed forces made their way over the mountains to come to the aid of President Karmal, who had been recently installed after a coup in which the former leader, President Amin, was killed.

In retaliation for the Soviet invasion, President Carter called for a boycott of grain shipments to the Soviet Union and of U.S. participation in the Moscow summer Olympics. The UN Security Council condemned the invasion by a 13–2 vote and demanded a pullout of the Soviet troops. In a series of statements by Tass, Pravda, and Izvestia in early January 1980, the Soviet action was vigorously defended by the government.

Feeling the pressure of world opinion against the Afghanistan intervention, Chairman Brezhnev, as early as two weeks following the invasion, found it necessary to give a major foreign policy reply to a Pravda correspondent so that his views and "the real motives of the foreign policy of the Soviet Union" would be known. On January 13, 1980, he defended his government's military action in an eight-page answer to the question, "How do you evaluate the present international situation, especially in light of the US Administration's latest moves?"[7]

Brezhnev's rhetorical response to the situation may be titled "The Preservation of Détente," reflecting his perception of the Soviet Union's goal in world affairs. The response is developed around three themes: (1) the opponents of peace and détente have engaged in a path of hostility, (2) the Soviet Union responded to assist Afghanistan in its revolution for independence, and (3) the deterioration of the international situation is not due to Afghanistan but to Washington's desire to return to the Cold War.

Brezhnev's response is not structured as a carefully reasoned brief with supporting claims and evidence but as a narrative of what happened in Afghanistan and how those events connect with the broader world scene. He wants to tell a larger story so that Afghanistan can be seen in its proper light. He begins with a description of the Soviet "imaginative policy of peace, détente, and disarmament," and then points the finger of blame at President Carter for "whipping up war psychosis" and "acting on the international stage as if it were [his] own private turf."

Approximately the next third of the response is then devoted to Brezhnev's version of "what actually did happen in Afghanistan." The final third of his remarks on Afghanistan is a description of the United States as "colonialists," "imperialist," "engaged in saber-rattling," "an absolutely unreliable partner in interstate ties," and guilty of having a "dangerous destabilizing impact" on world affairs. In reconstructing the events in Afghanistan as an effort to battle "external aggression" and to repel imperialism, Brezhnev makes the story consistent with the party line and with the transcendent value of fighting "the opponents of peace."

Brezhnev's rhetoric is structured in a narrative form with unfolding scenes that together create a plot where the villains are going back to the Cold War while the heroes are attempting to preserve détente and peace in the world. The story is a global one, not a regional episode between neighboring nations.

The metaphors used by Brezhnev create a picturesque style of earthiness and ordinary things. In reference to the enemy, they include "path of hostility," "mountains of lies," "military bridgehead," "another Chile," the imperialists' "card . . . was trumped," "unreliable partner," the unilateral measures of the United States are like "boomerangs" that will "hit their initiators." The metaphor that serves his purpose best for his opponents is that of "acting on the international stage as if it were their own private turf," referring to the United States' "deeply ingrained habit of treating other states in a cavalier fashion." Brezhnev sees President Carter's behavior as that of an actor treating the world as his own stage. The metaphor, though chosen to restate an older reality for Brezhnev about the United States, actually discloses the nature of his own rhetoric—he has acted toward Afghanistan as if it were his stage or turf. It is reflexive rhetoric, though it was designed to describe the enemy. The descriptive term used for the Soviet action is the positive one of preserving "détente." The linguistic contrast is that Brezhnev says he advocates "peace" but Carter wants more "turf."

Thatcher and the Falklands

The situation in the Falkland Islands was different from that of Afghanistan because England had to reconquer the islands following

Argentina's takeover, not prevent rebels from taking over. Though there were conflicting claims over the sovereignty issue from years before, Prime Minister Thatcher immediately took a strong position. When Parliament met on April 3, 1982, she addressed the nation in a tone of restraint. Two days later, however, the task force set sail for the Falklands. Because it would take a few weeks for the task force to reach its destination, there was time to attempt to negotiate a settlement. Throughout the month of April, the British government continued to seek a peaceful solution with Argentina through the mediation of Secretary of State Alexander Haig. On April 14, Thatcher told the House of Commons, "The eyes of the world are now focused on the Falkland Islands; others are watching anxiously to see whether brute force or the rule of law will triumph."[8]

Thatcher gave her major address on this issue in the House of Commons on May 20, 1982, following weeks of negotiations and consideration of numerous proposals offered by both Britain and Argentina as well as by UN Secretary General Perez de Cuellar. The "Falkland Speech" is a carefully detailed narrative of the political events as interpreted by Thatcher.[9] She begins, "Mr. Speaker, seven weeks ago today, the Argentine Foreign minister summoned the British Ambassador in Buenos Aires and informed him that the diplomatic channel was now closed." That act, described in the opening sentence, symbolizes the British view of the entire drama. The plot is a series of acts by Argentina characterized by "obduracy and delay, deception and bad faith" in order "to confuse and prolong the negotiations while remaining in illegal possession of the islands." This series is contrasted with Britain's numerous proposals for a peaceful settlement, all rejected by Argentina.

The villain is clearly the government in Buenos Aires and the hero is in London. Thatcher uses the term "rejected" or its equivalent in reference to Argentina's response to her proposals no less than sixteen times in fifty-six paragraphs. She traces the events from the beginning to the present in chronological order, providing names, dates, places, article numbers of the proposals, documents, clauses, and current points in dispute. The structure is essentially a story, not an argumentative brief. She constructs events in a manner that permits the listener only one conclusion—that her "case is just" and that the government has "been doing everything reasonable to secure a negotiated settlement." Near the end of the speech she deliberately reminds her audience that "the negotiations do not close any military options," the one claim that all the previous scenes led toward.

The address is important for its narrative dimension because it carries the appearance of factual truth, as if the political reality is the objective reality, thus giving her final conclusion the force of ultimate terms, holding both narrative probability and fidelity. What Thatcher thus constructs in this text is a superb example of what Zarefsky says about the Lincoln-Douglas debates: "Public argument is situated not only in chronological time but in symbolic, narrative time as well." This may be seen in the narrative dimensions of plot, heroes and villains, and movement through past, present, and future.[10] Thatcher warns her listeners that the future holds the potential for serious military action.

The style of Thatcher's language is very matter-of-fact, subdued, uncolorful, and tonally heavy. Three times in the opening paragraphs she identifies the crisis as "a new and even more serious phase," "of the utmost gravity," and "this very serious situation." In the final paragraphs she refers to "the gravity of the situation" and says that "difficult days lie ahead." These somber constructions, which begin and end the speech, though not laced with colorful metaphors, are held together by the juxtaposition of the positive label of success and the negative symbol of aggression. She says, "Aggression must not be allowed to succeed." Thatcher uses the image of "aggression" succeeding rather than "the principles of democracy and the rule of law" succeeding with the hope that it will create a readiness in her audience to accept the government's choice of military invasion of the islands. The image of aggression succeeding, a veiled reference to Hitler, easily reminds the listeners of a time when their own islands were threatened by the success of aggression.

In her discussion of Argentina's refusal to accept Britain's proposals, she concludes: "Had the Argentines accepted our proposals, we should have achieved the great prize of preventing further loss of life." The great prize metaphor clearly suggests that winning was the image of choice for Thatcher. In placing blame for future casualties on Argentina, she demonstrates Edelman's point that "any affirmation of an origin for a problem is also an implicit rejection of alternative origins."[11] Because Argentina did not accept the proposals, "the great prize" will not be won, and it will be Argentina's fault. The alternative origin is that it is Britain's fault, which must be rejected.

Finally, Thatcher repeats her clear reference to the success of the Allies in World War II in the last paragraph: "Britain has the responsibility towards the Islanders to restore their democratic way of life. She has a duty to the whole world to show that aggression will not succeed and to uphold the cause of freedom." That "the aggression succeeding" image is a deliberate construction to symbolize the Falklands may be seen in the later text of her reply on May 24 to Pope John Paul II on his appeal for a cease-fire. She uses exactly the same language: "Aggression must not be allowed to succeed."[12]

This repeated use of language suggests that Thatcher wants her audience to think of Argentina as a negative symbol, in contrast to the House of Commons as a positive symbol of a people who did *not* allow aggression to succeed. In an obvious reference to the wars in Europe and in the Pacific, she says in her reply to the pope, "The world has seen too often in this century the tragic consequences of failure to defend the principles of justice, civilized values and international law."[13] Her language, of course, discloses the nature of her own intentions— to settle the matter by Britain's own attempt to succeed at a military reconquest.

Begin and Lebanon

On June 6, 1982, the Israeli Defense Force (IDF) moved into Lebanon in what was called the "Peace for Galilee Operation." Within a week Beirut was surrounded and a cease-fire announced. The goal was "to uproot the terrorist PLO and its commands and bases from Lebanon."[14] Israeli officials announced that their simple objective was "to liberate northern Israel from the shells and rockets of Palestinian forces by securing a zone 25 miles north of the border."[15]

The policy of the Israeli government was immediately criticized by many, including the United States. President Reagan sent Prime Minister Begin a firm message, calling for him to stop the fighting and pull out.[16] A journalist for the *New York Times* wrote that "the idealism that made it such a special country" had been sapped by Israel's "trauma of living under siege." He concluded, "Fear breeding hate led to the grotesquely disproportionate assault on Lebanon."[17] The Israeli action was termed "a criminal act of genocide" by the *New York Times,* and Tass demanded that "this brazen aggression be stopped" because "Lebanon's fate as an independent and undivided state is threatened."[18]

Begin and Defense Minister Sharon defended their plan in a full-
scale debate in the Knesset on June 29, 1982.[19] Begin's major address
in this debate is constructed in narrative form in two main sections.
The first section, which includes a story from World War I about
England's decision to bomb Germany, helps explain why Israel is
justified in bombing its targets in Lebanon. Begin tells his audience
why he went into Lebanon by recounting conversations he had had
with President Reagan and others. To demonstrate that his story is a
campaign for the "truth" against "lies," he asks the question, "Mr.
Speaker, what did we find in Lebanon?" He then narrates what they
found, including stockpiles of weapons.

In the second section of his speech Begin explains "what happened
from the day we made the decision about the Peace for Galilee Operation until today." This explanation includes a detailed account, from
his point of view, of the communications between him and Reagan.
Continued fighting after the IDF had reached its twenty-five miles was
necessitated by the failure of the "terrorists" and the Syrians to observe
the cease-fire. Begin says, "I described the facts to you with the help
of the documents I read to you." He concludes the address with a
picture of what the government is ready to do: "Let them [the 7,000
'murderers'] leave with their personal weapons; we will let them pass
safely but they must leave, all of them." He then envisions a free
Lebanese government that will have a modern army. Israel will then
be able to sit down with Lebanon to sign "the second peace treaty
between Israel and an Arab state."

Begin's narrative includes time past, time present, and time future.
It includes the villains, the PLO "terrorists" who brought "this plague"
and "murder and rape to Lebanon." Israel, of course, is the hero who
"brought liberation and human dignity to Lebanon." ?

Both at the formal level and the deeper meaning level, the narrative
produces a law-enforcement image to help "interpret" the "facts" from
Begin's perspective. Begin describes the Peace for Galilee Operation as
a defensive campaign to "disarm" the "destroyer," creating the image
of a police officer taking a revolver away from a would-be murderer.
In the opening paragraphs he quotes Thomas Carlyle on the French
Revolution: "Upon encountering a lie which depresses you, remove it."
His speech seeks to remove "the malice of lies" about what Israel is
doing in Lebanon. It is not "genocide and massacre" as is claimed, but
"liberation of a motherland." The disarming process, carried out in the

interest of peace, is "to make them lay down their arms, drive them away, to get our settlements out of the range of their diabolic fire." Begin calls the PLO "armed gangs" who must be forced to "lay down their arms," their "katyushas" and "Kalashnikovs," and be removed because they are "animals." The metaphor of "disarming," which in this instance has both literal and symbolic meaning, is used again in the final paragraph to bring closure to the argument of his narrative:

> Mr. Speaker, blessed be the people that has such an army, blessed be the army that is commanded by a man like Raful [chief of Staff Lt. Gen. Refa'el Eytan's nickname] and blessed be the country whose defense minister is a man like Ari'el Sharon. I am saying this with all my heart and with all the strength of my belief. If we stand together we will be able to withstand all and to assure peace for our people and our country. To our sons and brothers we will bequeath a golden rule: he who sets out to destroy you, you should anticipate him and *disarm* [emphasis added] him.

Mitterand and Chad

Chad, a multicultural nation in north-central Africa, was formerly a French colony. A civil war between the north and the south was fought there from 1969 to 1972, and again in the late 1970s and in 1983. Libya, to the north of Chad, intervened on behalf of the north, and France did so on behalf of the Chadian government, which was in control of the south where most of the population and production are centered.

In early August 1983, France sent more troops to Chad to help control the civil war because Libya at that time occupied the northern half of the territory. In what was described as "his first full exposition of policy since fighting flared" in June,[20] President Mitterand responded to questions about the crisis in Chad in a lengthy interview published in *Le Monde* on August 26, 1983, titled "The explanations of Mr. Mitterand on the crisis in Chad."[21] He defends his policy of military intervention by telling his version of the story, taking his readers back fifteen years to recount the various scenes that had unfolded in that civil war. His primarily narrative structure provides a clear picture of why France had now increased its troops beyond numbers that would serve merely instructional and logistic purposes. He says his armed soldiers are there as "a dissuasive role" against those who would want to approach the southern zone where they were stationed.

In answer to a question regarding why France waited so long in June 1983 to respond with more troops, Mitterand makes sure his audience understands his position by responding with two other questions. "Should we strike a preventive war against Libya as soon as we hear of preparations they are making?" "Was it necessary to engage our army as soon as one soldier or a Libyan plane appeared at Chad's border?" His answer to both is No. His reasons are grounded in what he believes to be a proper understanding of international relations and an acceptable construction of the African story.

"First," says Mitterand, "the idea of launching a conflict before a characterized external aggression takes place is contrary to my conception of international life." The second reason is that not striking first should make it clear "to the eyes of all the countries of the world, and particularly the formerly colonized countries," that "the will of war and of domination was that of Libya and not that of France." In other words, the involvement of France is only to defend the independence of "a friend." The third reason is that France does not have to arbitrate strictly internal conflicts between Chadians. All three reasons demonstrate Mitterand's desire to be perceived as respecting national independence.

As in the Afghanistan, Falklands, and Lebanon cases, the Chad narrative includes a villain (Libya), a hero (France), and a plot (long-term civil war changed into an international conflict with an uncertain outcome). It is a movement with a past, a present, and a future, a future that excludes partition as a solution. Mitterrand says the partition plan called for by some would be contrary to law, would plunge Chad and all of Africa into "a tragic period of general instability," and would threaten the preservation of "often fragile unity" within newly independent countries. He sees a future where all Chadians "would reunite around a table" and aim for "unity, sovereignty, and independence."

Two primary arguments from history emerge out of Mitterrand's construction of events: (1) France has a historic obligation to preserve the independence of Chad, and (2) France has a unique responsibility in helping maintain "the African equilibrium." Throughout his remarks Mitterrand repeatedly stresses that France's military presence is due solely to the principle of French politics that all states must be permitted independence, sovereignty, and integrity. This is especially true of

Chad, where France has had "particularly historic and contractual" obligations. Furthermore, France sees itself as having a special responsibility in Africa to maintain an international equilibrium. Libya's intervention required France's intervention, lest the proper order in military, moral, and political affairs in Africa be upset.

Mitterrand uses numerous metaphors in his explanation of the Chadian crisis. He talks about "launching" a conflict, "a preventive war," "an automatic war," being invited to do a bombing as if it were "a promenade," "this infernal game," "the wear and tear of time," "plunge" into instability, "setting aflame the African Islam," and "the eyes of all the countries." Another metaphor is "the mesh." He refers to France's involvement as getting stuck; the French word used is *l'engrenage*, which literally means "a chaining up of circumstances from which one cannot disengage oneself." These are stylistic terms to influence his audience negatively regarding what the villain is doing.

Probably the most forceful and pervasive metaphor used by Mitterrand, however, is the code word "equilibrium." He wants to see "an equilibrium" restored, a "harmonizing" of actions; he sent forces "to help this country find peace" that would "reunite the Chadians around a table" and bring about a "departure of [all] the foreign armies." He speaks of "the African equilibrium" as a special duty France has in that continent. This same metaphor is also a major one in his address to the UN General Assembly on September 30, 1983. He says, "Peace can last only in equilibrium. . . . Such is the teaching of history." He continues:

> It is by respecting this golden rule that we establish the rights of one another to have independence and security. To establish these equilibriums or to restore them when they are broken, to guarantee their stability, to reduce progressively the forces to lower and lower levels and to verify continually the furnished information, there is the approach, the only possible approach to the problems that are posed to us.[22]

This metaphor has within it the implicit "Transcendent issue" of Libya's destroying the equilibrium in Africa by its invasion of Chad, which justifies France's military intervention to reestablish the equilibrium. Because France has a foreign policy tradition of being committed to maintaining "a more legitimate and stable international order,"[23] Mitterrand is communicating to a receptive audience with this "good reason." As Edelman reminds us, "it is not creativity that wins an audience in such cases [as Roosevelt's and Churchill's "stylistic felicities"], but rather telling people what they want to hear in a context that makes the message credible."[24] — so ?

Reagan and Grenada

In October 1983, U.S. troops landed on the small island of Grenada in the Caribbean "to restore order and democracy" to a country that had gone from being "a friendly island paradise for tourism" to "a Soviet-Cuban colony being readied as a military bastion to export terror and undermine democracy."[25] These descriptions are from President Reagan's speech given on October 27, 1983, over nationwide television, only days after the savage massacre of U.S. Marines in Beirut. Reagan talked about both incidents, explaining why the United States was in Beirut and had to go to Grenada. The Grenada invasion was felt by some to be a staging of certain success in the wake of a stunning defeat in Beirut. As I have argued elsewhere, "In Grenada, though the military accomplishment was secure, it was generally acknowledged that the outcome was more important for Reagan politically than it was for hemispheric security."[26]

Reagan, like the other leaders we have described, uses the narrative form to construct events as he wants his audience to see them. A story is less easily rebutted than a brief, so Reagan is on safer ground to reconstruct terminology that *shows* rather than *argues*. He uses the story to create *his* political reality rather than another's, such as that of the press. When he calls the villains "thugs," "a military force" of "Cubans," "Soviet advisors," and other such devil terms, he wants an emotive response beyond acceptance of "facts."

By focusing on the "success" of Grenada, Reagan is able to put out of focus for his audience the failure in Beirut.[27] Knowing that deployment of U.S. troops on foreign soil can be a risk for a president, especially when it is a surprise move with no public deliberation and examination of the facts of the case, Reagan needed to act rhetorically with dispatch. His speech was given within days of the invasion. Edelman describes the importance of using political language to create political reality:

> The critical element in political maneuver for advantage
> is the creation of meaning: the construction of beliefs

about events, policies, leaders, problems, and crises that rationalize or challenge existing inequalities. The strategic need is to immobilize opposition and mobilize support. While coercion and intimidation help to check resistance in all political systems, the key tactic must always be the evocation of interpretations that legitimize favored courses of action and threaten or reassure people so as to encourage them to be supportive or to remain quiescent.[28]

Reagan's Grenada story is an interpretation for political purposes that holds two "good reasons." First, the United States needed to confront the enemy in that island nation to preserve freedom and bring democracy to the people, including the safety of a thousand U.S. citizens. Second, the United States needed to act in its self-interest there, or "the enemy" might continue to expand "through a network of surrogates and terrorists." To respond to the request by members of the Organization of Eastern Caribbean States to "join them in a military operation to restore order and democracy to Grenada" was to act in self-defense, according to Reagan.

Reagan's speech to the American people closes with an emotional story from General Kelly of the Marine Corps that in itself is a metaphor for Reagan's Lebanon-Grenada story. General Kelly made a hospital visit to a young marine who lay with tubes in his body and wrote "semper fi" on a pad of paper. The Marine motto—"semper fidelis"— is Reagan's compressed language—his metaphor—for the story of America. Reagan's mission is America's mission, "to give to others that last best hope of a better future." "We cannot," Reagan concludes, "and will not dishonor them now and the sacrifices they made by failing to remain as faithful to the cause of freedom and the pursuit of peace as they have been."

IMPLICATIONS

I have shown in this comparative examination of the foreign policy rhetoric of national leaders that the rhetoric of intervention follows certain patterns. These patterns show similarities in three areas: structure, style, and strategy. I will now consider eight implications that grow out of these similarities.

1. The common structure in these five international texts was narrativity. The speakers wanted to construct the rhetorical story according

to their political interpretation. The stories in all cases reconstructed events as they occurred in time and place. The plot included villains, called "rebels" in Afghanistan, Argentine forces in the Falklands, "terrorists" in Lebanon, "rebels" in Chad, and "rebels" in Grenada, who conspired with outside forces (except the Argentines) to overthrow "legitimate" authority. The heroes were the stronger, big power (if not superpower) nations who came to the rescue by request (in most instances) to stop the usurper or aggressor. In a narrative the crucial questions are, Does it make sense? and Is it true? The narratives constructed by these world leaders asserted Yes to both.

2. The narrative structure permitted the rhetor to place the action within a larger world scene that gave the appearance of his or her wanting to preserve peace and freedom. Though use of the narrative form is not the only way to place an event in a larger picture, it is a compelling way because of the story's ability to show that there may be different actors, or other villains and heroes, beyond the ones identified by the "enemy." Naming military intervention as a means to achieve the transcendent value of world peace is more easily accomplished by the "mystification" of a story where facts, relevance, consequence, and consistency can be blended with the audience's values and traditions.[29] Brezhnev pointed to the deterioration of international détente that he wanted to stop with his intervention. Thatcher placed her story in the larger cause of the preservation of the principles of democracy. Begin was able to show that his forces in Lebanon were only part of the story; PLO "armed bands" were also on foreign soil there, as were Syrian forces. He was ready to leave Lebanon if all other foreign elements left simultaneously. Israeli forces in Lebanon were also only a "slice of reality" in his view because the PLO was viewed as modern-day Nazis. Begin, a former member of the Jewish freedom fighters called the *irgun,* was obliged by his background and philosophy to see a continuing narrative of potential holocaust. Mitterrand placed the Chad situation in the larger picture of "the African equilibrium" and France's responsibilty for it. Reagan's narrative was only one scene in the ongoing, historic, and never-ending saga of America's mission to bring freedom and peace to the world.

3. Using metaphor and terms of compressed language to clothe and close the narrative's argument was a common characteristic of these international leaders. Though several of them, such as Brezhnev, Begin, and Reagan, used metaphors more freely than others, all at-

tempted strategic use of verbal images. Brezhnev said he was "preserving" détente for the world against Carter's treating the world as his stage or turf. Thatcher spoke of "stopping the success of aggression." Begin repeatedly called his invasion a mission of peace to "disarm." Mitterrand's troops were bringing "an equilibrium" to both Chad and Africa. Reagan's choice metaphor was the Marine Corps motto, "semper fidelis." In one symbolic term, these rhetors tried to move their auditors along a continuum of thinking and feeling about the situation being described. As Fernandez argues, the metaphor serves as a strategy to make a "shift in feeling tone—of adornment and disparagement" by "tak[ing] their subjects [in these cases military interventions on sovereign soil] and mov[ing] them along a dimension or a set of dimensions," which were "domains" with very positive connotations and acceptable meanings. In this manner, says Fernandez, "persuasive metaphors situate us and others with whom we interact" in what amounts to "a cultural quality space."[30] The rhetors in question, in dealing with potentially controversial political problems that had both domestic and foreign policy implications, were highly motivated to move their national audiences into "cultural" or "semantic space" that would provide "cultural integration" instead of cultural "disintegration."[31]

4. All speakers used political language that inverted what Edelman calls "the value hierarchies implicit in the actions" described in their narratives. In his discussion of political language as deconstruction, Edelman calls attention to this important use of such language:

> Political language can win or maintain public support or acquiescence in the face of other actions that violate moral qualms and typically does so by denying the premises on which such actions are based while retaining traces of the premises.
> The most compelling way, then, in which political language undermines itself is through inversions of the value hierarchies implicit in the actions and in the other language with which it is associated. To wage war is to foster peace.[32]

Not unexpectedly, every one of these leaders undermined certain humane social values (respect for life, for sovereignty, and for independence) in order to serve other, purportedly higher values (peace, freedom, security) that in ordinary times would not be violated by

202 D. Ray Heisey

unacceptable tactics such as bombing villages, killing civilians, or sending troops onto foreign land. The speakers can succeed in these efforts
because the inversions are not imposed upon so much as drawn from
the audience. The "good reasons" used by the speakers for their nations'
actions disclose more about "the problems, aspirations, and social
situation" of the audience than they do about "the cogency of its
argument."[33]

5. Based on analysis of these rhetorical events, interventionist
rhetoric may also be characterized as dramatistic in nature. Dramatistic rhetoric contributes to the unfolding of a movement, defined
by Griffin as

> a dialectical progression through the stages of incep-
> tion, crisis, and consummation: a progress that begins
> when the discontented, drawn by a perfecting myth,
> the dream of an ideal New Order, rise up and say No—
> a negative that provokes the emergence of a counter-
> movement and hence the possibility for crisis, the ren-
> dering of a public judgment, a judgment which, if
> favorable, results in the movement's consummation.[34]

Though such a movement is generally not associated with the established power elite, functionally a government can create a movement
in the public consciousness. The established government of one nation
can find itself going through the three stages in order to bring change
to another nation by intervention. Because the social or political order
in Afghanistan, for example, did not conform to Brezhnev's vision, he
rose up and said No to the rebels, as did Thatcher to the Argentines,
Begin to the PLO, Mitterand to the Libyan-backed rebels in northern
Chad, and Reagan to the Cuban-backed rebels in Grenada. The military
intervention was the (political) acting out of the rhetorical No, thus
creating the crisis. These leaders then said Yes to the new order they
wanted to establish in the interest of peace, freedom, or security. The
movement, in Griffin's terms, was consummated because in each of
the five cases the intervening leader announced a victory—the achievement of the desired goal. If the prime mover of events in the drama
perceives a victory, then consummation has occurred.

Six months after the Afghanistan invasion, Brezhnev claimed that
Moscow's side had won against the "interventionists" (note the inverted
label), who had suffered a "serious defeat." He told the Central Committee that Moscow "will further help Afghanistan build a new life and

preserve the gains" begun by the Karmal regime.[35] But it was nine years later when Gorbachev finally removed Soviet troops in a move that was considered in most circles an admission of defeat. On the eve of the Soviet pullout in early February 1989, ABC World News Tonight showed a twenty-year-old Soviet soldier leaving Afghanistan, saying, "A Brezhnev mistake."[36] In the Falklands it was less than four weeks until Thatcher proclaimed victory, concluding, "The battle of the Falklands was a remarkable military operation, boldly planned, bravely executed and brilliantly accomplished."[37]

Less than a week after the June 1982 Lebanon invasion, Defense Minister Sharon proclaimed Israeli victory by announcing that all major military objectives had been achieved and that there were no plans to enter Beirut. That picture changed rapidly. A year later Israeli troops were still in Lebanon. Begin reiterated at that time that he would bring Israel's sons home from Lebanon on the condition that "both the Syrians and terrorists will leave."[38] Since that did not happen as soon as Begin had hoped, the Israelis became more enmeshed in Beirut until the discovery of the tragic massacre in Beirut shifted public sentiment against the government. Sharon became the scapegoat, and eventually Begin's adventurism cost him much personal and political grief. The Begin intervention received much criticism at home and abroad. A journalist writing in the *Jerusalem Post* a little over a month following the invasion concluded, "Militarily we have been successful." Then he asked, "But do we really aspire to conduct relations with our neighbors—especially the Palestinians—using power as the central factor?"[39] Earlier that summer Begin's speech to the UN was boycotted by two-thirds of the delegates. One of the three (out of ten) Common Market delegates who was present said, "It was a demonstration of displeasure over what is happening in Lebanon."[40] The Arab League issued a statement saying Begin "personifies the ghettoization of the Israeli psyche, the institutionalization of Israel's self-destructive racial paranoia and fascistic Zionist militarism."[41]

6. Another similarity in the interventionist rhetoric of these cases is that it distances the "enemy" rhetorically by accusation and attempts an identification with the "home" audience by justification. The narratives were built so as to place clear blame on the rebel-backed powers, portraying them as the "interventionists." Language can be used to create distance between peoples, Burke reminds us, just as surely as it can be used to close distances and bring people closer together. In the

same way, these leaders attempted to identify with the values of their national audiences by appealing to the Soviet pride in "preserving world détente," to the British history of standing up to "aggression," to the Israeli need for stamping out threats to its security, to the French focus on bringing a balance to the international disequilibrium, and to the American dream of bringing liberation to friends overtaken by a common enemy. The linguistic style is to label the other as guilty of international "sin" while identifying oneself with the noble ends held sacred by the constituency—ends higher in the values hierarchy than the actions being committed in their name.

The justification also takes a common form. Either "we were asked to help" or "we have an obligation to help" is the explanation and, further, "we are committed to perserving some grander principles at stake here than even the lives of our young men." In such situations, national leaders are obviously fulfilling their expected role, which is to persuade toward a certain point of view to meet the national agenda, not raise the level of understanding of complex issues. "Political understanding," says Edelman, "lies in awareness of the range of meanings political phenomena present and in appreciation of their potentialities for generating change in actions and beliefs. It does not spring from designating some one interpretation as fact, truth, or scientific finding."[42]

7. Further, to borrow the concept of "rhetorical trajectories" that Griffin uses in the analysis of the assassination of President Kennedy, interventionist rhetoric symbolizes "the convergence of trajectories, both spatial and rhetorical, in the lives of the [intervenor] and the [intervened]." Griffin argues that Kennedy, like Lincoln, died "because of the ideological movement that he symbolized, a movement whose rhetorical trajectory had long been signalled by his words and deeds." The act of assassination was both a final "summation of that rhetoric and a message to his audience." In Oswald's case, says Griffin, it was to help bring about his "dream of an ideal New Order."[43]

To complete the application to the rhetoric of these international incidents, I would argue that all five cases were ideologically driven, and not pragmatically or even economically motivated. These leaders confronted forces that threatened their national dreams and so ordered their troops to "assassinate" those threats in massive and collective action. Though at the macro level, these dreams, like Oswald's and Kennedy's, were "moral, a striving for salvation, perfection, the 'good.'"[44] Griffin continues his explanation by noting that these two men used god terms such as "justice" and "peace" and devil terms such as "opposition." We have noted earlier that the same god terms of "peace," "justice," "freedom," and devil terms of "enemy," "armed bands," "rebels," and "terrorists" were used by the international leaders in their rhetorical support for intervention.

Though it is beyond the scope of this essay, the evidence strongly suggests that in each case the military intervention could have been predicted because, as Griffin says of Oswald, the "progression had long been signalled by the trajectory of words and deeds."[4] Without question this was true in the Falklands case, where Thatcher had talked much of working out a settlement with Argentina but always reminded her listeners that the military option was held open. Begin had often made strikes into Lebanon and warned the PLO that he would not tolerate continued attacks on his citizens. Mitterrand had announced that he did not want to get militarily involved in Chad but finally relented. He had gone in before in earlier years, so the words and deeds on this occasion were consistent. Even the two superpowers, who did make "surprise" interventions, had a history of such moves, and Brezhnev and Reagan especially were ideologues who could have been expected to go in the direction they did.

The rhetorical trajectories, then, may be identified in the rhetoric of the national leaders. The assassination took the form of military intervention. If viewed together, it is possible that just as Oswald may have had an imaginary movement in his mind, so these five nations formed a subconscious worldwide movement—an international nation-state interventionist movement, if you will—from five different areas of the globe by the "haves" of the establishments against the "have-nots" of the third world.

8. The interventionist rhetoric in these cases can be traced to a resurgence of an earlier national vulnerability, issuing from traditional ideology. Although the decade of the 1980s closed with an emphasis on economics, not ideologies, in international affairs, the 1980s opened with nations very much preoccupied with their ideological agendas. All five interventions were by world leaders who seized opportunities within a brief period in the early part of the decade to "flex" their national muscles before a global audience. By the end of the decade, this world audience had generally agreed that there were serious questions about the wisdom or necessity of these adventures.

The Soviets found themselves in Afghanistan as a last gasp of their previous vulnerability in intervening in Eastern bloc countries. The pledge by Gorbachev that the Soviets would never invade another country was perhaps more a statement about their economic priorities than about their ideology. In the Falklands case, Thatcher had to give one more bugle call for the British empire before that emphasis would be laid to rest. Begin's invasion was also a deliberate act representing a former mentality that said security is waged by preemptive strikes. This mentality, of course, was a natural outgrowth of a lifetime of survival, both personally and nationally. As Rowland argues in *The Rhetoric of Menachem Begin,* Begin's "myth of holocaust and redemption" explains why he sees every event in terms of Israel's historic destiny. The PLO is viewed as "a modern-day Nazi organization" determined to destroy the Jewish people. This myth, says Rowland, "is an all-encompassing world view shaping [Begin's] policies and rhetoric."[46]

Mitterrand's invasion may be seen as a throwback to De Gaullism and the French vision of world grandeur. The French president followed in the path of Giscard d'Estaing's policy of preventing "destabilization" in Africa.[47] Reagan, of course, came into office on a conservative philosophy that stressed the United States' historic mission to be "a shining city on a hill" for all the world. Grenada was simply one of the battles to keep that mission alive.

What we see happening in these instances of international intervention is a contemporary expression of each nation's vulnerable past. It was, as it were, not only a final act of nostalgic ritual to demonstrate the glory that once was, but also a slice of their history. The final decade of this century will probably be more concerned with economic priorities as Yeltsin promises "new economic links" to Asia, as 1992 changed the economic face of Europe, and as the coming of 1997 will conclude the last outpost of Britain's former empire in Hong Kong.[48] The Lebanon invasion, furthermore, in the opinion of some analysts, "may turn out to be the last Arab-Israeli war, though certainly not the last war in the Middle East or the Persian Gulf."[49] If these five interventions are viewed as being in any way connected, they represent what Edelman calls "social problems as texts," where "each action or term carries the trace of others, constructing an exploding set of scenes and signs that move in unpredictable directions and that radiate endlessly."[50]

CONCLUSION

This essay began by asking whether rhetoric plays as crucial a role in "defining, shaping and responding to international crises" for foreign leaders as it does for the United States. If it does, what are the similarities and differences in the rhetoric of intervention among world leaders?

The analysis of five major rhetorical transactions by world leaders defending their military intervention in a regional crisis showed similarities in the structure, style, and strategy of their rhetoric. They all used the narrative structure, the strategy of metaphor and verbal images, and a dramatistic style of political language. Though from different histories and cultures, these leaders engaged in "defining, shaping and responding" to crisis situations judged to be within their political sphere of influence in remarkably similar ways, rhetorically.

The international rhetorics examined conform not only to each other but also to what Cherwitz and Zagacki describe as the similarities between justificatory and consummatory presidential rhetoric: reminding "the public of its deep ideological commitments," uniting "the country around a single theme," and assuming "that countries get along with each other by following pre-established international laws and codes of action."[51] My analysis has shown that each intervention produced a reminder to the audience of the commitment it had nationally to its own past and its own beliefs. There was, in each case, a single theme around which the leader asked the people to rally. Also, in each case the rhetor mentioned international agreements to which adherence was necessary for world peace.

Two of the unique characteristics Cherwitz and Zagacki attribute to justificatory rhetoric are also attributable to international interventionist rhetoric. Such rhetoric is "irrevocable, direct and decisive" and is similar to "the speech act of *announcing*." That is, it is the "end-point" of a crisis, allowing the next move to be up to the opponent.[52] Brezhnev said he would withdraw if the rebels stopped fighting. Thatcher said she would not attack if Argentina withdrew. Begin said he would withdraw if Syria and the PLO withdrew simultaneously. Mitterrand said he would not attack if the rebels did not cross the line. And Reagan implied that he would not need to attack any more areas if the Cubans and Soviets stopped their spreading of colonies.

Several of the unique characteristics that Cherwitz and Zagacki identify with justificatory rhetoric, however, do not pertain to international crisis rhetoric. They argue that justificatory rhetoric does not employ arguments issuing from a higher moral ground, does not stress so much the indicting of perpetrators, and does not imply as much of a global audience.[53] The evidence from the international cases is not conclusive on these points by any means. Even though intervention rhetoric would have to be placed within the justificatory category, the Soviet, British, and French responses did argue from a higher moral ground. Also, in every one of the five cases studied, the rhetor went to great pains to indict the perpetrators of the crisis, calling them "rebels," "terrorists," or "occupying forces." The blame was clearly leveled at the enemy. Regarding the implied global audience, again each speaker invoked a world audience by mentioning the UN or other world powers such as the United States, China, the Soviet Union, or more general terms such as "imperialists," "the East," "the West," and "internationalization" of the problem. More research in this area needs to be done before conclusive characteristics can be identified.

The final point to be made is that while the structure, style, and strategy of interventionist rhetoric appeared to be more similar than different when internationally compared, the substance of the arguments did differ from case to case. I refer here to the resurgent national ideology disclosed in the rhetoric and the way it related to the "higher moral ground" to which the rhetor appealed.

In my previous analysis of the interventionist rhetoric used by Mitterrand and Reagan, I concluded that "national leaders can be expected to use arguments and images for justifying military action that are consistent with their own nation's culture and history." Further, I argued that victimage rhetoric worked well for Reagan in "creating appearances" and that transcendent rhetoric worked for Mitterrand.[54] The present analysis of five cases confirms those preliminary findings where only the two were compared.

In comparing the ideology revealed in each case, Brezhnev argued transcendence, as did Thatcher and Mitterrand. Brezhnev called his ideology of "expansionism" a preserving of international détente, a higher moral ground than simply helping a neighbor, Afghanistan, in distress. Thatcher called her ideology of "empire" a preserving of democracy, also a higher moral ground than simply installing British administrators on the Falkland Islands. Mitterrand argued for transcendence when he invoked the higher principle of "equilibrium" over against assisting a former colony in a continuing civil war.

On the other hand, Begin and Reagan drew a much sharper picture of the "enemy" as repulsive and terroristic. This conforms to the image of savagery and the creating of victimage rhetoric. Both Begin's and Reagan's responses are within this tradition. As shown by Ivie, victimage rhetoric is established in U.S. presidential discourse,[55] and Reagan's rhetoric has been characterized, as far as the Grenada speech is concerned, as belonging to that category.[56] As for Begin, Rowland has shown that the Israeli Prime Minister was influenced in his decision to invade Lebanon by the all-encompassing worldview of his "myth of return," which sees the PLO as modern Nazis and Yassir Arafat as a contemporary Hitler out to destroy Israel.[57] Begin called the PLO "terrorists" and "murderers," and the issue under debate was "Jewish blood." The Begin rhetoric was based on the Israeli ideology of survival, past and present. The Reagan rhetoric was grounded in the American ideology of victimage, in world wars, in cold war, or from communist domination and the "Evil Empire."

The rhetorical substance, then, differed among these international rhetors in the early 1980s, while other dimensions of their rhetoric were more similar. Where there were differences, they may be attributed to cultural and historic aspects of the nations involved.

One of the significant contributions made by Leland Griffin was his expansion of the boundaries of rhetorical criticism to include analysis of rhetorical movements within society and, more recently, within a person's mind. In a similar way, exploring dimensions of international rhetoric on a comparative level to bring into focus similarities and differences among cultures and national traditions on a given theme is an effort to expand the boundaries even further.

The purpose here has been to add to our understanding of foreign policy rhetoric with the international leadership dimension included. As the nations of the world continue to become more and more interdependent, the need for rhetorical analysis of international rhetoric will grow. If interventionist rhetoric may be considered a type of crisis rhetoric within the foreign policy genre, the challenge for critics is to generate additional insights on this as well as other categories that will enable the building of a theory of crisis rhetoric appropriate to both individual nations and global considerations.

[handwritten annotations: "ignores the aural component that contributes a number to the forms"; "rhetorical vs. aesthetic reaction / appeal"]

THE CONSTRUCTION OF APPEAL IN VISUAL IMAGES: A HYPOTHESIS

Sonja K. Foss

[handwritten annotation: "ambitious, provocative"]

I was moved almost to tears by the Vietnam Veterans Memorial in Washington, D.C., surprised at the memorial's appeal for me because I knew no one killed in Vietnam and, in fact, protested the war. After watching the Talking Heads' film *Stop Making Sense,* with no prior knowledge of the group or its music, I became a Talking Heads' fan. I was amused and delighted when I encountered the Wonder Bread building in Rock Springs, Wyoming—its shape a loaf of bread, its exterior covered with the yellow, red, and blue dots of the familiar bread wrapper. These are not uncommon experiences in a culture where myriad visual images beckon and cajole, compel and coach us into new attitudes and actions. Reflection on the process by which various visual images appeal to me—some of them images to which I did not expect my response to be positive—led me to the question that was the impetus for this essay: How is appeal constructed in visual images? In other words, how do viewers come to see images as attractive and interesting—to assign a positive evaluation to them?

I am aware that my interest in the topic of visual images makes me somewhat suspect in the discipline of speech communication; in fact, one of my goals in this essay is to encourage a greater acceptance of such work in our field. The committee on rhetorical criticism at the National Conference on Rhetoric recommended in 1970 that the scope of rhetorical criticism be expanded to include nondiscursive subjects such as architecture, rock music, and ballet.[1] But even the recommendations of this prestigious committee had little effect on scholarship on visual imagery in speech communication. The committee's call for expansion led primarily to debates on the appropriateness of such expansion rather than to substantial numbers of studies of nondiscursive phenomena.

Representative of those in opposition to enlargement of the scope of rhetorical criticism to include visual symbols was Baskerville, who suggested that the study of nondiscursive symbols by rhetorical critics made all knowledge our province and put critics "in danger of biting off more than we can conveniently chew."[2] Lack of training in visual phenomena is cited as another reason for lack of work in this area by rhetorical scholars. Rhetorical critics are less familiar with the dimensions of and appropriate terminology for studying visual symbols, as Braden suggested: "I argue that by inclination and training most of us are best qualified to study the speech or rhetorical act."[3]

One of the most persuasive arguments against the study of nondiscursive symbols deals with theory development and was particularly well articulated by Hart. The goal of rhetorical criticism, he suggested, is the accumulation of theoretical statements about rhetoric. When nondiscursive forms such as visual images are the object of criticism, "the *immediate* implementation of the theoretical threads derived in previous studies of . . . verbal interchanges" is more difficult simply because of the differences between discursive and nondiscursive phenomena.[4] I believe that theory building is not only possible as a result of the criticism of nondiscursive rhetoric but that it may be enhanced and facilitated through such criticism simply because nondiscursive symbols often offer data that are richer and more complex than words alone.

But I have another reason for working in the area of visual rhetoric. Images presented through media such as advertisements, television, MTV, films, signs, and building exterior and interior design constitute a major part of our rhetorical environment. As much as scholars who work in the area of public address may feel nostalgia for a culture in which public speeches had a primary impact, that culture is gone; visual images now have the significance that public speeches once did. To study only verbal discourse, then, is to study a minute portion of the symbols that affect us daily. To understand and influence culture, to teach students to respond critically to the symbols around them, and to discover how to create effective messages, an understanding of the process by which visual images appeal is necessary.

My effort to understand the construction of appeal in visual imagery is related to Leland Griffin's work in two ways. First, the study of nondiscursive forms stretches boundaries, as did Griffin's early essay, "The Rhetoric of Historical Movements."[5] At a time when the conventional techniques of rhetorical analysis and appraisal focused on the individual great orator, Griffin expanded the scope of our data by suggesting that movements are appropriate for analysis and broadened the methods of rhetorical analysis by proposing how to isolate and analyze movements. My interest in examining the boundaries constructed around efforts to analyze and evaluate rhetoric—in this case, a boundary defined by a focus on discursive symbols—and the effects these boundaries have on critical products and resulting theories, then, has roots in Griffin's work.

This essay is a continuation of Griffin's work in yet another way. In a 1960 essay, "The Edifice Metaphor in Rhetorical Theory,"[6] Griffin dealt with connections between rhetoric and architecture and outlined two relationships between them. The germinal relation is a reciprocal, creative connection in which discourse is the means through which a building is constructed; that structure then may inspire discourse. The second relation, the analogic relation, links rhetorical theory with the edifice metaphor from architecture as a way of conceptualizing and discussing rhetorical theory. Griffin traces the edifice metaphor in the work of rhetorical theorists from classical to contemporary times, showing how this metaphor introduced into a rhetorical theory a concern not only with arrangement but with its aesthetic dimensions. Griffin's work in this area pointed, as I attempt to do in this essay, to the importance of studying the place of nondiscursive forms in rhetorical theory.

I began my investigation of the question of how appeal is constructed in visual images by turning to the speech communication literature. I was not surprised to discover that little has been done on this topic in our field. The body of work that is beginning to emerge on this subject is characterized by two primary approaches.

Some rhetorical scholars use visual imagery as data to investigate questions related to the nature and function of rhetoric. In such studies, visual images constitute artifacts to use in illustrating, explaining, or investigating rhetorical constructs developed from the study of discursive rhetoric. Visual images, in this approach, are assumed to have essentially the same characteristics as discursive symbols. An example is Rosenfield's analysis of Central Park in New York City, in which he studies the park as an example of epideictic or celebratory rhetoric.[7]

Another example is my study of Judy Chicago's work of cooperative art, *The Dinner Party,* in which I use the piece to identify strategies used by women to empower and accord legitimacy to their own perspective.[8] Other studies in which visual data are used to illustrate or explore rhetorical constructs include Rushing's analysis of the mythic evolution of "The New Frontier" using space fiction films;[9] Haines's analysis of the Vietnam Veterans Memorial to demonstrate the process of sight sacralization, in which attributes formerly reserved for holy places are ascribed to tourist attractions;[10] Campbell's study of the strategy of enactment using Peter Weir's film, *The Year of Living Dangerously;*[11] and Olson's study of the epideictic, deliberative, and apologetic functions of Benjamin Franklin's commemorative medal, *Libertas Americana.*[12]

A second approach to the study of visual imagery from a rhetorical perspective is the investigation of the rhetorical features of visual images themselves. The assumption of scholars who adopt this approach is that visual images are significantly different from discursive symbols, and their concern is with the discovery of how the particular nature of visual symbols themselves affects audiences' responses. Images, for example, do not express a thesis or proposition in the way that verbal messages do—the thesis is usually uncertain and ambiguous. Neither can visual images depict the negative—they cannot say something is *not* something else—as words can. In addition, the elements of visual images are presented simultaneously, in contrast to the linear, successive order of words.[13]

Examples of this second approach to the study of visual imagery, in which the unique features of visual images are investigated in order to develop richer and more comprehensive explanations of symbol use, include Kaplan's work on visual metaphors, which resulted in a description of three characteristics that distinguish visual metaphors from language-based metaphors.[14] My study of the Vietnam Veterans Memorial is another example; it is an investigation of ambiguity in visual phenomena and the process by which it persuades.[15] My examination of body art, in which artists use their bodies as their primary means of expression, also investigates the process by which ambiguous visual messages function, with an emphasis on how unconventional referents are interpreted by an audience.[16] Rhetorical scholars, then, are beginning to investigate the rhetorical characteristics of images, although focused and coherent theories of the process by which appeal is constructed in imagery have yet to be formulated.

Oddly enough, other disciplines—ones that might be expected to deal with the question of the appeal of visual imagery—do not provide much more information. A review of the literature of the disciplines of aesthetics, art history, architecture, art education, studio art, cognitive psychology, leisure studies, marketing, and advertising revealed very little attention to the process by which visual images come to be viewed as appealing. I found snippets of explanations—for example, what constitutes style in visual imagery,[17] how unity functions in an image,[18] the nature of representation,[19] the role of intention in the interpretation and evaluation of visual images,[20] what constitutes truth in visual images,[21] and the differences between visual and verbal symbols.[22] Some of these dimensions are a part of the process of the construction of appeal in visual images, but they are not examined for the creation of a theory that describes this process. Even the semiotics literature, which I suspected would offer useful explanations of the process of visual appeal, was disappointing. Semiotics provides explanations of how signs generate meaning,[23] but the next step—the one in which my interest lies—of how the interpretation of meaning constitutes appeal is rarely of concern.

Even prescriptive essays and textbooks in areas such as retailing and advertising, which I felt certain would present information about how to create appealing images that elicit positive evaluations, contained virtually no explanation of the process. Typical were admonitions such as one from retailing, which suggested that the "image of a store must be in accordance with its merchandise."[24] In advertising, the advice is only slightly more helpful: "When persuasive images are too abstract or conceptual, too indirect and even elliptical, they lose the capacity to provoke response."[25] The author of one advertising textbook gave these suggestions: illustrations in advertisements "should attract attention," "emphasize a fact about the product or its use," "reinforce the image of the package," and "stimulate the audience's desire for the product."[26] These prescriptions may result in the creation of visual images that are appealing, but they lack a theoretical base that explains how such appeal is constructed and why it works.

Because my review of what I believed would be relevant literature was of little assistance in discovering how visual images persuade, I turned to specific visual images to use as data to begin to identify features of this process. I chose to study images in both two and three dimensions, including paintings, prints, photographs, drawings, sculpture, furniture, and the interior and exterior design of buildings. I selected images in a variety of media so that any notions I formulated would not be limited by the particular characteristics of one medium. The images that constituted my data also were unaccompanied by verbal texts that might suggest specific interpretations to the viewer and were limited to ones new to an audience and appealing at their initial encounter. Images repeatedly encountered by an audience and that gradually develop appeal as a result of increased familiarity were not included. Finally, I confined my inquiry to images that have been labeled *visual art, art pictures,* or *pictorial denotation;* their distinctive feature is that the access point or central emphasis of the images is visual. In the images with which I was concerned, their visual structures or forms are less obviously the bearers of ideas and register more as visual arrangements.[27]

HYPOTHESIS OF VISUAL APPEAL

From my analysis of various images, I formulated a hypothesis of how appeal is constructed in visual images. My hypothesis, in brief, is this: A novel technical aspect of the image violates viewers' expectations; this violation functions both to sustain interest in the image and to decontextualize it. Connotations commonly associated with the technical aspect then provide an unexpected but familiar context in which to interpret the image. The result is appeal of the image, which I am defining as arousal of interest in, attraction of viewers to, and assignment of a positive evaluation to the image.

I see visual images that appeal to be characterized by elements that are presented to the viewer virtually simultaneously. The feature that appears to trigger the process, however, is technical novelty; some dimension of the form, structure, or construction technique of the image stands out as exceptional or extraordinary. This element may be exquisite detailing, superb craftsmanship, or a finely finished surface—elements that stand out in this age of mass-produced and often poorly crafted objects. The technical novelty may result from a different scale than usual—miniature or grand—so that it generates awe and admiration. Perhaps its design is refreshing or innovative and thus stands apart from most of the images in the environment—images that are, as Krier labels them, "an insult to our aesthetic sensibilities."[28] Viewers may wonder how a particular effect was achieved or marvel at the process that produced it. For whatever reason, viewers are drawn to focus on a technical aspect of the image that is unusual or special in some way.

The technical novelty of the image surprises or violates viewers' expectations. The element of the image that is characterized by technical novelty suggests that expectations for the image are incorrect; viewers discover that the context in which they attempt to interpret the image is not appropriate. The image is defamiliarized;[29] consequently, the coding system viewers expected to use in their interpretation of the image is not appropriate.

The violation of expectations and lack of context in which to place an image could generate confusion and frustration for viewers, making abandonment of the effort to understand the image likely. Were this to occur, viewers would not be susceptible to the potential of the image to appeal. But the element of technical novelty makes abandonment of the image by viewers unlikely. They want to resolve the tension created by the technical novelty—to understand the proper context in which to place the image. In the face of the image's displacement from the expected context, then, they are inclined to react critically to the image, to seek places in which to position it, and thus to restore familiarity to their world.

Images that appeal do not simply abandon viewers at the point of tension generated by the technical novelty. They help viewers comprehend the image by clearly referencing associations that point to contexts with positive connotations for them. These associations may be generated by the form of the image, the content of the image, or both. They suggest to viewers familiar contexts of events, objects, and qualities they are likely to associate with delight, affection, nostalgia, or other positive attributes.

The positive associations elicited by the image function in two ways. First, they provide a context in which viewers can interpret the image. This context is different from the one in which they initially tried to interpret the image, but it is familiar to them. The tension felt is at least partially resolved for viewers, who have found a place in which the image becomes sensible.

A second function served by these positive associations clustered around the technical novelty is that they accord a degree of credibility to the image. The frustration or irritation that may occur because of the violation of expectation that results from the technical novelty makes a negative perception of the image likely. Credibility is reclaimed for the image in its association with a positive and familiar context.

To summarize: Construction of appeal in a visual image is triggered by an element of technical novelty that results in a displacement of the image from its usual interpretive context. Association of the image with contexts that are positive for and known to the viewer—but different from the context originally expected—places the image in a new context. Interpretation of the image in this context is likely to result in assignment of a positive meaning to it.

THE HYPOTHESIS SUPPORTED

To illustrate and support my hypothesis of how appeal is constructed in visual images, I provide in this section three case studies of different types of visual images that appeal: a piece of furniture, the *Beverly* sideboard from the Memphis furniture collection; a work of environmental art, Christo's *Valley Curtain*; and an interior space, the pool room in Elvis Presley's home, Graceland.

Beverly Sideboard

Memphis is a style of furniture designed by a loose consortium of about thirty designers centered in Milan, Italy. Its name comes from a Bob Dylan song, "Stuck Inside of Mobile with the Memphis Blues Again," which was playing during an early planning session of the group. The Memphis designers later came to appreciate the allusions of the name "to both the ancient capital of Egypt and the birthplace of Elvis Presley—a juxtaposition of the ancient and exotic and the contemporary and banal."[30] Appropriately described as "amiably batty,"[31] the chairs, sofas, tables, bookcases, storage units, beds, teapots, and vases created by Memphis designers usually are characterized by wild colors and patterns, asymmetry, incongruous shapes and forms, hard surfaces, and use of plastic laminates and industrial materials.[32]

I have selected one piece of Memphis furniture to illustrate my hypothesis of how appeal is constructed in visual images—the *Beverly* sideboard.[33] Designed by Memphis's founder, Ettore Sottsass, Jr., for the first Memphis collection in 1981, the sideboard consists of a cabinet base constructed of light green laminate with a front inset of a dense, abstract, print design in green and yellow. On top of the cabinet is a

wooden, ladderlike structure that leans to the left. Connected both to
the ladder structure and to the top of the cabinet is a curved metal
pipe from which juts a red light bulb. Projected from the left of the
cabinet are three rectangular blocks of different sizes in black, green,
and red.

A combination of elements of the *Beverly* sideboard constitutes the
technical novelty of the image. The materials of which the piece is
constructed—plastic laminates, wood, and metal—are not typical materials from which home furnishings are created. The color of the
furniture is also unusual. The amount of color is one source of this
novelty; furniture for the home tends not to be intensely colored. But
the novelty of the sideboard's color continues in the juxtaposition of
red, green, and a print design in green and yellow. Rather than harmonizing with each other, these colors are placed in simple proximity
without apparent regard for conventional color relationships. The result is brilliant vibration suggestive of the colors of public spaces such
as Burger Kings, neon signs, motels, and K-Marts. These are not the
soft, warm, and soothing colors expected in a home.

Yet another technical element that is unusual in the sideboard is
its structural independence. It is not organized according to a clear
theme—such as a stylistic period or a particular function—as traditional furniture is. Instead, the sideboard appears to have been designed and constructed by assemblages, clusters, and deposits of forms
that overlap and intersect. The principles uniting the slanted pieces of
lumber, curved chrome tube, and red, green, and black blocks are not
clear and suggest "a series of accidents that come together by chance"[34]
rather than any kind of unity or coherence.

The technical novelty of the *Beverly* sideboard—materials, color,
and structural independence—subverts the context of traditional home
furniture, leaving viewers unclear of a relevant context for interpretation. At the same time, the technical aspects of the sideboard that
violated viewers' expectations function to suggest alternative contexts
in which it can be interpreted. The various uncommon technical elements of the sideboard incorporate objects or designs that refer to
contexts likely to be known to viewers and invite them to use those
contexts to select meanings for the furniture.

One context suggested is that of a downtown strip of bars, restau-
rants, theatres, video arcades, stores, and gas stations, characterized by
their industrial materials and paints, juxtapositions of color, disparate

graphics, giant illuminated and neon signs, and spraypainted graffiti. It brings to the interpretation of the sideboard a sense of infinite choices and possibilities—a sense that everything is available; adventure; and a night on the town that includes a touch of raunchiness. The context of the child's world of play is also referenced in the sideboard through the incorporation of the red, green, and black blocks—the child's toys— and the plastic laminate—a material likely to appear in a child's room. These contexts suggest that the seriousness and status usually associated with home furnishings should be replaced by the qualities of adventure, exploration, joy, lightheartedness, and fun.

Through the associations viewers are encouraged to make between novel technical elements in the sideboard and familiar contexts, they are provided with means for interpreting the piece in a positive manner. The introduction of the contexts of the strip and childhood play into the *Beverly* sideboard suggests that viewers are to reference, in combination, the vitality of the strip and the joy of the child's play. Associated with these contexts, the sideboard appeals in its reminder of contexts in which viewers once spent a great deal of time—days spent in play as a child and nights spent exploring the strip as an adolescent and young adult. Both are contexts in which viewers relished the discovery of the world and its infinite possibilities. But the sideboard pushes viewers beyond simple nostalgia for their earlier ways of living and asks that they question the routine, repetitive ways in which they currently live. It asks viewers to become subversive agents, transforming their humdrum, everyday routines into deliberate new ways of living that incorporate the adventure and joy that have been lost.

Valley Curtain

Christo's *Valley Curtain* provides an image framed in the context of the visual arts with which to illustrate the hypothesis of how appeal is constructed in visual images. Bulgarian-born artist Christo [Javacheff] is known for art works in which he drapes or wraps common objects. He has wrapped Chicago's Museum of Contemporary Art in a dark brown tarp; covered a million square feet of coastal rocks with polypropylene near Sydney, Australia; erected twenty-four miles of white fence through the hills of Sonoma and Marin counties in California; wrapped three miles of paths in a park in Kansas City, Missouri, in nylon; and wrapped Florida's Biscayne Islands in hot pink polypropylene.

While any of Christo's projects could be used to illustrate my hypothesis, I have chosen his *Valley Curtain,* completed in 1972, which consisted of the hanging of an orange nylon curtain between the two mountainsides of Rifle Gap, seven miles north of Rifle, Colorado. The curtain hung from the top of the mountains down to the valley floor, broken only by a hole, 100 feet wide by 20 feet high, cut in the curtain to permit uninterrupted traffic flow on Highway 325, which lay in the curtain's path. The curtain was shredded (and the art work thus dismantled) twenty-seven hours after its unveiling by a freak forty-mile-per-hour wind.

Clearly, the technical novelty that is the trigger for the process I am describing is present in the *Valley Curtain.* A curtain hanging across a valley is uncommon: "Billowing in the midst of a country so majestic, yet so wild and craggy, stood this perfectly clean, perfectly manufactured, orange nylon curtain. It was mind-boggling."[35] The technical novelty is produced primarily through its huge size; the curtain measured 1,250 feet across and 200 feet long. Wonderment at the process used to construct and hang the curtain is a second source of novelty. These technical aspects of the curtain generate surprise and wonderment for viewers; they also confuse. How are viewers to interpret a curtain between two mountains? Certainly, a context of the wilderness is not appropriate, even though the object appears in that environment; the curtain is foreign to the mountains and trees that surround it.

Connotations referenced by the curtain provide guidelines for viewers about how to interpret the work. A number of contexts are suggested by associations generated by various aspects of the curtain. It is in the shape of a curtain and constructed of nylon, suggesting a shower curtain in a bathroom or home setting—a comfortable, private, interior space. Even a Halloween context is suggested both by the bright orange color and the smile-like shape, referencing the gaping smile of a jack-o-lantern. Interpreted in these familiar contexts, connected with comforts of the home and childhood fun, the curtain becomes nonthreatening. Another way in which the curtain may be read is through a framework of adventure. The orange color and the nylon fabric recall parachutes and life vests, suggesting that adventure, risk, and danger may be appropriate interpretive codes in the contexts suggested by these associations. The curtain shape also may generate images of a theatre, where the audience waits expectantly for the curtain to rise.

Associated with the contexts of home, childhood holidays, adventure, and entertainment, the *Valley Curtain* becomes familiar or at least knowable to viewers. The foreignness suggested when viewers attempt to interpret it within an art context disappears. The introduction of such notions as adventure and drama into viewers' interpretations of the *Valley Curtain* encourages them to see the curtain as fun, dramatic, invigorating, and stimulating.

Pool Room in Graceland   *issue of intentionality*

Elvis Presley's home in Memphis, Tennessee, which opened to the public after his death in 1977, offers a vast array of visual images for analysis: the exterior of the house and its landscaping; the carport with several of Presley's automobiles; the interior rooms of the house; various exhibitions of memorabilia in the house and souvenir shops; the rock wall around the house covered with messages from fans; and the Meditation Gardens, where Presley and his relatives are buried. While touring Graceland, I was struck particularly by my positive response to one room, the pool room, and I will use it as my third sample in support of the hypothesis of how appeal is constructed in visual images.

Centered in the room is a large pool table with a light blue playing surface and bright red sides. The carpet in the room is a bright royal blue. Above the pool table are two stained-glass lamps, patterned in a leaf-and-floral design in yellow, blue, and green. An odd assortment of furniture rings the walls of the room—bright red Naugahyde chairs, dressers and tables in the French provincial style, and ordinary, block-style sofas in a bold, patterned fabric of red, blue, and yellow. The major feature of the room is the fabric that completely covers all four walls and the ceiling of the room—the same fabric with which the sofas are covered. The fabric covering alone would be visually stunning, but it is made more so because it is pleated. Even folds only a few inches wide run vertically along the walls; on the ceiling, the pleats come together in a circle in the center of the ceiling.

In the pool room, the fabric is the element of technical novelty to which viewers are immediately drawn. The fabric signals that viewers are not to interpret the pool room in the expected pool-room contexts. Inappropriate is the casual, dark, smoky, perhaps dirty bar, where patrons huddle around the pool table, beer in hand. Equally inappropriate is the dank basement of a suburban home, where family members and friends infrequently and indifferently shoot a few games for casual amusement. The fabric surprise not only tells viewers what contexts are irrelevant to their interpretation of the room but compels them to wonder who devised the decorating scheme, how the pleats are held in the fabric, and how the fabric is attached to the walls and ceilings. Appreciation of the technical skill needed to accomplish the effect is part of viewers' responses to the room.

Interest in the technique of the fabric covering encourages viewers to attempt to make sense of the technique and thus the entire room— to discover an appropriate context in which to interpret them. The fabric itself provides the clue: it suggests the elaborate garden tents of eighteenth- and nineteenth-century Europe as well as the tents of the Great Gatsby and garden parties from U.S. cultural heritage. The yards of fabric enfold viewers, closing them off from the external world, creating a special world of richness, elegance, and elitism.

The fabric covering not only suggests a new interpretive context for the pool room but diminishes the impact of the elements that are incongruous with the fabric. The pool room's chairs are made of cheap and low-class Naugahyde. The royal blue of the carpet suggests an effort at communicating elegance by someone who doesn't know elegance and only is able to imitate its surface details. The apparently stained-glass lamp shades very well may be plastic. But these factors diminish in importance for viewers and are irrelevant to their interpretation of the room because of the technical novelty of the fabric. Viewers are guided to focus on the richness, taste, civility, and extravagant consumption associated with high-class, cultured social events and to use such associations to emancipate them from their routine, everyday, and middle-class lives. The pool room becomes, in viewers' interpretations, truly a room fit for the king.

EXTENDING THE HYPOTHESIS

The three examples of the *Beverly* sideboard, the *Valley Curtain*, and Elvis Presley's pool room have illustrated the features that I propose contribute to the construction of appeal in a visual image—technical novelty, decontextualization, and references to new interpretive contexts. I see the hypothesis I have proposed as only a bare outline for understanding the process of visual appeal, but it constitutes a starting place for scholars in speech communication who wish to explore this process. I would like to see the hypothesis extended in a number of areas so that it is able to describe the complexity of the construction of appeal in visual imagery.

Research needs to be done to test the hypothesis. While the hypothesis explains the process of appeal in the visual images I examined, its application to other images will suggest whether it provides a relevant and useful explanation of the processes in other situations. In particular, images that show how the hypothesis accounts for lack of appeal of images need to be analyzed. The jungle room in Graceland provides one such example. A family room of sorts, this room includes a fake waterfall, furniture covered with fuzzy fabric, and lacquered burl tables. The room as an image fails to meet a stipulated feature of the hypothesis: the connotations suggested by the uncommon technical dimensions of the fuzzy fabric and burl wood do not elicit connotations that have positive associations for most viewers. The fabric and the tables suggest polyester, cheapness, and tackiness. This image, then, disappoints—it neither intrigues nor attracts viewers. Exploration of other such examples where images fail to create appeal will be particularly useful in refining and modifying the hypothesis.

The hypothesis needs to be extended, as well, so that the process by which appeal is constructed can be explained in other types of visual images. The hypothesis applies to visual images that are limited in important ways—are unaccompanied by verbal text and have a visual rather than a verbal focus, for example. Many types of images are not covered by the hypothesis, and a delineation of various types of images, perhaps on a continuum from diagrams to abstract art, with a detailing of the differences in the processes of appeal involved, is needed.

The relationship between the features of the process I have described and other characteristics of images needs to be pursued in an extension of the hypothesis. A start can be made in this area by proposing relationships on the basis of the literature that offers explanations of other aspects of visual images. Questions useful to investigate in this way, for example, might be: How does style relate to the process of visual appeal? Are different processes involved when images differ stylistically? Style is only one of the issues that have been explored in other disciplines concerning the nature and function of visual symbols; connection and integration of the literature of those disciplines on such issues will turn the bare outline that is the current hypothesis into a more useful explanatory device.

it's argued

The audience is not taken into account in the current hypothesis, and inquiry into the role of the audience in the process of visual appeal is vital. In the hypothesis, I simply <u>assume</u> that how I view an image is how others view it and that what is appealing to me appeals to all viewers. What is needed is an exploration of the requirements or conditions that must be met by an audience in order for the image to be seen as appealing. Is there, for example, a particular level of visual literacy that the hypothesis requires of viewers if appeal is to occur? Is knowledge of particular cultural contexts necessary? How does the hypothesis account for the cultural diversity that exists among potential viewers of an image? What is the role of personal taste in this process?

I would like to see an exploration of the history and sources of the features that the hypothesis suggests characterize visual appeal. My suspicion is that the process described by the hypothesis is a relatively recent one. The element of technical novelty as the trigger feature seems to be an element that would not necessarily have characterized visual images even half a century ago; it now seems required perhaps because of the visual technical effects to which contemporary viewers are accustomed through the mass media. Have the mass media—particularly television—created as a requirement for visual appeal technical novelty? Are contemporary viewers no longer able to be influenced by the commonplace? Does appeal result only from the spectacular, the uncommon, and the exceptional? If so, what are the implications for cultural change in the construction of visual appeal, and how should the changes that have occurred be evaluated?

novel?

The research area involved in the study of the process by which appeal is constructed in visual images is vast. Recognition of its scope almost seems to trivialize the contribution I have attempted to make in this essay because I have described only a small part of the process by which appeal is constructed in visual images. I hope, however, that the hypothesis I have formulated will serve as a starting point for others who recognize that our current rhetorical theory is largely inarticulate about visual symbols and who want to help it address both verbal and visual symbols.

Notes on Contributors

Ann E. Burnette is Assistant Professor of Speech Communication, Southwest Texas State University, where she teaches and conducts research in rhetorical criticism. Her doctoral dissertation, currently in progress, examines the rhetoric of "massive resistance" employed by segregationists in response to the civil rights movement during the 1950s.

Thomas B. Farrell is Professor of Communication Studies, Northwestern University, and a longtime colleague of Professor Griffin. His research focuses on rhetorical theory and criticism. He is the author of numerous awardwinning essays in communication journals and a book, *Norms of Rhetorical Culture*, published by Yale University Press. He received the Speech Communication Association's Woolbert Award for research that has stood the test of time.

Royce E. Flood is Professor of Speech Communication at Butler University. His master's and doctoral degrees are from Northwestern. He served as director of debate at Butler and over the past decade has developed interests in general education and film studies. Among his publications are several texts on public speaking and debate. His research interests focus on midwestern public address (specifically such figures as David Crockett and Elihu Washburne) and on film history, especially the American studio period of the 1930s.

Sonja K. Foss is Associate Professor of Communication at Ohio State University. Her research and teaching areas are contemporary rhetorical theory and rhetorical criticism, with specialties in the application of feminist perspectives to communication and the study of the visual image as rhetoric. She is the coauthor of *Contemporary Perspectives on Rhetoric* and *Women Speak*. Professor Griffin directed her dissertation about the debate on the Equal Rights Amendment.

Charles J. G. Griffin is Associate Professor of Rhetoric and Communication, Kansas State University. In addition to his interest in the rhetoric of social movements, his research interests include the rhetoric of religion in America and the rhetoric of the presidency. He has published previously in *Quarterly*

225

Journal of Speech, Communication Studies, and the *Southern Speech Communication Journal.*

D. Ray Heisey is Professor and Director, School of Communication Studies, Kent State University. His teaching and research interests include history and criticism of public address, with special attention to presidential rhetoric and the discourse of world leaders in the context of cultural conflicts. Recent publications include essays on the Iranian revolution and the Iran-Contra affair. He completed his doctoral dissertation under Professor Griffin's guidance in 1964.

John Lee Jellicorse is Dean of the School of Communication at Hong Kong Baptist College. His doctoral dissertation was completed under Professor Griffin's supervision. After serving on the faculty at Northwestern, where he was promoted to Associate Professor in 1968, he has spent his career as an administrator and curriculum developer, including fourteen years as Head of the Department of Communication and Theatre at the University of North Carolina at Greensboro. In addition to articles on Whitman, Jellicorse has published extensively on administrative and curricular issues in the field of communication.

Thomas F. Mader is Associate Professor of Communications at Hunter College of the City University of New York, where he teaches courses in critical thinking, rhetorical criticism, and interpersonal communication. He is co-author of *Understanding One Another: Communicating Interpersonally* and of an essay in the *Handbook of Rhetorical and Communication Theory.* His research on the cultural implications of rhetorical sensitivity has taken him to exchange professorships at the University of Puerto Rico and the Lehman-Hiroshima Center in Chiyoda, Japan. He remembers the day Lee Griffin gave him back a paper on Martin Buber and casually remarked, "I think you'd find Kenneth Burke worth reading."

Edward Schiappa is Associate Professor of Communication at Purdue University, where he teaches and conducts research in classical and contemporary rhetorical theory. His work has appeared in such journals as *American Journal of Philology, Rhetoric Review, Quarterly Journal of Speech, Philosophy and Rhetoric,* and *Communication Monographs.* He is the author of *Protagoras and Logos: A Study in Greek Philosophy and Rhetoric* (University of South Carolina Press, 1991), and is currently working on *The Disciplining of Discourse: Rhetoric and Dialectic in Ancient Greece.* Schiappa's doctoral dissertation, which won a Dissertation Award from the Speech Communication Assocation, was one of the last supervised by Professor Griffin before his retirement.

David Waite is Professor and Head of the Department of Speech Communication, Butler University. From 1966 to 1973 Professor Griffin stimulated and encouraged his interest in nineteenth-century American public address, especially the antislavery movement. Additional research interests include business and professional speaking and the American comic book. He is the coauthor of *Public Speaking: A Rhetorical Approach* and *The Business and Professional Communicator: Theory and Applications.*

David Zarefsky is Dean of the School of Speech and Professor of Communication Studies, Northwestern University. He teaches and conducts research in argumentation and the history of American political discourse. Among his publications are *President Johnson's War on Poverty: Rhetoric and History* and *Lincoln, Douglas, and Slavery: In the Crucible of Public Debate,* both of which won the Winans-Wichelns Award of the Speech Communication Association. He is the 1993 President of the SCA. His dissertation was completed under Professor Griffin's direction in 1974.

◆　　◆　　◆

NOTES

THE BEGINNINGS OF GREEK RHETORICAL THEORY

1. George A. Kennedy, *Classical Rhetoric and Its Christian and Secular Tradition from Ancient to Modern Times* (Chapel Hill: University of North Carolina Press, 1980), 6. For the variety of cultures demonstrating self-conscious oratory, see Maurice Bloch, *Political Language and Oratory in Traditional Society* (London: Academic Press, 1975). On the early dating of Greek oratory, see Walter Donlan, "The Dark Age Chiefdoms and the Emergence of Public Argument," Paper presented at the annual Speech Communication Association Convention in New Orleans, LA, November, 1988.

2. An important exception is Thomas Cole's new work, *The Origins of Rhetoric in Ancient Greece* (Baltimore: Johns Hopkins University Press, 1991).

3. Theresa Enos, "The Course in Classical Rhetoric: Definition, Development, Direction," *Rhetoric Society Quarterly* 19 (1989): 45–48. As Michael Gagarin recently noted, Kennedy is "the most important contemporary scholar of Greek rhetoric writing in English" ("The Nature of Proofs in Antiphon," *Classical Philology* 85 [1990]: 23 n. 3).

4. Robert J. Connors, [Review of] *"The Muse Learns to Write* By Eric A. Havelock," *The Quarterly Journal of Speech* 74 (1988): 379–81.

5. Eric A. Havelock, *The Greek Concept of Justice* (Cambridge: Harvard University Press, 1982), 2. I discuss criticisms and attenuations of Havelock's and Ong's treatment of the cognitive effects of literacy in chapter two of *Protagoras and Logos: A Study in Early Greek Philosophy and Rhetoric* (Columbia: University of South Carolina Press, 1991).

6. Walter J. Ong, *Orality and Literacy: The Technologizing of the Word* (London: Methuen, 1982), 39.

7. Havelock, *Greek Concept,* 2.

8. Eric A. Havelock, *Preface to Plato* (Cambridge: Harvard University Press, 1963), 197–233.

9. See Ong, 53–57.

10. Robert J. Connors, "Greek Rhetoric and the Transition from Orality," *Philosophy and Rhetoric* 19 (1986): 38–65.

11. Eric A. Havelock, *The Literate Revolution in Greece and Its Cultural Consequences* (Princeton: Princeton University Press, 1982), 224.

228

12. Richard Rorty, "The Historiography of Philosophy: Four Genres," *Philosophy in History: Essays on the Historiography of Philosophy,* ed. Richard Rorty, J. B. Schneewind, and Quentin Skinner (Cambridge: Cambridge University Press, 1984), 63. See also Stephen Makin, "How Can We Find Out What Ancient Philosophers Said?" *Phronesis* 33 (1988): 121–32.

13. Eric A. Havelock, "The Linguistic Task of the Presocratics," in *Language and Thought in Early Greek Philosophy,* ed. Kevin Robb (La Salle, Ill.: The Hegeler Institute, 1983), 57.

14. Havelock, *Literate Revolution,* chapter 11; Havelock, "Linguistic Task."

15. Havelock, "Linguistic Task," 8, emphasis added. See also Havelock, *Preface to Plato,* 300–301.

16. Kennedy, *Classical Rhetoric,* chapters 1 through 4.

17. Edward Schiappa, "Did Plato Coin *Rhētorikē?*" *American Journal of Philology* 111 (1990): 457–70. See also Edward Schiappa, "*Rhētorikē:* What's in a Name? Toward a Revised History of Early Greek Rhetorical Theory," *Quarterly Journal of Speech* 78 (1992): 1–15.

18. Thomas S. Kuhn, *The Essential Tension* (Chicago: University of Chicago Press, 1977), 165–77.

19. Kennedy, *Classical Rhetoric,* 18–19.

20. D. A. G. Hinks, "Tisias and Corax and the Invention of Rhetoric," *Classical Quarterly* 34 (1940): 61–69; D. L. Clark, *Rhetoric in Greco-Roman Education* (N.Y.: Columbia University Press, 1957), 25; George A. Kennedy, *The Art of Persuasion in Greece* (Princeton: Princeton University Press, 1963), 58–61; Donald C. Bryant, *Ancient Greek and Roman Rhetoricians* (Columbia, Mo.: Artcraft Press, 1968), 30–31; W. K. C. Guthrie, *The Sophists* (Cambridge: Cambridge University Press, 1971), 178–79; James J. Murphy, *A Synoptic History of Classical Rhetoric* (N.Y.: Random House, 1972), 6–7.

21. A. W. Verrall, "Korax and Tisias," *Journal of Philology* 9 (1880): 197–210; Bromley Smith, "Corax and Probability," *The Quarterly Journal of Speech* 7 (1921): 15; R. C. Jebb, *The Attic Orators from Antiphon to Isaeos,* vol. 1, 2d ed. (N.Y.: Russell & Russell, 1893, reprinted 1962), cxxi.

22. Stanley Wilcox, "The Scope of Early Rhetorical Instruction," *Harvard Studies in Classical Philology* 46 (1942): 127. See F. Hiller von Gaertringen, ed., *Inscriptiones Graecae,* vol. 1, ed. minor (Berlin: De Gruyter, 1924), 45, line 21; Marcus N. Tod, ed., *Greek Historical Inscriptions,* new ed. (Chicago: Ares Publishers, 1985), 88–90. For the origins of *rhētorikē* in Plato's *Gorgias,* see Schiappa, "Did Plato Coin *Rhētorikē?*"

23. H. N. Fowler's translation of Plato, *Phaedrus* 267a6–b2 (Cambridge, Mass.: Loeb Classical Library, 1914).

24. G. J. De Vries, *A Commentary on the Phaedrus of Plato* (Amsterdam: Adolf M. Hakkert, 1969), 222–23.

25. 273c7–9, translated by Fowler.

26. *Panegryicus* ¶8, trans. George Norlin, *Isocrates,* vol. 1 (Cambridge, Mass.: Loeb Classical Library, 1928).

27. Ronna Burger, *Plato's Phaedrus: A Defense of a Philosophical Art of*

Writing (University: University of Alabama Press, 1980), 115–26; R. L. Howland, "The Attack on Isocrates in the *Phaedrus*," *Classical Quarterly* (1937): 151–59.

28. H. G. Liddell and R. Scott, *A Greek-English Lexicon,* 9th ed., revised and augmented by H. S. Jones (Oxford: Clarendon Press, 1940), s.v. *eikos,* 484–85.

29. On the conceptual significance of the neuter singular construction see Havelock, "Linguistic Task," 55; Bruno Snell, *The Discovery of the Mind,* trans. T. G. Rosenmeyer (Oxford: Basil Blackwell, 1953), chapter 10.

30. See [Anaximenes] *Rhetoric to Alexander* 1433b33–37; 1445a37–38.

31. K. H. Waters, *Herodotus the Historian: His Problems, Methods and Originality* (London: Croom Helm, 1985). On the scarcity of books in the late fifth century B.C. see E. G. Turner, *Athenian Books in the Fifth and Fourth Centuries B.C.,* 2d ed. (London: H. K. Lewis, 1977); Rosalind Thomas, *Oral Tradition and Written Record in Classical Athens* (Cambridge: Cambridge University Press, 1989).

32. Aristotle, *Rhetoric* 1402a17–28, trans. George A. Kennedy, *Aristotle: On Rhetoric* (N.Y.: Oxford University Press, 1991), 210.

33. Tony M. Lentz, *Orality and Literacy in Hellenic Greece* (Carbondale: Southern Illinois University Press, 1989), chapter 6.

34. Havelock, "Linguistic Task," 69–70.

35. Harold Cherniss, *Aristotle's Criticism of Presocratic Philosophy* (N.Y.: Octagon Books, 1935). See also J. B. McDiarmid, "Theophrastus on the Presocratic Causes," *Harvard Studies in Classical Philology* 61 (1953): 85–156. For a defense of Aristotle see W. K. C. Guthrie, "Aristotle as Historian," *Journal of Hellenic Studies* 77 (1957): 35–41.

36. Edward Schiappa, *Protagoras and Logos,* 103–16.

37. C. J. Classen, "Aristotle's Picture of the Sophists," in *The Sophists and their Legacy,* ed. G. B. Kerferd (Wiesbaden: Franz Steiner, 1981), 7–24.

38. Aristotle, *Sophistical Refutations* 183b25–34, translation adapted from that by W. A. Pickard-Cambridge in Jonathan Barnes, ed., *The Complete Works of Aristotle,* vol. 1 (Princeton: Princeton University Press, 1984).

39. For Thrasymachus see the fragments collected and translated in R. K. Sprague, *The Older Sophists* (Columbia: University of South Carolina Press, 1972). For Theodorus see Kennedy, *Art of Persuasion,* 58–61.

40. 2.2.6, translated by H. M. Hubbell, *Cicero, Vol. II* (Cambridge, Mass.: Loeb Classical Library, 1949), 171.

41. Ibid., vii; George A. Kennedy, *The Art of Rhetoric in the Roman World* (Princeton: Princeton University Press, 1972): 103–10.

42. A. E. Douglas, "The Aristotelian *Synagōgē Technōn* after Cicero *Brutus* 46–48," *Latomus* 14 (1955): 536–39.

43. Ibid., though Douglas's criticism is more with ¶48 than ¶46.

44. Kennedy, *Art of Rhetoric,* 247.

45. Richard Leo Enos, *The Literate Mode of Cicero's Legal Rhetoric* (Carbondale: Southern Illinois University Press, 1988), 20. See also Neal Wood, *Cicero's Social and Political Thought* (Berkeley: University of California Press,

1988), 53. Wood's chapter 3 makes clear that Cicero was not a democratic reformer, however.

46. *Institutio Oratoria* 3.1.8; cf. 2.17.7. Translated by H. E. Butler, *Quintilian* (Cambridge, Mass.: Loeb Classical Library, 1921).

47. Stanley Wilcox, "Corax and the *Prolegomena*," *American Journal of Philology* 64 (1943): 1–23.

48. Christianus Walz, *Rhetores Graeci* (Stuttgart: J. G. Cottae, 9 volumes, 1832–1836); Hugo Rabe, *Prolegomenon Sylloge, Rhetores Graeci*, XIV (Leipzig: Teubner, 1931).

49. See Rabe, #4, p. 245, translation by Vincent Farenga, "Periphrasis on the Origin of Rhetoric," *Modern Language Notes* 94 (1979): 1035.

50. Wilcox, "Corax and the *Prolegomena*," 19.

51. Ibid., 20–23. Wilcox's logic is as follows: (1) Dionysius of Halicarnassus and Diodorus Siculus both relate the story of Gorgias's first visit to Athens. (2) Since Dionysus says that his source is Timaeus, Timaeus must also be Diodorus's source. (3) Since Timaeus the Sicilian glorified his homeland by recording and embellishing the Gorgias story, it is likely he would have recorded the story of Corax and Tisias. (4) Since Diodorus's account of Sicilian history is similar to Rabe #4, Timaeus must be the source for both. Steps 2 and 3 in the argument are obviously non sequiturs. Step 4 would tend to disprove the assertion Timaeus was the basis of Rabe #4 since Diodorus does not mention Corax or the invention of rhetoric—a remarkable omission by a proud fellow Sicilian historian.

52. "Mit Korax und Tisias hat sie gar nichts zu tun." Hermann Mutschmann, "Die Älteste Definition der Rhetorik," *Hermes* 53 (1918): 443. See E. R. Dodds, *Plato's Gorgias* (Oxford: Clarendon Press, 1959), 203.

53. Rabe #17, p. 270, translated by Farenga, "Periphrasis on the Origin of Rhetoric," 1035–36.

54. See Wilcox, "The Scope of Early Rhetorical Instruction"; "Corax and the *Prolegomena*," D. A. G. Hinks, "Tria Genera Causarum," *Classical Quarterly* 30 (1936): 170–76; George A. Kennedy, "The Earliest Rhetorical Handbooks," *American Journal of Philology* 80 (1959): 169–78.

55. For Theodorus see Plato, *Phaedrus* 266d7–e6. For Protagoras see H. Diels and W. Kranz, *Die Fragmente der Vorsokratiker*, 6th ed. (Dublin/Zurich: Weidmann, 1951), 80 A1. Diels and Kranz hereafter cited as *DK*.

56. *DK* 87 A2: Translated by J. S. Morrison in Sprague, *Older Sophists*, 115.

57. Eric A. Havelock, *The Liberal Temper in Greek Politics* (New Haven: Yale University Press, 1957), chapter 8.

58. Richard Garner, *Law and Society in Classical Athens* (N.Y.: St. Martin's Press, 1987); Martin Ostwald, *From Popular Sovereignty to the Sovereignty of Law: Law, Society, and Politics in Fifth-Century Athens* (Berkeley: University of California Press, 1986). Though it is beyond the immediate scope of this essay, I believe the better candidates for the beginnings of the technical tradition are found in the fourth century B.C., and would include Aristotle's influential *Rhetoric*.

59. Kennedy, *Classical Rhetoric,* 19. On the subject of sophistic *technai,* see Cole, *Origins of Rhetoric,* 71–112.

60. Kennedy, *Classical Rhetoric,* chapter 3.

61. Ibid., 25.

62. Kennedy, *Art of Persuasion,* 26, emphasis added.

63. In Sprague, *Older Sophists,* 70–71.

64. C. J. Classen, "The Study of Language Amongst Socrates' Contemporaries," *The Proceedings of the African Classical Association* 2 (1959): 43, emphasis added.

65. Kennedy, "Earliest Rhetorical Handbooks," 170.

66. B. A. Kimball, *Orators and Philosophers: A History of the Ideal Liberal Education* (N.Y.: Columbia University Teachers College Press, 1986), 17.

67. G. B. Kerferd, ed., *The Sophists and Their Legacy* (Wiesbaden: Franz Steiner, 1981); G. B. Kerferd, *The Sophistic Movement* (Cambridge: Cambridge University Press, 1981).

68. It should be kept in mind that use of the word *philosopher* to denote a specific group of serious thinkers originates with Plato. Prior to that time one with wisdom (*sophia*) would have been called a sophist. See Havelock, "Linguistic Task."

69. Havelock, *Preface to Plato,* 290.

70. Ibid., 285–86.

71. Ostwald, 213–29.

72. Schiappa, "Did Plato Coin *Rhētorikē?*"

73. Kerferd, *Sophistic Movement,* 83.

74. Havelock, "Linguistic Task," 80.

75. Havelock, *Preface to Plato,* 29.

76. Ibid., 43.

77. See note 14 above.

78. W. K. C. Guthrie, *A History of Greek Philosophy,* vol. 4 (Cambridge: Cambridge University Press, 1975), 227; C. C. W. Taylor, *Plato, Protagoras: Translated with Notes* (Oxford: Clarendon Press, 1976), 141–48.

79. Taylor, 141.

80. *DK* 80 A25, translated in Sprague, *The Older Sophists,* 16.

81. *DK* 22 B57. See Charles H. Kahn, *The Art and Thought of Heraclitus* (Cambridge: Cambridge University Press, 1979).

82. See Isocrates, *Panathenaicus* ¶18.

83. See Schiappa, *Protagoras and Logos, passim.*

84. *DK* 80 A1. For thoughtful treatments of the "man-as-measure" fragment, see Guthrie, *The Sophists,* 188–92; Mario Untersteiner, *The Sophists,* trans. K. Freeman (Oxford: Basil Blackwell, 1954), 77–91; Lazlo Versenyi, "Protagoras' Man-Measure Fragment," *American Journal of Philology* 83 (1962): 178–84.

85. Michael Gagarin, "Plato and Protagoras" (Ph.D. diss., Yale University, 1968), 122; Scott Austin, *Parmenides: Being, Bounds, and Logic* (New Haven: Yale University Press, 1986), 120; Guthrie, *The Sophists,* 47; Kerferd, *Sophistic Movement,* 92.

86. For Protagoras see J. S. Morrison, "The Place of Protagoras in Athenian

Public Life," *Classical Quarterly* 35 (1941): 1–16; for Parmenides see E. L. Minar, "Parmenides and the World of Seeming," *American Journal of Philology,* 70 (1949): 41–53.

87. Charles H. Kahn, *Anaximander and the Origins of Greek Cosmology* (N.Y.: Columbia University Press, 1960), 119–65.

88. See, for example, "Breaths," in W. H. S. Jones, *Hippocrates,* vol. 2 (Cambridge: Loeb Classical Library, 1923), 229.

89. A. T. Cole, "The Relativism of Protagoras," *Yale Classical Studies,* 22 (1972): 19–45.

90. Lane Cooper, *The Rhetoric of Aristotle* (Englewood Cliffs, N.J.: Prentice-Hall, 1932), 177.

91. See O'Brien's translation of the weaker/stronger *logoi* fragment in Sprague, *Older Sophists,* 13; Cole, "Relativism of Protagoras"; G. B. Kerferd, "Protagoras," in *The Encyclopedia of Philosophy,* vol. 6 (N.Y.: Macmillan, 1967), 506.

92. Kennedy, *Classical Rhetoric,* 31.

93. Charles H. Kahn, "The Greek Verb 'To Be' and the Concept of Being," *Foundations of Language* 2 (1966): 245–65; Charles H. Kahn, *The Verb 'Be' in Ancient Greek* (Dordrecht, Holland: D. Reidel, 1973).

94. Kahn, *Verb 'Be' in Ancient Greek,* 366–70.

95. Kerferd, *Sophistic Movement,* 93, based on DK 82 B3.

96. Ibid., 93–99.

97. Charles P. Segal, "Gorgias and the Psychology of the Logos," *Harvard Studies in Classical Philology* 66 (1962): 104.

98. Edward Schiappa, "Neo-Sophistic Rhetorical Criticism or the Historical Reconstruction of Sophistic Doctrines?" *Philosophy and Rhetoric* 22 (1990): 192–217.

99. My thanks to David Zarefsky for his helpful criticisms of earlier drafts of this essay. Any remaining deficiencies are entirely my responsibility. This paper extends ideas originally developed in my dissertation at Northwestern University, *Protagoras and Logos: A Study in Early Greek Rhetorical Theory* (1989), directed by Leland M. Griffin. A revised version of the dissertation has been published as *Protagoras and Logos: A Study in Greek Philosophy and Rhetoric* (Columbia: University of South Carolina Press, 1991). Professor Griffin's support and enthusiasm for my sometimes heretical work was always there when I needed it the most. My gratitude cannot be expressed in words.

RHETORIC IN DEFENSE OF THE DISPOSSESSED

1. Stuart Stiffler, "Davy Crockett: The Genesis of Heroic Myth," *Tennessee Historical Quarterly* 16, no. 2 (1957):134.

2. Kenneth S. Lynn, *Mark Twain and Southwestern Humor* (Boston: Little, Brown, 1959), 36–37; quoted in Robert G. Gunderson, "The Southern Whigs," in *Oratory in the Old South,* ed. Waldo Braden (Baton Rouge: Louisiana State University Press, 1970), 115.

3. Jackson [Tenn.] *Southern Statesman,* February 12, 1831.

4. Richard Hofstadter, *Anti-Intellectualism in American Life* (New York: Alfred A. Knopf, 1970), 164.

5. Robert V. Remini, *Andrew Jackson and the Course of American Democracy* (New York: Harper & Row, 1984), 252–53.

6. Vernon L. Parrington, *Main Currents in American Thought* (New York: Harcourt Brace & Company, 1927), 178.

7. Gunderson, 114–17.

8. Emma Lazarus, "The New Colossus," engraved on the base of the Statue of Liberty.

9. Robert H. Bremner, *From the Depths* (New York: New York University Press, 1956), 16.

10. See Thomas P. Jones, "The Public Lands of Tennessee," *Tennessee Historical Quarterly* 27 (September 1968): 13–36.

11. See Frederick Jackson Turner, *The Frontier in American History* (New York: Henry Holt & Co., 1920).

12. Samuel Cole Williams, *Beginnings of West Tennessee* (Johnson City, Tenn.: Watauga Press, 1930), 175.

13. Francis S. Philbrick, *The Rise of the West, 1754–1830* (New York: Harper & Row, 1965), 300.

14. Thomas P. Abernathy, *From Frontier to Plantation in Tennessee* (Chapel Hill: University of North Carolina Press, 1932), 236.

15. Williams, 175.

16. Ibid.

17. Joseph Gales and William W. Seaton, *Register of Debates in Congress,* V (Washington, 1831), 162.

18. For detailed accounts of Crockett's life see James A. Shackford, *David Crockett: The Man and the Legend* (Chapel Hill: University of North Carolina Press, 1956), and the series of articles by Stanley Folmsbee and Anna Catron in vols. 28–30 (1956–1958) of *East Tennessee Historical Society Publications.*

19. Shackford, 5.

20. David Crockett, *The Life of Davy Crockett* (New York: Signet, 1955), 25 (hereafter cited as *Life*). This is a modern one-volume compilation of Crockett's three autobiographical works.

21. Shackford, 22–23.

22. See note 4 above.

23. Gales and Seaton, *Register of Debates,* VI, i, 583.

24. Ibid., V, 163.

25. Ibid.

26. Ibid., VI, i, 583.

27. Ibid., V, 163.

28. Ibid., VI, i, 583.

29. Ibid., V, 163.

30. Ibid., 164.

31. Ibid., IV, ii, 2519.

32. Ibid.

33. Ibid., 2520.

34. Ibid., V, 162.

35. Ibid., IV, ii, 2520.

36. Ibid., V, 162.

37. Richard Hofstadter, *The Paranoid Style in American Politics and Other Essays* (New York: Vintage Books, 1967).

38. Charles U. Larson, *Persuasion: Reception and Responsibility,* 6th ed. (Belmont, Calif.: Wadsworth, 1992), 216.

39. Gales and Seaton, *Register of Debates,* V, 163.

40. Ibid., 164.

41. *Jackson* [Tenn.] *Gazette,* February 7, 1829.

42. *Jackson* [Tenn.] *Gazette,* March 21, 1829.

43. This concept is explored thoroughly by Daniel Katz in his article, "The Functional Approach to the Study of Attitudes," *Public Opinion Quarterly* 24 (1960): 163–204.

44. G. Thomas Goodnight and John Poulakos, "Conspiracy Rhetoric: From Pragmatism to Fantasy in Public Discourse," *Western Journal of Speech Communication* 45 (Fall 1981): 300.

45. Gales and Seaton, *Register of Debates,* V, 163.

46. Ibid.

47. David Crockett, *An Account of Colonel Crockett's Tour to the North and Down East* (Philadelphia: Cary & Hart, 1835), 151 (hereafter cited as *Tour*).

48. *Jackson* [Tenn.] *Gazette,* March 14, 1829.

49. For a compelling examination of this tradition in Southern society, see Edward L. Ayres, "Legacy of Violence," *American Heritage* 42, no. 6 (October 1991): 102–9.

NULLIFICATION IN VERMONT, 1844

1. *Vermont House Journals,* 1844, 27.

2. The most useful study of Union sentiment is Paul C. Nagel, *One Nation Indivisible: The Union in American Thought, 1776–1861* (New York: Oxford University Press, 1964).

3. Ernest G. Bormann, *Forerunners of Black Power: The Rhetoric of Abolition* (Englewood Cliffs, N.J.: Prentice Hall, 1971), 20–29.

4. George Campbell, *Republicanism* (Haverhill, N.H.: John R. Reding, 1840), 7–8; J. T. Marston, Montepelier *Vermont Patriot,* April 8, 1843. In Vermont newspapers of the period, use of page numbers is rare. Most political stories are found on page 2 or 3.

5. David Ludlum, *Social Ferment in Vermont, 1791–1850* (New York: AMS Press, 1966), 147–49.

6. Rowland T. Robinson, "Fifth Annual Report of the Anti-Slavery Society of Ferrisburgh and Vicinity," cited in Ludlum, *Social Ferment,* 174–75.

7. Wilbur H. Siebert, *Vermont's Antislavery and Underground Railroad Record* (Columbus, Ohio: Spahr and Glenn Co., 1937), 37–39; Anonymous

letter to the Middlebury *Free Press,* August 8, 1837, as quoted in Charles A. Morse, *William Slade: Congressional Career, 1831–43* (Master's thesis, University of Vermont, 1965), 27.

8. William Slade, *Speech of Mr. Slade, of Vermont, on the Right of Petition; the Power of Congress to Abolish Slavery and the Slave Trade in the District of Columbia; the Implied Faith of the North and South to Each Other in Forming the Constitution; and the Principles, Purposes and Prospects of Abolition* (Washington, D.C.: Gales and Seaton, 1840); Ludlum, *Social Ferment,* 175.

9. John Mattocks, letter to Theodore Weld, as quoted in Siebert, *Vermont's Antislavery Record,* 37–38.

10. *Vermont House Journals,* 1843, 22.

11. Bennington *Vermont Gazette,* October 24, 1843.

12. *Vermont House Journals,* 1843, 143.

13. Resolves of a meeting at Lunenberg printed in the Danville *North Star,* April 15, 1844; resolves of the Whig State Convention printed in the *Rutland Herald,* July 11, 1844.

14. Bennington *Vermont Gazette,* May 14, 1844; *Vermont Gazette,* July 30, 1844; *Augusta* (Maine) *Age,* as quoted in the *Vermont Gazette,* July 30, 1844; Danville *North Star,* August 19, 1844.

15. William Slade, letter to the New Haven (Connecticut) *Palladium,* March 26, 1842, as quoted in Ludlum, *Social Ferment,* 182–83.

16. Whig State Convention as quoted in the *Rutland Herald,* July 10, 1845.

17. Siebert, *Vermont's Antislavery Record,* 39.

18. R. L. Morrow, "The Liberty Party in Vermont," *New England Quarterly* 2 (April 1929): 243.

19. *Vermont House Journals,* 1844, 15–30. All subsequent quotations from this address are noted parenthetically.

20. Benjamin Labaree, *A Sermon on the Death of General Harrison, Delivered in Middlebury, Vermont, on the Day of the National Fast* (Middlebury, Vt.: E. Maxham, 1841), 22.

21. Ernest Lee Tuveson, *Redeemer Nation: The Idea of America's Millennial Role* (Chicago: University of Chicago Press, 1968), uses two terms to express this concept of Unionism: "New Rome" (96) and "New Israel" (312). Nagel uses the term "nation's triumph" (147).

22. George Perkins Marsh, *The Goths in New-England* (Middlebury, Vt.: J. Cobb, 1843), 39.

23. Vermont Domestic Missionary Society, *Twenty-Eighth Annual Report: With the Treasurer's Report, and the Minutes of the Annual Meeting at Middlebury, June 18, 1846* (Windsor, Vt.: Chronicle Press, 1846), 14.

24. "New Eden" or "New Eden-Sparta" is Tuveson's term (131–32); Nagel uses "liberty's harbinger" (147–73).

25. Nagel, 39.

26. E. P. Walton, "Congressional Speech," Irasburg *Orleans Independent Standard,* March 15, 1861.

27. William Slade, "Speech of William Slade at the Whig State Convention," *Rutland Herald,* August 1, 1844.

28. Slade, *Right of Petition*, 20–21.

29. Slade, "Speech at the Whig State Convention."

30. Danville *North Star*, November 4, 1844; Bennington *Vermont Gazette*, October 29, 1844; *Rutland Herald*, December 26, 1844; Montpelier *Vermont Patriot*, April 23, 1846.

31. Slade, *Right of Petition*, 21.

32. John Wheeler, *Address before the Porter Rhetorical Society* (Andover, Mass.: n.p., 1836), 7–8.

33. James R. Andrews, "Reflections of the National Character in American Rhetoric," *Quarterly Journal of Speech* 58 (October 1971): 317.

34. Vermont Antislavery Society, *Fourth Annual Report of the Vermont Antislavery Society* (Brandon, Vt.: W. G. Brown, 1838), 18–19.

35. Danville *North Star*, June 9, 1845.

36. See Kenneth Burke, *A Rhetoric of Motives* (New York: G. Braziller, 1955), 291–93: "The representatives of Babylon are members of an alien and menacing order. Rhetorically their perverseness offers some justification for continuing the torture" (293).

37. *Vermont House Journals*, 1845, 29.

38. William Slade, *Letters of Hon. William Slade upon Free Soil and the Presidency* (n.p., n.d.), 9.

39. Slade, *Letters*, 15.

40. Ludlum, *Social Ferment*, 198.

41. Montpelier *Vermont Patriot*, August 8, 1850; "Resolves of the Whig Convention," *Middlebury Register*, July 30, 1850; *Burlington Courier*, March 24, 1850.

42. *Vermont House Journal*, 1851, 24–26.

43. Montpelier *Green Mountain Freeman* and *Bellows Falls Gazette*, quoted in the *Burlington Courier*, April 3, 1851.

PERSUASION OF THE UNCONSCIOUS WILL

Travel assistance in conducting research for this essay was provided by Hong Kong Baptist College.

1. Whitman, as quoted by Horace L. Traubel, in *With Walt Whitman in Camden*, vol. 4, ed. Sculley Bradley (Philadelphia: University of Pennsylvania Press, 1953), 145 (hereafter cited as *WWWC*). In citations from this and similar works in which Whitman is directly quoted, quotation marks in the original are included in the citation.

2. Walt Whitman, *Comprehensive Reader's Edition of Leaves of Grass*, ed. Harold W. Blodgett and Sculley Bradley (New York: New York University Press, 1965), 563 (hereafter cited as *RLG*). See also Walt Whitman, *Prose Works 1892*, ed. Floyd Stovall, vol. 2 of *Collect and Other Prose* (New York: New York University Press, 1964), 713 (hereafter cited as *PW*).

3. "Walt Whitman[:] The Centennial Conference" (Conference brochure, 1991), 1.

4. The presentations were by James E. Miller, Jr., on "Whitman's Multitudinous Poetic Progeny," George Hutchinson on "The Whitman Legacy and the Harlem Renaissance," and Kenneth Price on "Whitman, Dos Passos, and 'Our Story Book Democracy.'" A session on "The Political Whitman" dealt with Whitman's political thought, but audience sympathy clearly was with M. Wynn Thomas's conclusion that Whitman was a "muddled figure" of interest not for his political ideas but as a "great poet."

5. For documentation of this phenomenon see John Lee Jellicorse, "The Poet as Persuader: A Rhetorical Explication of the Life and Writings of Walt Whitman" (Ph.D. diss., Northwestern University, 1967), vi–x (hereafter cited as Jellicorse).

6. *WWWC*, vol. 1 (Boston: Small, Maynard, 1906), 98.

7. *WWWC* 1:58.

8. *WWWC* 4:454.

9. Whitman, as quoted by William Roscoe Thayer, "Personal Recollections of Walt Whitman," *Scribner's* 65 (June 1919): 678. For a discussion of the differences between Whitman's approach and those of modern literary theories, and some of the distortions created when the latter are applied to the former, see John Lee Jellicorse, "Walt Whitman and Modern Literary Criticism," *American Transcendental Quarterly* 12 (Fall 1971): 4–11.

10. *WWWC* 4:41.

11. This is illustrated by Kenneth Burke's criticism of Whitman, which is esoteric and totally inaccurate from the standpoint of Whitman's clearly stated intentions. See especially "Policy Made Personal: Whitman's Verse and Prose—Salient Traits," in *Leaves of Grass One Hundred Years After,* ed. Milton Hindus (Stanford: Stanford University Press, 1955), 74–108. For a recent summary see William H. Rueckert, "Kenneth Burke's Encounters with Walt Whitman," *Walt Whitman Quarterly Review* 6 (Fall 1988): 61–90.

12. Walt Whitman, *Complete Writings of Walt Whitman,* ed. Richard Maurice Bucke, Thomas B. Harned, and Horace L. Traubel (New York: G. P. Putnam's Sons, 1902), 9:34 (hereafter cited as *CW*).

13. *WWWC* 4:4. See Jellicorse, vi–xi.

14. *PW* 2:475.

15. One of many examples of the heart/understanding/will mental philosophy concept common in Whitman's day, cited by Thomas C. Upham, *Mental Philosophy: Embracing the Three Departments of the Intellect, Sensibilities, and Will* (New York: Harper & Brothers, 1869), 1:55–57.

16. See, for example, Walt Whitman, *The Gathering of the Forces,* ed. Cleveland Rodgers and John Black (New York: G. P. Putnam's Sons, 1920), 2:11–12, 274, 290–91 (hereafter cited as *GF*). There are some striking similarities between Whitman's early concept of education and his later theory of persuasion, however. For a summary of his conception of "the psychology of learning" as revealed in his early editorials, see Florence B. Freedman, "'The Reporter's Lead Flies Swiftly,'" in Walt Whitman, *Walt Whitman Looks at the Schools,* ed. Florence B. Freedman (New York: Columbia University Press, 1950), 50–60 (hereafter cited as *Schools*).

17. Ricardo Quintana, "*The Deserted Village,* Its Logical and Rhetorical Elements," *College English* 26 (December 1964): 206.

18. Kate Sanborn, *Memories and Anecdotes* (New York: G. P. Putnam's Sons, 1915), 163.

19. See especially the 1847 notebook entries that begin with "Be simple and clear.—Be not occult." Walt Whitman, *The Uncollected Poetry and Prose of Walt Whitman,* ed. Emory B. Holloway (Garden City, N.Y.: Doubleday, Page & Co., 1921), 2:63–69 (hereafter cited as *UPP*).

20. This aspect of Whitman's endeavors was given special emphasis by his followers and disciples. See Jellicorse, 938, n. 7.

21. For commentary see, for example, Frank Thilly, *A History of Philosophy,* revised by Ledger Wood (New York: Henry Holt & Co., 1957), 86–87, 102, 194–99; Aristotle, *The Rhetoric of Aristotle,* trans. Lane Cooper (New York: D. Appleton & Co., 1932), 56–57, 8–9; M. H. Abrams, *The Mirror and the Lamp: Romantic Theory and the Critical Tradition* (New York: Oxford University Press, 1958), 157, 160–61, 171.

22. See Upham, 1:51, 54–60. Compare Richard Ohmann, "In Lieu of a New Rhetoric," *College English* 26 (October 1964): 17.

23. See, for example, Abrams, 158.

24. See, for example, Upham, 1:57–58, quoting Henry Home [Lord Kames].

25. John Locke concluded in *An Essay Concerning Human Understanding,* "And thus, by a due consideration, and examining any good proposed, it is in our power to raise our desires in a due proportion to the value of that good, whereby in its turn and place it may come to work upon the will and be pursued. For good, though appearing, and allowed ever so great, yet till it has raised desires in our minds, and thereby made us uneasy in its want, it reaches not our wills. . . ." (New York: Valentine Seaman, 1824), 1:239. And David Hume acknowledged, "IT [sic] seems evident, that reason, in a strict sense, as meaning the judgment of truth and falsehood, can never, of itself, be any motive to the will, and can have no influence but so far as it touches some passion or affection." *Four Dissertations* (London, 1756), 170 (spelling modernized). See also, for example, James Mackintosh, *The Miscellaneous Works of the Right Honourable Sir James Mackintosh,* ed. R. J. Mackintosh (Philadelphia: A. Hart, 1852), 131, 146, 122.

26. For elaboration see Dale C. Hesser, "The Religion of Walt Whitman" (Ph.D. diss., University of Kansas, 1957), 110–16.

27. See, for example, C. M. Bowra, *The Romantic Imagination* (New York: Oxford University Press, 1961), 1–24; Thilly, 285–383.

28. "Practical" reason is "practical," according to Kant, because it directly influences the will and determines behavior, but "Pure" reason can also be practical. Immanuel Kant, *Critique of Practical Reason and Other Works on The Theory of Ethics,* trans. Thomas Kingsmill Abbott, 6th ed. (New York: Longmans, Green & Co., 1909), 131; see also 182–84.

29. See, for example, Thilly, 146–55, 263–64, 381–83; and Bowra, 2–3, 8. For the Transcendentalists' view, see Stephen E. Whicher, "Transcenden-

talism," *Dictionary of World Literature,* ed. Joseph T. Shipley (New York: Philosophical Library, 1953), 423–24.

30. See, for example, Bowra, 24, 1, 7; Abrams, 101, 313, 21–26, 71; Thilly, 399. For specific examples drawn from William Hazlitt, Samuel Taylor Coleridge, Ralph Waldo Emerson, and Henry David Thoreau, see Jellicorse, 940–41.

31. See Abrams, 47–56, et passim.

32. See Bowra, 19, 22. For examples based on Kant and William Wordsworth, see Jellicorse, 941–42, n. 35.

33. See Douglas Ehninger, "Campbell, Blair, and Whately Revisited," *Southern Speech Journal* 28 (Spring 1963): 169–82.

34. One of the best discussions of the conviction-persuasion dichotomy remains that of Lester Thonssen and A. Craig Baird, *Speech Criticism* (New York: Ronald Press Co., 1948), 368–78. See also Ehninger, 174–75.

35. See Ehninger, 180–82.

36. A detailed but extremely biased summary of nineteenth-century anti-intellectualism is Richard Hofstadter's *Anti-Intellectualism in American Life* (New York: Knopf, 1964). Antirationalism and the anti-intellectualism that it encouraged produced good results as well as affronts to those who had college degrees. The list of "highbrow antirationalists" (Nietzsche, Sorel, Bergson, Emerson, Whitman, William James, Blake, D. H. Lawrence, and Hemingway) excluded from Hofstadter's study could be expanded to include most of the great American and British figures from John Adams (see, for example, MS. in *John Adams & the Prophets of Progress* by Zoltan Haraszti [Cambridge, Mass.: Harvard University Press, 1952], 72) to William Butler Yeats. See also Richard Ellmann, *The Identity of Yeats* (New York: Oxford University Press, 1954), 121; Abrams, 21.

37. See Bowra, 8–10; Abrams, 177–83. Re Samuel Taylor Coleridge, who made some of the most famous declarations of the primacy of the imagination, see James D. Boulger, *Coleridge as Religious Thinker* (New Haven, Conn.: Yale University Press, 1961), 2.

38. See, for example, Sir Philip Sidney, "The Defense of Poesie," in *Literary Criticism: Plato to Dryden,* ed. Allan H. Gilbert (Detroit: Wayne State University Press, 1962), 406–14.

39. See, for example, Abrams, 298–335; Bowra, 7; Percy Bysshe Shelley, "A Defence of Poetry," *English Romantic Poets,* ed. James Stephens, Edwin L. Beck, and Royall H. Snow (New York: American Book Company, 1952), 526–27.

40. See especially Ralph Waldo Emerson, "The Poet," in *The Complete Works of Ralph Waldo Emerson,* ed. Waldo Emerson Forbes (New York: Houghton Mifflin, 1903–4), 3:3–42; "Eloquence," 7:61–100; "Eloquence," 8:111–33. See also Abrams, 21, 29.

41. This tendency is less clear in the major rhetorics (Campbell, Blair, and Whately) than in popular rhetorics and histories of oratory. For a sample of the praise of *vis oratoris,* see E. L. Magoon, *Living Orators of America* (Cincinnati: H. W. Derby & Co., 1849), and *Orators of the American Revolution,* 5th ed. (New York: Scribner, 1859); William Mathews, *Oratory and Orators,*

12th ed. (Chicago: Scott, Foresman & Co., 1896).

42. See Abrams, 7–23; Henry David Thoreau, *The Writings of Henry David Thoreau*, ed. Bradford Torrey (New York: Houghton Mifflin, 1906), 1:365; Charles R. Metzger, *Thoreau and Whitman: A Study of Their Esthetics* (Seattle: University of Washington Press, 1961), 20–35, 62–69, 105.

43. "One Power alone makes a Poet: Imagination, The Divine Vision." William Blake, *Poetry and Prose of William Blake*, ed. Geoffrey Keynes (New York: Nonesuch, 1939), 821. See especially John Stafford, *The Literary Criticism of "Young America": A Study in the Relationship of Politics and Literature, 1837–1850* (Los Angeles: University of California Press, 1952), 71.

44. Abrams, 101, 298–99; James Craig La Driere, "Poetry and Prose," Shipley, ed., 315–16.

45. Abrams, 335; Bowra, 3; and Leslie A. Marchand, *The Athenaeum: A Mirror of Victorian Culture* (Chapel Hill: University of North Carolina Press, 1941), 235.

46. *CW* 9:6. For a discussion of the biblical indexing in the 1860 edition of *Leaves of Grass*, see Jellicorse, 166–67. An example is presented in the text of this essay at note 109.

47. Stafford, 54–94; quoted passages from 58, 92.

48. *CW* 10:16. These notes derive from Frederich von Schlegel's *Lectures on the History of Literature*; see Floyd Stovall, "Notes on Whitman's Reading," *American Literature* 26 (November 1954): 361. For Whitman's notes on oratory that reveal his exposure to the understanding-imagination distinction, see William L. Finkel, "Walt Whitman's Manuscript Notes on Oratory," *American Literature* 22 (March 1950): 35, 42, 45–48, 50–51.

49. *GF* 1:61. See Jellicorse, 944, n. 59, for more on the background of Whitman's understanding of rhetoric based on Whately as received through a speech by Charles Murray Nairne.

50. *CW* 8:254, from a passage in Thomas Sheridan, *Lectures on the Art of Reading*, vol. 1 (London, 1775); see Finkel, 44–45; 45, n. 58.

51. *PW*, vol. 1: *Specimen Days* (New York: New York University Press, 1963), 270; Metzger for detailed comparisons of Whitman and Thoreau; and Hesser. See also Olive W. Parsons, "Whitman the Non-Hegelian," *PMLA* 58 (December 1943): 1073–93.

52. *CW* 9:176; see also 175–84.

53. MS. in Henry Seidel Canby, *Walt Whitman, an American* (Boston: Houghton Mifflin, 1943), 357. The importance of Whitman's affinity for the Quakers has been pointed out by almost all of his major biographers and critics. See especially Walter B. Fulghum, Jr., "Quaker Influences on Whitman's Religious Thought" (Ph.D. diss., Northwestern University, 1943). Metzger also presents thorough proof that Whitman's conception of soul was derived from "the Pietist doctrine of inner Light" (Metzger, 43; see also 41–42, 50).

54. *PW* 2:638, 644; see also 631–47.

55. *UPP* 1:196.

56. See "Walt Whitman [at Dartmouth]" in Bliss Perry, *Walt Whitman*, 2d ed. (New York: Houghton Mifflin, 1908), 208; *CW* 9:98; *PW* 2:648. The soul

or unconscious will is "'the conscience of consciences'" to which the lesser consciences (especially the literary) are subordinate (*WWWC*, vol. 5, ed. Gertrude Traubel [Carbondale, Ill.: Southern Illinois University Press, 1964], 398). See also *Schools,* 211–12.

57. *PW* 2:538; Whitman's note, 486–88.

58. *PW* 2:532.

59. See *CW* 9:3; *PW* 2:537–38; *WWWC* 1:468.

60. *CW* 8:252 (note based very indirectly on Nairne; see Finkel, 42).

61. *CW* 8:252; Walt Whitman, *Walt Whitman's Workshop,* ed. Clifton Joseph Furness (Cambridge, Mass.: Harvard University Press, 1928), 34 (latter hereafter cited as *WWW*). See Finkel, 42.

62. *PW* 2:486–88; *CW* 1:lvi.

63. Ms. in Feinbeng, quoted in Jellicorse, 356; *CW* 1:lvi; *PW* 2:770. In Whitman's day "psychological" referred to the laws of the mind (psyche). In the passage cited Whitman uses the term "physiological" for what today would be termed "psychological."

64. *CW* 1:lvi.

65. See Jellicorse, 396, 679–88.

66. *PW* 2:546. See also *PW* 2:486–88, 551; *PW* 1:257–58.

67. *PW* 1:289.

68. *PW* 1:292.

69. *PW* 2:516.

70. *CW* 9:142–43.

71. See *PW* 2:639; *WWW,* 66.

72. *CW* 9:161.

73. *CW* 9:153–54.

74. *CW* 9:15.

75. See, for example, *PW* 1:150, 174–75, 183, 200, 243, 246–47, 253, 271, 277, 284; 2:398–99, 415–16, 486.

76. See, for example, *CW* 1:lvi; 9:38, 42, 173, 182, 192; *WWW,* 49, 52, 80. See also the Preface to Walt Whitman, *Leaves of Grass* (Brooklyn, 1855), xi (*Leaves of Grass* hereafter cited as *LG* with city and year).

77. *LG* (Brooklyn, 1855), vi.

78. *WWWC* 1:254; 4:241. Whitman stated this belief early in his career and maintained it throughout his life. See, for example, Walt Whitman, *Walt Whitman of the New York Aurora,* ed. Joseph Jay Rubin and Charles H. Brown (State College, Pa.: Bald Eagle Press, 1950), 99–100; *CW* 9:107; *GF* 1:62–64, 69, 144–45; *WWWC* 4:429; 5:53, 137–38.

79. *CW* 9:4.

80. The youthful Henry Ward Beecher, for example, wrote in his diary for May 4, 1837, that ". . . you can gain men easily if you get round their *prejudices* and put truth in their minds; but *never* if you attack *prejudices.*" Quoted in William C. Beecher and Samuel Scoville, *A Biography of Rev. Henry Ward Beecher* (New York: C. L. Webster & Co., 1888), 158.

81. Techniques that are "indirect and therefore more effective" (*CW* 9:197). See also, for example, *CW* 9:8–9; *PW* 1:292; *WWW,* 34.

82. *WWWC*, vol. 2 (New York: D. Appleton & Co., 1908), 269. See also *PW* 2:383; *WWWC* 1:363; 2:186; 4:476–77. "'What the world calls logic is beyond me . . . ,'" he told Horace Traubel (*WWWC* 1:149). See also *WWWC* 1:110–11, 430, 439–40; 2:190–91, 323–24, 398, 460; vol. 3 (New York: Michael Kennerley, 1914), 124, 207, 324.

83. *CW* 9:5. This is one of Whitman's most frequently articulated doctrines. For extensive examples see Jellicorse, 949, n. 102.

84. See, for example, *GF* 2:332–33; *PW* 2:557, 559–60, 750; *UPP* 1:115; *WWWC* 4:416.

85. See, for example, *PW* 2:635.

86. Whitman underlined the following passage in an article (dated 1848) on Tennyson's *The Princess:* "A poet, by becoming openly didactic, would deprive his work of that essential quality of suggestiveness by which activity on the part of the reader is absolutely demanded. . . ." (Trent Collection, reported by Roger Asselineau, *The Evolution of Walt Whitman* [Cambridge, Mass.: Belknap Press of Harvard University Press, 1962], 2:355–56, n. 29). In addition, see *CW* 9:37–38; *PW* 2:627; *WWWC* 3:357–58. Cf. Stafford, 89–93.

87. *UPP* 2:64 (in the notebook dated 1847). See also MS. in Jacob Schwartz, *Manuscripts, Autograph Letters, First Editions and Portraits of Walt Whitman* (New York: American Art Association; Anderson Galleries, Inc., 1936), 29, item no. 102 (among manuscripts toward the 1855 Preface).

88. *PW* 2:598.

89. *PW* 2:565. See also *PW* 1:138–39.

90. See Jellicorse, 177–249.

91. MS. in Edward G. Bernard, "Some New Whitman Manuscript Notes," *American Literature* 8 (March 1936): 61. See also, for example, *PW* 1:174–75; 2:497; *WWW*, 47.

92. *PW* 1:211. See also *PW* 1:183. Marion Harris has pointed out Whitman's belief that sensory experience can prompt "affective experience" (intuitive knowledge), allowing one to perceive "the relation of the individual to the eternal, spiritual world" ("Nature and Materialism: Fundamentals in Whitman's Epistemology," *Walt Whitman Review* 9 [December 1963]: 88).

93. *CW* 9:31; *LG* (Brooklyn, 1855), ix; *CW* 9:152. See also *Schools*, 171, 192.

94. *PW* 2:659. See also *CW* 9:30.

95. *LG* (Brooklyn, 1855), vii; see also v.

96. "Greater than wires of iron or treaties, or even strong mutual interests is Sympathy" (MS. [1854] in Emory Holloway, "A Whitman Manuscript," *The American Mercury* 3 [December 1924]: 476).

97. "'. . . men nearer realize what they are through what they see in others'" (*WWWC* 3:510).

98. *PW* 2:643.

99. Walt Whitman, *The Early Poems and the Fiction*, ed. Thomas L. Brasher (New York: New York University Press, 1963), 99 (hereafter cited as *EPF*).

100. See *Schools*, 100, 150, 162; *UPP* 1:71; *GF* 1:139.

101. *EPF*, 327–30; 330.

102. *CW* 9:30. Emory Holloway dated the earliest extant notebook towards *Leaves of Grass* as 1847 (*UPP* 2:63, n. 1).

103. *WWW*, 93.

104. *WWW*, 35.

105. MS. in Schwartz, 28, item no. 98.

106. *RLG*, 155. See also *PW* 2:771, 53, 644–45. The Romantics and Transcendentalists also emphasized the use of archetypes and illustrations. See, for example, Bowra, 10–12.

107. For a few of a very large number of potential examples, see *CW* 8:248; *PW* 1:260–61, 281; 2:401, 467, 552, 560, 595, 659, 690, 726–27; *WWWC* 1:100; 3:7; 4:502; 5:130.

108. See, for example, *CW* 9:159–60, 196; *PW* 2:570, 597, 635–36, 642–44; *WWWC* 4:165–66; 5:151–52.

109. *LG* (Boston: Thayer and Eldridge, 1860–61), 400; *RLG*, 390–91.

110. See, for example, *CW* 9:39, 64, 104–5, 149, 162; *PW* 2:486, 731, 751; *WWW*, 109.

111. For typical examples, see *CW* 10:50; *PW* 1:294–95; 2:524; *LG* (Brooklyn, 1855), v–vii; *PW* 2:486.

112. See *CW* 9:127 for a typical statement. For a further treatment of the divine literatus, see Jellicorse, 403–15.

113. See Jellicorse, 415–39, for a full treatment of this topic.

114. For Whitman's analysis of his audience see Jellicorse, 345–71. In his notes for lectures he prophesied, "Men like me—also women, our counterparts, perfectly equal—will gradually get to be more and more numerous—perhaps swiftly, in shoals" (Walt Whitman, *An American Primer*, ed. Horace L. Traubel [Boston: Small, Maynard, 1904], 21 [hereafter cited as *AP*]).

115. *WWW*, 66; *RLG*, 348. See also *RLG*, 346–48, 480–81, 487; *CW* 3:247. Whitman also affirmed poetically that the literatus's success is to be measured by "results" (*RLG*, 351).

116. *PW* 1:276; *WWWC* 4:396. See also *WWWC* 2:489; 4:351; *PW* 2:486, 653, 726; *WWW*, 67–68.

117. See, for example, Roy S. Azarnoff, "Walt Whitman's Rhetorical Theory and Practices" (Ph.D. diss., University of Missouri, 1965). This topic is also dealt with more extensively in Jellicorse, 415–42. C. Carroll Hollis has also written extensively on this subject and presented new aspects of his studies in "Whitman's Poetic Orality" at the 1992 Whitman Centennial Conference.

118. See, for example, *CW* 8:252. See also Edmund Reiss, "Whitman's Debt to Animal Magnetism," *PMLA* 78 (March 1963): 86–87.

119. *PW* 2:674. See also, for example, *CW* 8:254; *PW* 2:597; *UPP* 1:257; *WWWC* 4:265; 5:152, 174, 454–55, 463.

120. Whitman, writing through Richard Maurice Bucke [and Walt Whitman], *Walt Whitman* (Philadelphia: David McKay, 1883), 185 (see Schwartz, 74, item no. 190).

121. *PW* 2:366. See also, for example, *PW* 2:591; *Schools*, 143.

122. See especially *PW* 2:490; also 2:721; *WWW*, 168.

123. *CW* 9:172.

124. *PW* 1:230. See also, for example, *RLG,* 635, 658; *UPP* 2:76.

125. *PW* 2:520.

126. And the audience member is a "reader or hearer." Use of this terminology can be found on almost every page of Whitman's poetry and prose.

127. *PW* 2:519.

128. *UPP* 2:76 (pre-1855 notebook).

129. *WWW,* 40; *PW* 2:558. See also, for example, *LG* (Brooklyn, 1855), x–xi; *PW* 2:672; *WWW,* 53, 171–72, 214, n. 57. Whitman's concept of persuasion through indirection has also been explicated by Azarnoff, 98–103.

130. Walt Whitman, *An 1855–56 Notebook Toward the Second Edition of Leaves of Grass,* ed. Harold W. Blodgett (Carbondale, Ill.: Southern Illinois University Press, 1959), 6–7. See also *CW* 9:8.

131. *CW* 9:185 (in note re Fichte); 182; see also 170.

132. *GF* 2:269.

133. See, for example, *GF* 2:314–15; *PW* 2:660; *UPP* 1:69.

134. See, for example, *PW* 2:541–42; *AP,* 21.

135. *PW* 2:735; in Rollo G. Silver, "Whitman in 1850: Three Uncollected Articles," *American Literature* 19 (January 1948): 306. See also *CW* 9:199.

136. *PW* 2:726.

137. *PW* 2:761.

138. *CW* 9:103, 190; *WWW,* 65. See also *GF* 1:112–13; *AP,* 3.

139. *PW* 2:666; 574; 473; *LG* (Brooklyn, 1855), v.

140. *PW* 2:555.

141. *WWWC* 2:185. See also *LG* (Brooklyn, 1855), vi; *CW* 9:38; *PW* 2:671.

142. Quoted in Thayer, 685.

143. In his notes on story writing, for example, he wrote "*A strong beginning to arouse curiosity*" (*WWW,* 188, n. 11).

144. See, for example, *CW* 10:12, 53, 97–98, 158–59; *PW* 2:496–97; *UPP* 1:42–43.

145. See, for example, *CW* 9:38; *PW* 2:398–99, 473; *Schools,* 72.

146. *CW* 9:229; 117; *UPP* 2:65 (early notebook). See also, for example, *CW* 1:lvi; 9:10, 97–98, 117–18.

147. Best explicated by noting Whitman's practice in *Leaves of Grass.* See Jellicorse, 584–619.

148. Letter to John Burroughs, dated Feb. 14, 1874, Walt Whitman, *The Correspondence of Walt Whitman,* vol. 2: 1868–1875, ed. Edwin H. Miller (New York: New York University Press, 1961), 278 (latter hereafter cited as *CWW*). See also *WWWC* 3:562.

149. *PW* 2:682; MS. in Schwartz, 12, item no. 26. See also, for example, *CW* 9:120.

150. See, for example, *CW* 9:5; *WWWC* 4:288, 293. For Whitman's methods of promotion, see Jellicorse, 620–718.

151. *CW* 8:250.

152. Blake, *Poetry and Prose,* 442.

153. Emerson, *Complete Works* 7:372 (p. 98, n. 1); Ralph Waldo Emerson, *Journals of Ralph Waldo Emerson,* ed. Edward Waldo Emerson and Waldo

Emerson Forbes (New York: Houghton Mifflin, 1912), 9:85. Cf. *CW* 9:159; *PW* 2:516; *WWWC* 4:293.

154. *CW* 9:193; letter to John Parker Hale, dated Aug. 14, 1852, *CWW*, vol. 1: 1846–1867 (New York: New York University Press, 1961), 39–40. See also, for example, *CW* 9:4, 7; 10:32; *GF* 1:72; *WWWC* 4:469; 5:381.

155. See, for example, *UPP* 2:95; *WWWC* 4:149–50. Cf. Azarnoff, 83, 91–92.

156. *CW* 9:121 (in notes re Schlegel). See also, for example, *CW* 9:4, 5, 139–40, 161; *PW* 1:281–82; 2:378–79, 546–47, 659; *UPP* 1:46–47.

157. See, for example, *CW* 9:160, 192.

158. *PW* 1:326. See also *RLG*, 702 (unused MS.), 58–59; *CW* 3:114; *PW* 2:362–63; *UPP* 1:221.

159. *GF* 2:282–83; *CW* 10:34–35; 9:7. See also, for example, *CW* 9:37–38; *PW* 2:398–99, 415, 638; *UPP* 1:140; *WWW*, 36.

160. *PW* 2:482. See also *CW* 9:121–22; *PW* 1:340; *WWWC* 3:27, 70. Cf. Stafford, 98.

161. *PW* 1:178; 2:473. See also *CW* 8:250; 9:172; *PW* 2:663, 724–25, 738; *WWW*, 137, 170, 172. See also Azarnoff, 104–6.

162. Asselineau, 2:355–56, n. 29 (in Trent Collection); *CW* 9:31; 191. See also *CW* 9:175.

163. *PW* 2:425. The "agonistic arena" phrase appears to have been derived from Whitman's study of Nairne. See *WWW*, 37; Finkel, 38–39. See also, for example, *WWW*, 256, n. 272; *CW* 8:251; Finkel, 41.

164. See Jellicorse, 461–71.

165. MS. in Feinberg Collection, Library of Congress, quoted in Jellicorse, 981, n. 451. See also *WWW*, 47–48.

166. *CW* 9:188. See also *CW* 9:94–95, 187–88; *WWWC* 4:293–94.

167. Letter to Wiliam D. O'Connor, dated Dec. 17, 1882, *CWW*, vol. 3: 1876–1885 (New York: New York University Press, 1964), 320.

168. *PW* 2:716.

169. *CW* 8:252–53; Whitman's note, *PW* 2:485. See also, for example, *PW* 2:656, 729, 735; *AP*, 16.

170. (Austin, Texas: University of Texas Press, 1964), 60–61.

171. Abrams, 22. See also 24.

172. "Tally" and "tallying" are Whitman's frequently used terms. In its broadest use, "to tally" means to join man and nature. *PW* 2:421. See also Azarnoff, 92–98, 131–33.

173. *LG* (Brooklyn, 1855), ix; *CW* 3:227; *LG* (Brooklyn, 1855), iii, ix. See also, for example, *CW* 3:227–28; 9:158–59, 222; 10:82; *PW* 2:563; *RLG*, 386, 599; *UPP* 1:121–22; *WWWC* 4:53; "Letters" in Silver, 315–16. For a summary of Whitman's many statements against the use of ornaments, see Jellicorse, 454, 983, n. 465.

174. *CW* 9:229; see also, for example, 8, 91–92.

175. Whitman's use of the important phrase "elliptical & idiomatic" can be traced to "Words," his manuscript notebook collection of material for a new dictionary. See C. Carroll Hollis, "Whitman and the American Idiom,"

Quarterly Journal of Speech 43 (December 1957): 409. See also *CW* 8:248; Finkel, 48–50; *WWW*, 35.

176. See *PW* 2:416; *RLG*, 228.

177. *PW* 2:419; see also, for example, 404, 461. For examples of Whitman's poetic affirmation of the duty of the persuader to absorb and present "the essences of real things, old times and present / times," see *RLG*, 344; 6, 353, 518.

178. *AP*, 12.

179. MS. in Hollis, "Idiom," 420, and a slight variant is in *AP*, 21.

180. *AP*, 8; *WWWC* 4:220.

181. Charles E. Feinberg, *Walt Whitman: A Selection of the Manuscripts, Books, and Associated Items, Gathered by Charles E. Feinberg, Catalogue of an Exhibition Held at the Detroit Public Library*. Prepared by Frances J. Brewer (Detroit: Detroit Public Library, 1955), 6, item no. 15 (from "Words"); *PW* 2:573. See, for example, *AP* (esp. 6, 18–20); *PW* 1:332–33; 2:550, 572–77; *UPP* 2:45–46, 274–75; *WWWC* 3:123; 4:96–97, 105.

182. *WWWC* 2:521; William Swinton [and Walt Whitman], *Rambles among Words: Their Poetry, History and Wisdom* (New York: Charles Scribner, 1859), 290 (see C. Carroll Hollis, "Whitman and William Swinton: A Co-operative Friendship," *American Literature* 30 [January 1959]: 440, n. 40). See especially *AP*, 33–34; also *PW* 2:544; *WWWC* 3:211.

183. *AP*, 14. See also *WWW*, 47; *PW* 2:572; *RLG*, 220, 635, 348, 349; Ernest Rhys, *Everyman Remembers* (New York: Cosmopolitan Book Corp., 1931), 125.

184. See Jellicorse, 555–58.

185. The most famous example being, of course, the narration for Pare Lorentz's *The River* (1937).

186. Swinton [and Whitman], 291 (see Hollis, "Swinton," 440, n. 40); *PW* 2:572–75; 573; *AP*, 8; 1. Whitman did not rule out entirely the use of metaphors whose meanings were not dependent upon spiritual analogies, but he did not stress their use in his statements of theory.

187. *AP*, 18; 34; 18; *PW* 2:419. See also, *PW* 1:32; *CW* 9:141; *UPP* 2:84 (early notebook).

188. See, for example, *WWWC* 2:314; 533; 3:93–94.

189. *AP*, 27.

190. *CW* 9:162; *PW* 1:182; *CW* 9:48; *PW* 2:769; *GF* 2:302. See also, for example, *CW* 10:34; Schwartz, 22, items no. 65, 66; *WWWC* 4:145, 324; *PW* 2:563, 566, 655; *WWW*, 34.

191. Letter to Franklin B. Sanborn, dated Nov. 14, 1892, *CWW* 3:316; *PW* 2:735, 660. See also letter to the Editors of *Harper's Magazine*, dated Jan. 7, 1860, *CWW* 1:46; letter to John Burroughs, dated Dec. 23–25, 1878, *CWW* 3:144; *PW* 2:537.

192. *WWW*, 36. See, for example, MS. in Bernard, 61–62; *CW* 8:248–50; *GF* 2:274–75; *PW* 2:550, 723; *WWW*, 36, 37; *WWWC* 3:458. This emphasis of brevity was in accord with contemporary belief that literature for the masses should be short. See Stafford, 72–73.

193. *CW* 9:141. See also, for example, *CW* 9:3, 47, 141; *PW* 2:68. These

concepts are best considered in terms of Whitman's practice rather than his theory. See Jellicorse, 547–66.

194. *PW* 2:615. See also letter to Harry Stafford, dated May 28, 1879, *CWW* 3:155; *PW* 1:302; 2:566.

195. *WWWC* 2:5.

196. For more specific suggestions on approaching the reading of Whitman from his own standpoint, see Jellicorse, "Whitman and Modern," 8–9.

197. See Jellicorse, 1194, n. 567.

198. "Book Reviews," *American Literature* 35 (May 1963): 246.

199. *LG* (Philadelphia: David McKay, 1892), 79.

LINCOLN AND DOUGLAS RESPOND TO THE ANTISLAVERY MOVEMENT

1. This approach to studying movements is explained in Leland M. Griffin, "The Rhetoric of Historical Movements," *Quarterly Journal of Speech* 38 (April 1952): 184–88; Leland M. Griffin, "A Dramatistic Theory of the Rhetoric of Movements," in *Critical Responses to Kenneth Burke,* ed. William H. Rueckert (Minneapolis: University of Minnesota Press, 1969), 456–79.

2. Thomas B. Farrell contended that as an argument is generated in response to a progression of historical events, it addresses at once the specific historical exigency that called it forth and the "diachronic succession of frames in history itself." Thomas B. Farrell, "Knowledge in Time: Toward an Extension of Rhetorical Form," *Advances in Argumentation Theory and Research,* ed. J. Robert Cox and Charles Arthur Willard (Carbondale, Ill.: Southern Illinois University Press, 1982), 128.

3. Griffin developed the concept of "rhetorical trajectory" in Leland M. Griffin, "When Dreams Collide: Rhetorical Trajectories in the Assassination of President Kennedy," *Quarterly Journal of Speech* 70 (May 1984): 111–31.

4. Ibid., 127.

5. See Kathleen Diffley, "'Erecting Anew the Standard of Freedom': Salmon P. Chases's 'Appeal of the Independent Democrats' and the Rise of the Republican Party," *Quarterly Journal of Speech* 74 (November 1988): 404.

6. Joel H. Silbey, *The Partisan Imperative: The Dynamics of American Politics Before the Civil War* (New York: Oxford University Press, 1985), 91.

7. John S. Wright, *Lincoln and the Politics of Slavery* (Reno: University of Nevada Press, 1970), 25.

8. Avery Craven, *The Coming of the Civil War* (1942; rpt. Chicago: University of Chicago Press, 1966), 226.

9. Eric Foner, *Politics and Ideology in the Age of the Civil War* (New York: Oxford University Press, 1980), 44.

10. Wright, 54.

11. The two texts are Stephen A. Douglas, Letter to Twenty-five Chicago Clergymen, April 6, 1854, *The Letters of Stephen A. Douglas,* ed. Robert W. Johannsen (Urbana: University of Illinois Press, 1961), 300–322 (hereafter cited as *DL*); Abraham Lincoln, Speech at Peoria, Illinois, October 16, 1854, *The*

Collected Works of Abraham Lincoln, vol. 2, ed. Roy P. Basler (New Brunswick, N.J.: Rutgers University Press, 1953), 247–83 (hereafter cited as *LS*).

12. Ronald Deane Rietveld, "The Moral Issue of Slavery in American Politics, 1854–1860" (Ph.D. diss., University of Illinois, 1967), 47.

13. See Wright, 64–65.

14. For a discussion of the conspiracy argument as used by Lincoln, see David Zarefsky, *Lincoln, Douglas, and Slavery: In the Crucible of Public Debate* (Chicago: University of Chicago Press, 1990), 68–110. See also David Brion Davis, *The Slave Power Conspiracy and the Paranoid Style* (Baton Rouge: Louisiana State University Press, 1969).

15. Paul M. Angle, ed., *The Complete Lincoln-Douglas Debates of 1858* (Chicago: University of Chicago Press, 1991), 375 (hereafter cited as *Debates*). The Angle edition is the most accessible text of the seven debates. This is a reissue, with a new foreword, of the edition published in 1958 on the occasion of the centennial of the debates.

16. Gerald M. Capers, *Stephen A. Douglas: Defender of the Union* (Boston: Little, Brown, 1959), 120.

17. On Douglas's use of the creation story, see Rietveld, 65. As Lincoln pointed out during the Senate campaign, however, man was *not* given a choice but was commanded not to eat of the forbidden fruit (Genesis 2:17). Similarly, in Deuteronomy, the Israelites were told, "I have put before you life and death, blessing and curse," but then were commanded, "Choose life" (Deuteronomy 29:19).

18. Douglas struck the same theme in the debates at Jonesboro and Alton.

19. The quotation is from Lincoln's "House Divided" speech.

BURKEAN RITES AND THE GETTYSBURG ADDRESS

1. Leland M. Griffin, "A Dramatistic Theory of the Rhetoric of Movements," in *Critical Responses to Kenneth Burke,* ed. Wm. H. Rueckert (Minneapolis: University of Minnesota Press, 1969), 478.

2. Leland M. Griffin, "When Dreams Collide: Rhetorical Trajectories in the Assassination of President Kennedy," *Quarterly Journal of Speech* 70 (May 1984): 111.

3. Barry Brummett is an exception. See, for example, his "Presidential Substance: The Address of August 15, 1973," *Western Journal of Speech Communication* 39 (Fall 1975): 249–59.

4. Thomas B. Farrell, "Critical Models in the Analysis of Discourse," *Western Journal of Speech Communication* 44 (Fall 1980): 300.

5. The most recent analysis in the communication field is Barbara Warnick, "A Ricoeurian Approach to Rhetorical Criticism," *Western Journal of Speech Communication* 51 (Summer 1987): 227–44. See also Garry Wills, *Lincoln at Gettysburg: The Words That Remade America* (New York: Simon & Schuster, 1992).

6. Aristotle, *Rhetoric,* trans. W. Rhys Roberts (New York: Modern Library, 1954), 1354a1.

7. Kenneth Burke, *A Rhetoric of Motives* (1950; reprint, Berkeley: University of California Press, 1969), 46 (hereafter cited as *Motives*).

8. Kenneth Burke, *Language as Symbolic Action* (Berkeley: University of California Press, 1968), 482–84.

9. Kenneth Burke, *Permanence and Change*, 3d ed. (Berkeley: University of California Press, 1984), 274 (hereafter cited as *Permanence*).

10. Kenneth Burke, *The Rhetoric of Religion* (Boston: Beacon Press, 1961), v (hereafter cited as *Religion*).

11. Kenneth Burke, *A Grammar of Motives* (1945; reprint, Berkeley: University of California Press, 1969), 69 (hereafter cited as *Grammar*).

12. See also Paul Ricoeur, *The Symbolism of Evil* (New York: Harper & Row, 1967), esp. "Conclusion: The Symbol Gives Rise to Thought," 347–57.

13. Thomas F. Mader, "A Problem with Johnstone's *Self*," *Philosophy and Rhetoric* 18 (1985): 94–95.

14. James George Frazer, *The Golden Bough* (1890; abridged ed., New York: Macmillan, 1947), 569.

15. Hugh D. Duncan, *Communication and Social Order* (London: Oxford University Press, 1970), 337–39.

16. J. Buchler, *The Concept of Method* (New York: Columbia University Press, 1961), 133.

17. Kenneth Burke, *Counter-Statement* (1931; reprint, Los Altos: Hermes, 1953), 153.

18. Kenneth Burke, *The Philosophy of Literary Form* (1941; reprint, New York: Vintage, 1961), 9.

19. Burke, *Permanence and Change* (1935; reprint, New York: Bobbs-Merrill, 1965), 50.

20. Ibid., 52.

21. Henry W. Johnstone, Jr., "Some Reflections on Argumentation," in *Philosophy, Rhetoric, and Argumentation*, ed. Maurice Natanson and Henry W. Johnstone, Jr. (University Park: Pennsylvania State University Press, 1965), 6.

22. Susanne K. Langer, *Philosophy in a New Key* (1942; reprint, Cambridge: Harvard University Press, 1973), 44.

23. Ibid, 51.

24. See also Leland M. Griffin, "The Rhetorical Structure of the New Left Movement: Part I," *Quarterly Journal of Speech* 50 (April 1964): 114–16.

25. On the distinction between "presence" and "existence," see Thomas F. Mader, "On Presence in Rhetoric," *College Composition and Communication* (December 1973): 375–81.

26. Henry W. Johnstone, Jr., *Philosophy and Argument* (University Park: Pennsylvania State University Press, 1959), 127.

27. Gilbert Highet, "The Gettysburg Address," in *Readings in Speech*, ed. Haig A. Bosmajian (New York: Harper & Row, 1965), 240–47.

28. Burke, *Permanence and Change* (1965 ed.), 274–94.

Manifesting Perspectives

1. Leland M. Griffin, "A Dramatistic Theory of the Rhetoric of Movements," in *Critical Responses to Kenneth Burke*, ed. William H. Rueckert (Minneapolis: University of Minnesota Press, 1969), 456–79.

2. The modern equivalent of this defense is explored in Thomas B. Farrell, "Knowledge, Consensus, and Rhetorical Theory," *Quarterly Journal of Speech* 62 (1976): 1–17.

3. Griffin, *Dramatistic Theory*, 460–64.

4. Ibid., 478.

5. Renato Poggioli, *The Theory of the Avant-garde*, trans. Gerald Fitzgerald (Cambridge, Mass.: Belknap Press, 1968), 18–21.

6. Robert Cumming, "The Literature of Extreme Situations," in *Aesthetics Today*, ed. M. Philipson and P. Gudel (New York: New American Library, 1980).

7. Nikos Stangos, ed., *Concepts of Modern Art* (New York: Harper & Row, 1981), p. 9.

8. See note 5.

9. Marjorie Perloff, *The Futurist Moment: Avant-Garde, Avant-Guerre, and the Language of Rupture* (Chicago: University of Chicago Press, 1986).

10. I have, in the text, paraphrased Poggioli's four moments as a kind of grid. See his discussion of the sequence in Poggioli, 25–40.

11. Leland M. Griffin, "The Rhetoric of Historical Movements," *Quarterly Journal of Speech* 38 (1952): 184–88.

12. Marjorie Perloff, "'Violence and Precision': The Manifesto as Art Form," *Chicago Review* 34, no. 2 (1984).

13. Perloff, *Futurist Moment*, chaps. 2–5.

14. Ibid., 6.

15. Marjorie Perloff, "Why Futurism Now?" *Formations* 4 (1988): 1–11.

16. Griffin, "Historical Movements," 184–88.

17. Wendy Steiner, *The Colors of Rhetoric: Problems in the Relation Between Modern Literature and Painting* (Chicago: University of Chicago Press, 1982), 35–36.

18. Ibid., 5.

19. James Breslin, "William Carlos Williams and Charles Demuth: Cross-Fertilization in the Arts," *Journal of Modern Literature* 6 (1977): 248–63.

20. Edgar Wind, *Art and Anarchy* (Evanston: Northwestern University Press, 1985), 47–63.

21. Elizabeth Gilmore Holt, ed., *The Triumph of Art for the Public, 1785–1848: The Emerging Role of Exhibitions and Critics* (Princeton: Princeton University Press, 1983), 9–11. See also Erich Auerbach, *Mimesis: The Representation of Reality in Western Literature*, trans. W. R. Trask (Princeton: Princeton University Press, 1968), 520–54.

22. Holt, 226.

23. Holt, 228.

24. Leo Tolstoy, *What is Art?* (Cambridge: Oxford University Press, 1929).

25. Edward F. Fry, ed., *Cubism* (New York: Oxford University Press, 1978), 30–32.

26. Norbert Lynton, "Futurism," in Stangos, 99.

27. F. T. Marinetti, "Manifesto of Futurism," *Le Figaro*, Feb. 20, 1909, 1.

28. Ibid.

29. Richard Huelsenbeck, "En Avant Dada: A History of Dadaism, 1920," trans. R. Manheim, in R. Motherwell, ed., *The Dada Painters and Poets* (New York: Wittenborn, Schulz, 1951), 24.

30. "Dadaist Manifesto," The Dadaist Revolutionary Central Council, German Group: Hausman, Huelsenbeck, in Huelsenbeck, 26.

31. "Berlin Dadaist Manifesto," in Robert Hughes, *The Shock of the New* (New York: Alfred A. Knopf, 1980), 70–71.

32. Ibid., 71.

33. Ibid.

34. Ibid.

35. Aristotle, *Rhetoric*, Book I, 1367a35.

36. Poggioli, 20.

37. "Berlin Dadaist Manifesto," 71.

38. Hugo Ball, "Dada Manifesto," in Stangos, 116–17.

39. "Berlin Dadaist Manifesto," 70–71.

40. Guillaume Apollinaire, "Cubism," *Les Soirees de Paris*, no. 20 (January 15, 1914).

41. Herschel Chipp, "Neo-Plasticism and Constructivism: Abstract and Non-Objective Art," *Theories of Modern Art: A Sourcebook by Artists and Critics*, ed. Chipp et al. (Berkeley: University of California Press, 1968), 309–13.

42. Naum Gabo and Anton Pevsner, "Constructivist manifesto," 1920 Moscow Constructivist Exhibit.

43. Ibid.

44. Aaron Scharf, "Constructivism," in Stangos, 160–68.

45. Ibid., 165.

46. A reference to the 1989 events in Tiananmen Square, Beijing. See "China Erupts: The Reasons Why," *New York Times Magazine*, June 4, 1989.

47. Margit Rowell and Angelica Zander Rudenstine, *Art of the Avant-garde in Russia: Selections from the George Costakis Collection* (New York: Solomon R. Guggenheim Museum, 1981).

48. Ibid., 305–18.

49. Dawn Ades, "Dada and Surrealism," in Stangos, 121–23.

50. See, for instance, Peter Bürger, *Theory of the Avant-Garde*, trans. M. Shaw (Minneapolis: University of Minnesota Press, 1984), 61–66.

51. Ades, 123.

52. Andre Breton, *Manifestoes of Surrealism* (Ann Arbor: University of Michigan Press, 1972), 42–43.

53. Ibid., 13–14.

54. Ibid., 14.

55. Antonin Artaud, "A Letter to the Chancellors of the European Universities," in Stangos, 123–24.

56. Theodor Adorno, "Looking Back on Surrealism," *The Idea of the Modern*, ed. Irving Howe (New York: Horizon Press, 1967), 220–24.

57. Breton, 22–27.

58. Kenneth Burke, *Counter-Statement* (Berkeley: University of California Press, 1968), 31.

59. All theories of invention assume some sort of play between dialogic forces, whether these be the accidents and definitions, subjects and predicates, problems and propositions, universals and particulars of Aristotle's *Topoi*, or the bisociated consciousness of Arthur Koestler, *The Act of Creation* (New York: Dell Publishing Company, 1973). I hazard the claim that the surrealists have presented us with the first and only genuinely subversive theory of creativity.

60. This seems to be Robert Hughes's claim, as well as the claim of postmodernists too numerous to mention. One implication of this essay is that the historicity of art does not necessarily cancel out or exhaust the aesthetic impulse. In this sense, it is doubly ironic that the postmodernist position, so indebted to aesthetic modernism for its own literary style, would try to hover outside the horizon for any historical accounting. If aesthetic theories may exhaust themselves, surely the same can be said for attitudes.

NARRATIVE AND METAPHOR IN INTERVENTIONIST RHETORIC

Mr. Heisey wishes to acknowledge the assitance of Rozell R. Duncan and David E. Powers in helping to obtain materials used in this research.

1. Richard A. Cherwitz and Kenneth S. Zagacki, "Consummatory Versus Justificatory Crisis Rhetoric," *Western Journal of Speech Communication* 50 (Fall 1986): 320, 309.

2. See, for example, the six articles, which include Cherwitz and Zagacki, in the Special Issue on the Rhetoric of Foreign Affairs in the *Western Journal of Speech Communication* 50 (Fall 1986), ed. Robert L. Ivie; Philip Wander, "The Rhetoric of American Foreign Policy," *The Quarterly Journal of Speech* 70 (November 1984): 339–61; Robert L. Ivie, "Images of Savagery in American Justifications for War," *Communication Monographs* 47 (November 1980): 279–94. These studies are of recent American rhetoric in response to international crises. The analysis of recent foreign policy rhetoric of international leaders by rhetorical critics is meager.

3. See D. Ray Heisey, "Reagan and Mitterrand Respond to International Crisis: Creating Versus Transcending Appearances," *Western Journal of Speech Communication* 50 (1986): 325–35.

4. The texts selected were: Leonid I. Brezhnev, "Replies to a *Pravda* Correspondent," given January 13, 1980, published in Brezhnev's book of translated speeches, *Peace, Détente, Cooperation* (New York: Consultants Bureau, 1981), 157–73; Margaret Thatcher, "Text of Falkland Speech by Prime

Minister Thatcher in House of Commons," *New York Times*, May 21, 1982, 10; Menachem Begin, "Menachem Begin Speech [on "Peace for Galilee Operation"]," FBIS Daily Report: Middle East and Africa, vol. 5, no. 126, June 30, 1982, Part I, 17–28; Francois Mitterrand, "The Explanations of M. Mitterrand on the Crisis in Chad," *LeMonde*, Aug. 26, 1983, 1, 4, translated by Alexander D. Heisey in six typescript pages with page number cited as from the typescript pages; Ronald Reagan, "Lebanon and Grenada," *Vital Speeches*, vol. 50, no. 3, November 15, 1983, 66–69.

5. Terrence Hawkes, *Metaphor* (London: Methuen & Co., 1972), 91.

6. Walter R. Fisher, "The Narrative Paradigm: An Elaboration," *Communication Monographs* 52 (December 1985): 349, 350.

7. Brezhnev, "Replies" (all subsequent quotations are from this text).

8. Margaret Thatcher, "Excerpts from Mrs. Thatcher's Talk," *New York Times*, April 15, 1982, 14.

9. Thatcher, "Falkland Speech" (unless otherwise indicated, all subsequent quotations are from this text).

10. David Zarefsky, "The Lincoln-Douglas Debates Revisited: The Evolution of Public Argument," *The Quarterly Journal of Speech* 72 (May 1986): 182.

11. Murray Edelman, *Constructing the Political Spectacle* (Chicago: University of Chicago Press, 1988), 18.

12. Thatcher, "Thatcher Answer to the Pope," *New York Times*, May 25, 1982, A13.

13. Ibid.

14. Ariel Sharon, "Ari'el Sharon Knesset Speech," FBIS Daily Report: Middle East and Africa, vol. 5, no. 126, June 30, 1982, Part I, 1.

15. *New York Times*, June 11, 1982, 1.

16. Ibid.

17. Ibid., June 14, 1982, A19.

18. Ibid., June 15, 1982, A20.

19. Begin, "Menachem Begin Speech" (all subsequent quotations are from this text).

20. *New York Times*, Aug. 26, 1983, 1.

21. Mitterrand, "The Explanations" (all subsequent quotations are from the English translation in typescript).

22. Mitterrand, "Excerpts from the Speech Before the General Assembly of the United Nations," *LeMonde*, Sept. 30, 1983, typescript 2.

23. Edward A. Kolodziej, *French International Policy Under de Gaulle and Pompidou* (Ithaca: Cornell University Press, 1973), 56.

24. Edelman, 113.

25. Reagan, "Lebanon and Grenada" (these and subsequent quotations are from this text).

26. D. Ray Heisey, "Reagan's Use of Peace/War Symbols Justifying Military Intervention," in *Within the Perfection of Christ: Essays on Peace and the Nature of the Church,* ed. Terry L. Brensinger and E. Morris Sider (Nappanee, Ind.: Evangel Press & Brethren in Christ Historical Society, 1990), 198.

27. See ibid., where I argue that "Reagan's use of peace/war symbols helps create force in his narrative by establishing a 'metaphorical field'" (200), based on Jeremy Rayner's essay "Between Meaning and Event: An Historical Approach to Political Metaphors," *Political Studies* 32 (1984): 537–50.

28. Edelman, 103, 104.

29. See Larry David Smith, "A Narrative Analysis of the Party Platforms: The Democrats and Republicans of 1984," *Communication Quarterly* 37 (Spring 1989): 91–99. To paraphrase what Smith says about the Party Platforms, I would argue that speeches of interventionism are continuing sagas that take military actions and cast them in terms of established points of view (98).

30. James W. Fernandez, *Persuasion and Performances: The Play of Tropes in Culture* (Bloomington: Indiana University Press, 1986), 12, 14.

31. Ibid., 24, 25.

32. Edelman, 115.

33. Ibid., 110.

34. Leland M. Griffin, "When Dreams Collide: Rhetorical Trajectories in the Assassination of President Kennedy," *The Quarterly Journal of Speech* 70 (May 1984): 111, 112. Victor Turner, also influenced by Kenneth Burke (as is Griffin), calls these progressions "social dramas" with four phases that he labels "breach, crisis, redress, and *either* reintegration *or* recognition of schism." See Victor Turner, "Social Dramas and Stories about Them," *Critical Inquiry* 7 (Autumn 1980): 141–68.

35. New York Times, June 24, 1980, A6.

36. ABC World News Tonight, Feb. 6, 1989.

37. *New York Times,* June 16, 1982, 24.

38. *New York Times,* June 2, 1983, A 11.

39. Alouph Hareven quoted in *World Press Review*, Sept. 1982, 42.

40. *New York Times*, June 19, 1982, 7.

41. Ibid.

42. Edelman, 123.

43. Griffin, 112, 113.

44. Ibid., 123.

45. Ibid., 113.

46. Robert C. Rowland, *The Rhetoric of Menachem Begin: The Myth of Redemption Through Return* (Lanham, Md.: University Press of America, 1985), 200, 236, 237.

47. J. R. Frears, *France in the Giscard Presidency* (London: George Allen & Unwin, 1981), 104.

48. See "When Ideology Bows to Economics," *U.S. News & World Report*, Feb. 6, 1989, 30, 31.

49. Amos Perlmutter, "Begin's Rhetoric and Sharon's Tactics," *Foreign Affairs* 61 (Fall 1982): 81.

50. Edelman, 36. Another way of viewing these interventions is through the metaphor that Wagner-Pacifici uses in the Aldo Moro case. She says the Moro affair "'stopped the clock' in Italy just long enough to provide a freeze-frame view of the long-term social and political malaise . . . out of which this

event erupted" (Robin Erica Wagner-Pacifici, *The Moro Morality Play: Terrorism as Social Drama* [Chicago: University of Chicago Press, 1986], 14).

51. Cherwitz and Zagacki, 317, 318.

52. Ibid., 310, 312.

53. Ibid., 312, 314, 316.

54. Heisey, "Reagan and Mitterrand," 332.

55. See note 2.

56. Heisey, "Reagan and Mitterrand," 327–29, 332.

57. Rowland, 208, 109.

THE CONSTRUCTION OF APPEAL IN VISUAL IMAGES

I wish to acknowledge the support of a summer research award by the Office of Research and Sponsored Programs of the University of Oregon for this project. I also thank the members of the Writing Group of the Speech Department at the University of Oregon, who helped me think more clearly about the process by which appeal is constructed in images.

1. Lloyd F. Bitzer and Edwin Black, eds., *The Prospect of Rhetoric: Report of the National Developmental Project* (Englewood Cliffs, N.J.: Prentice-Hall, 1971), 221.

2. Barnet Baskerville, "Rhetorical Criticism, 1971: Retrospect, Prospect, Introspect," *Southern Speech Communication Journal* 37 (Winter 1971): 116.

3. Waldo W. Braden, "Rhetorical Criticism: Prognoses for the Seventies—A Symposium: A Prognosis by Waldo W. Braden," *Southern Speech Journal* 36 (Winter 1970): 105.

4. Roderick P. Hart, "Forum: Theory-Building and Rhetorical Criticism: An Informal Statement of Opinion," *Central States Speech Journal* 27 (Spring 1976): 71–72.

5. Leland M. Griffin, "The Rhetoric of Historical Movements," *Quarterly Journal of Speech* 38 (April 1952): 184–88.

6. Leland M. Griffin, "The Edifice Metaphor in Rhetorical Theory," *Speech Monographs* 27 (November 1960): 279–92.

7. Lawrence W. Rosenfield, "Central Park and the Celebration of Civic Virtue," in *American Rhetoric: Context and Criticism,* ed. Thomas W. Benson (Carbondale: Southern Illinois University Press, 1989), 221–65.

8. Sonja K. Foss, "Judy Chicago's *The Dinner Party*: Empowering of Women's Voice in Visual Art," in *Women Communicating: Studies of Women's Talk,* ed. Barbara Bate and Anita Taylor (Norwood, N.J.: Ablex, 1988), 9–26.

9. Janice Hocker Rushing, "Mythic Evolution of 'The New Frontier' in Mass Mediated Rhetoric," *Critical Studies in Mass Communication* 3 (September 1986): 265–96.

10. Harry W. Haines, "'What Kind of War?': An Analysis of the Vietnam Veterans Memorial," *Critical Studies in Mass Communication* 3 (March 1986), 1–20.

11. Kathleen Campbell, "Enactment as a Rhetorical Strategy in *The Year*

of Living Dangerously," *Central States Speech Journal* 39 (Fall/Winter 1988): 258–68.

12. Lester C. Olson, "Benjamin Franklin's Commemorative Medal, *Libertas Americana:* A Study in Rhetorical Iconology," *Quarterly Journal of Speech* 76 (February 1990): 23–45.

13. For discussions of differences between visual and verbal symbols, see, for example: Dorothy Walsh, "Some Functions of Pictorial Representation," *British Journal of Aesthetics* 21 (Winter 1981), 32–38; David Novitz, *Pictures and Their Use in Communication* (The Hague, Netherlands: Martinus Nijhoff, 1977), 92–95; and Susanne K. Langer, *Philosophy in a New Key: A Study in the Symbolism of Reason, Rite, and Art* (1942; rpt. New York: Mentor/New American Library, 1951), 86–89.

14. Stuart Jay Kaplan, "Visual Metaphors in the Representation of Communication Technology," *Critical Studies in Mass Communication* 7 (March 1990): 37–47.

15. Sonja K. Foss, "Ambiguity as Persuasion: The Vietnam Veterans Memorial," *Communication Quarterly* 34 (Summer 1986): 326–40.

16. Sonja K. Foss, "Body Art: Insanity as Communication," *Central States Speech Journal* 38 (Summer 1987): 122–31.

17. See, for example, Harry Rand, "Style and Utility," *Arts Magazine* 57 (June 1983): 82–84.

18. Representative is an essay by Catherine Lord, "Kinds and Degrees of Aesthetic Unity," *British Journal of Aesthetics* 18 (Winter 1978): 59–65.

19. Nelson Goodman deals extensively with this issue in *Languages of Art: An Approach to a Theory of Symbols* (Indianapolis: Bobbs-Merrill, 1968).

20. See, for example, Ina Loewenberg, "Intentions: The Speaker and the Artist," *British Journal of Aesthetics* 15 (Winter 1974): 40–49.

21. Illustrative is an essay by Marcia Eaton, "Truth in Pictures," *Journal of Aesthetics and Art Criticism* 39 (Fall 1980): 15–26.

22. See Langer, note 13 above.

23. Excellent sources on semiotics include: Keir Elam, *The Semiotics of Theatre and Drama* (New York: Methuen, 1980); Roland Barthes, *Image Music Text,* ed. and trans. Stephen Heath (New York: Hill and Wang, 1977); Pierre Guiraud, *Semiology* (Boston: Routledge & Kegan Paul, 1975); Umberto Eco, *A Theory of Semiotics* (Bloomington: Indiana University Press, 1976); Arthur Asa Berger, *Signs in Contemporary Culture: An Introduction to Semiotics* (New York: Longman, 1984); and Sol Worth, *Studying Visual Communication,* ed. Larry Gross (Philadelphia: University of Pennsylvania Press, 1981).

24. Nory Miller, "Spaces for Selling," *AIA Journal* 67 (July 1978): 35–41.

25. Victor Margolin, "A Swedish Campaign to Combat Youth Alcoholism," *Mobilia* 11 (February 1984): 27.

26. Louis Kaufman, *Essentials of Advertising* (New York: Harcourt Brace Jovanovich, 1980), 357–58.

27. This distinction between types of images is made by: Dorothy Walsh, "Some Functions of Pictorial Representation," *British Journal of Aesthetics* 21

(Winter 1981): 32–38; Alwynne Mackie, "Modernism and the Language of Art," *Art International* 24 (August-September, 1981): 184–93; and Goodman, 5.

28. Rob Krier, "On Architectural Composition," *Architectural Design* 56 (1986): 60.

29. Fredric Jameson discusses defamiliarization in: *The Prison-House of Language: A Critical Account of Structuralism and Russian Formalism* (Princeton, N.J.: Princeton University Press, 1972), 54–64.

30. Richard Horn, *Memphis: Objects, Furniture, and Patterns* (Philadelphia: Running, 1986), 21.

31. Ibid., 35.

32. Two excellent sources on Memphis furniture are: Horn; and Barbara Radice, *Memphis: Research, Experiences, Results, Failures and Successes of New Design* (New York: Rizzoli International, 1984).

33. All Memphis furniture is named for hotels.

34. Radice, 87.

35. Mike Flanagan, "Out West," *Denver Post Magazine,* Oct. 16, 1983, 38.